U0887443

FAO/WHO Food Standards
CODEX alimentarius

国际食品法典标准

——畜禽产品卷

农业部农产品质量安全监管局
农 业 部 科 技 发 展 中 心 编译
国际食品法典中国联络处

中国农业科学技术出版社

图书在版编目(CIP)数据

国际食品法典标准——畜禽产品卷/农业部农产品质量安全监管局,农业部科技发展中心,国际食品法典中国联络处编译.—北京:中国农业科学技术出版社,2012.10

ISBN 978-7-5116-0972-4

Ⅰ.①国… Ⅱ.①农…②农…③国… Ⅲ.①食品卫生法-法规-汇编-世界②食品标准-汇编-世界③畜禽-肉品加工-食品卫生法-汇编-世界④畜禽-肉品加工-食品标准-汇编-世界 Ⅳ.①D912.109②TS207.2

中国版本图书馆 CIP 数据核字(2012)第 134233 号

责任编辑 闫庆健 李冠桥
责任校对 贾晓红

出 版 者 中国农业科学技术出版社
北京市中关村南大街 12 号 邮编:100081
电　　话 (010)82106632(编辑室) (010)82109704(发行部)
(010)82109709(读者服务部)
传　　真 (010)82106632
网　　址 http://www.castp.cn
经 销 者 各地新华书店
印 刷 者 北京科信印刷有限公司
开　　本 880 mm×1 230 mm 1/16
印　　张 14.375
字　　数 425 千字
版　　次 2012 年 10 月第 1 版 2012 年 10 月第 1 次印刷
定　　价 80.00 元

《国际食品法典标准——畜禽产品卷》

编译组

主　　编　周云龙　崔野韩

副 主 编　王　艳　郑蔚然　徐学万

翻译与审校（按姓氏笔画排序）

王　艳　王　媛　王　强　刘鹏程
孙彩霞　张志恒　李淑芳　杨桂玲
沈源源　陈本晶　张卫星　张　玲
邹　轶　周云龙　周海燕　郑蔚然
胡　莉　赵晓燕　徐学万　袁玉伟
崔野韩　董　飞　魏鹏娟

前　言

国际食品法典委员会（Codex Alimentarius Commission，简称 CAC），是专门制定国际食品标准的政府间工作组织，由联合国粮农组织（FAO）和世界卫生组织（WHO）于1963年联合成立，旨在通过建立国际协调一致的农产品及食品安全和质量标准、加工规范和准则，保护消费者的身体健康和生命安全，促进贸易公平。目前，CAC 已被世界贸易组织（WTO）确认为三个农产品及食品国际标准化机构之一，食品法典标准被认可为国际农产品及食品贸易仲裁的依据。截至目前，CAC 已经拥有遍布全球各洲的184个成员国和1个成员组织（欧盟），覆盖全球人口的98%。

中国作为 WTO 的成员，同时也是国际农产品及食品贸易大国，正在日益广泛而深入地参与国际活动。为全面系统地介绍国际食品法典标准，继《国际食品法典标准——果蔬与农药残留限量卷》和《国际食品法典标准——水产品及水产加工品卷》之后，我们组织相关专家对 CAC 畜禽产品标准进行了收集、整理，并编译成《国际食品法典标准——畜禽产品卷》，供我国读者参考使用。我们真诚地希望该书的出版能对从事农产品及食品生产、加工、检测、贸易、管理、研究、标准制定及其他感兴趣的人士提供有益帮助。

本书英文资料来源于 CAC 官方网站，资料收集截止时间是2012年5月。由于编译者水平和能力有限，本书在内容收集和文字翻译方面可能存在疏漏和不当之处，敬请各位读者批评指正！

编译者

2012年9月

目　录

咸牛肉标准

CODEX STANDARD FOR CORNED BEEF

(*CODEX STAN 88 – 1981 Rev. 1 – 1991*)

1 范围

本标准适用于标注为“咸牛肉”，罐装在密封容器内，经热处理至产品耐贮存的程度后，进行销售的罐装牛肉产品。

本标准不适用于有多种成分特征的熟火腿产品。相关产品的质量声明应该采用不会误导消费者，也不会因为产品采用本标准而产生混淆的适当方式来进行描述。

2 描述

咸牛肉是指源自牛类动物经切碎、腌制、剔骨的胴体肉，可以包括头部肉、内脏和牛筋肉。

产品应由经预烹饪后的粗碎牛肉，或者在经预烹饪牛肉中加入最大百分比为不超过5%的生牛肉组成的混合物制备而成；在其他情况下，肉应当在装入容器前或装入容器后进行腌制。

容器密封后，应当进行热处理，热处理应当充分保证产品耐贮藏，并且不存在公众健康风险。

附属定义

密封容器是指完全密封并且不渗漏的密封罐头，它由适合于本标准所涵盖产品的任何材料制成。

3 基本组成及质量指标

3.1 基本配料

——未腌制牛肉；

——腌制配料包括食用盐和亚硝酸钠或亚硝酸钾。

3.2 可选配料

——蔗糖、转化糖、葡萄糖（右旋糖）、乳糖、麦芽糖、葡萄糖浆（包括玉米糖浆）。

3.3 成分

成品的总蛋白质含量不能少于21%（质量比）。

3.4　基本的质量指标

3.4.1　原料

制作本产品所采用的牛肉应该达到食用的质量要求，并且没有令人不适的气味和滋味。

3.4.2　成品

成品应干净、无染色、无源自容器的污染。成品肉应均匀一致、腌制透彻，并且该产品在冷冻条件下可以切片。

4　食品添加剂

	最大添加量
4.1　防腐剂	
4.1.1　亚硝酸盐，钾盐和（或）钠盐	100mg/kg（以亚硝酸钠计）
	按成品总净含量计算的最大值
4.1.2　亚硝酸盐，钾盐和（或）钠盐	50mg/kg（以亚硝酸钠计）
4.1.3　氯化钾	**按照良好操作规范**
4.2　抗氧化剂	
4.2.1　抗坏血酸及其钠盐	300mg/kg（以抗坏血酸单体或复合物计）
4.2.2　异抗坏血酸及其钠盐	300mg/kg（以抗坏血酸单体或复合物计）

4.3　残留

按食品法典第1卷5.2所列示的添加剂，采用法则第三部分中关于食品添加剂的残留标准。

5　污染物

	最大限量
5.1　铅（Pb）	1mg/kg❶
5.2　锡（Sn）	
5.2.1　锡（Sn）：马口铁罐装产品	200mg/kg❶
5.2.2　锡（Sn）：其他容器包装的产品	50mg/kg❶

6　卫生

6.1　推荐采用《国际推荐肉禽产品加工卫生操作规程》［Ref. No. CAC/RCP 13－1976（Rev. 1，1985)］和《国际推荐低酸和酸化低酸罐头食品卫生操作规程》［Ref. No. CAC/RCP 23－1979（Rev. 1，1989)］，《食品卫生通则国际推荐标准》［Ref. No. CAC/RCP 1－1969（Rev. 2，1985)］和《鲜肉加工国际推荐规程卫生规范》（CAC/RCP 11－1976）进行操作。

---

❶ 暂定标准。

6.2 所有用于咸牛肉加工的肉都应是按照《鲜肉加工国际推荐规程卫生规范》要求生产，并按照《国际推荐动物宰前宰后检验及鉴定的操作规程》（CAC/RCP 41－1993）进行检验，通过质检人员检查其适合人类食用。肉类在经过检查后，不应该受污染，或者添加任何有害物质加工、处理，致使其不适于人类食用。

6.3 未加工或半加工的肉和咸牛肉应该在一定的设备中，按照一定的方式进行处理、分类或运输，以保护肉和咸牛肉不受污染和不变质。

6.4 咸牛肉应依照《国际推荐低酸和酸化低酸罐头食品卫生操作规程》第7.4条中的规定用密封容器包装。

6.5 咸牛肉应按照《国际推荐低酸和酸化低酸罐头食品卫生操作规程》中的第7.5条、第7.6.1款至7.6.7款（包含第7.6.7款）进行热处理。

6.6 被填充和密封的容器热处理后冷却应该按照《国际推荐低酸和酸化低酸罐头食品卫生操作规程》的第4.6.8款执行。

6.7 热处理之后，填充的、密封容器应该按照《国际推荐低酸和酸化低酸罐头食品卫生操作规程》的第7.7条处理。

7 标签

除了第5.2条（辐照食品）不相关外，应按照《预包装食品标签通用标准》（Ref. No. CODEX STAN 1－1985）的规定。同时还应标注：

7.1 食品名称

标签上标明食品的名称“咸牛肉”。

7.2 生产日期和贮存说明

对于有稳定货架期的咸牛肉罐头产品，保质期应该标注到年份。

7.3 非零售容器的标签

非零售容器按照零售产品需要的标注内容，将食品名称、生产日期、贮存说明，以及批检验合格证明、制造商、批发商名称、地址必须标注在容器上，除此之外的内容可以标识在容器上，也可以标明在产品附随的文件上。

批检验合格证和生产商或批发商的名称、地址可由一个识别标识所替代，但此识别标识须能在附随的文件中被明确地辨认。

8 分析方法

见食品法典第13卷

8.1 亚硝酸盐

推荐方法：ISO/DIS 2918。

8.2 铅

按照AOAC（1990，15th Edition，934.07），食品中铅的测定（双硫腙比色法）。

8.3 锡

按照 AOAC（1990，15th Edition，985.16），马口铁罐头食品中锡的测定（原子吸收分光光度法）。

CODEX STANDARD FOR CORNED BEEF

(*CODEX STAN 88 – 1981 Rev. 1 – 1991*)

1 SCOPE

This standard applies to canned beef products designated as "Corned Beef" and sold in hermetically sealed containers which have been heat treated after sealing to such an extent that the product is shelf-stable.

It does not apply to meat products of the type "Corned Beef" with compositional characteristics different from those specified. These products shall be designated with a qualifying statement which describes the true nature in such a way that it does not mislead the consumer and that it does not lead to confusion with products covered by this standard.

2 DESCRIPTION

Corned beef is chopped, cured, boneless carcase meat from animals of bovine species and may include head meat, heart meat and skirt meat.

The product shall be prepared from coarsely cut beef which has been precooked or a mixture of such precooked beef to which a maximum of 5% raw beef has been added; in either case, the meat shall be cured before or after filling into the container.

The heat treatment shall be applied after the container is sealed and shall be sufficient to ensure that the product is shelf-stable and that it presents no public health hazard.

Subsidiary Definition

Hermetically sealed container means a container which is completely sealed and impermeable and which is made of any appropriate material which is suitable for the product covered by the standard.

3 ESSENTIAL COMPOSITION AND QUALITY FACTORS

3.1 Essential Ingredients

- uncured beef;
- curing ingredients consisting of food-grade salt and sodium or potassium nitrite.

3.2 Optional Ingredients

- sucrose, invert sugar, dextrose (glucose), lactose, maltose, glucose syrup (including corn syrup).

3.3 Composition

The total protein content in the final product shall not be less than 21% m/m.

3.4 Essential Quality Factors

3.4.1 Raw Material

The meat from which the product is prepared shall be of a quality suitable for human consumption and free from objectionable odours and flavours.

3.4.2 Final Products

The final product shall be clean and substantially free from staining and contamination from the container. The meat shall be uniformly and thoroughly cured and the product shall be capable of being sliced, when chilled.

4 FOOD ADDITIVES

	Maximum Ingoing Amount
4.1 Preservatives	
4.1.1 Nitrite, potassium and (or) sodium salts	100mg/kg total nitrite expressed as sodium nitrite **Maximum level calculated on the total net content of the final product**
4.1.2 Nitrite, potassium and (or) sodium salts	50mg/kg total nitrite expressed as sodium nitrite
4.1.3 Potassium chloride	Limited by Good Manufacturing Practice
4.2 Antioxidants	
4.2.1 Ascorbic acid and its sodium salt	300mg/kg (expressed as ascorbic acid singly or in combination)
4.2.2 Iso-ascorbic acid and its sodium salt	

4.3 Carry-over

Section 3 of the Principle relating to the Carry-Over of Additives into Food, as set forth in Section 5.2, Volume 1 of the Codex Alimentarius, shall apply.

5 CONTAMINANTS

	Maximum Level
5.1 Lead (Pb)	1mg/kg❶
5.2 Tin (Sn)	
5.2.1 Tin (Sn): For products in tinplate	200mg/kg❶
5.2.2 Tin (Sn): For products in other	50mg/kg❶

❶ Temporarily endorsed.

6 HYGIENE

6.1 It is recommended that the Recommended International Code of Hygienic Practice for Processed Meat and Poultry Products [Ref. No. CAC/RCP 13 – 1976 (Rev. 1, 1985)], the Recommended International Code of Hygienic Practice for Low-Acid and Acidified Low-Acid Canned Foods [Ref. No. CAC/RCP 23 – 1979 (Rev. 1, 1989)], the Recommended International Code of Practice-General Principles of Food Hygiene [Ref. No. CAC/RCP 1 – 1969 (Rev. 2, 1985)] and the Recommended International Code of Hygienic Practice for Fresh Meat (CAC/RCP 11 – 1976) should apply.

6.2 All meat used in the manufacture of corned beef shall have been subjected to the inspection processes prescribed in the Code of Hygienic Practice for Fresh Meat and in the Code for Ante-Mortem and Post-Mortem Inspection of Slaughter Animals and for Ante-Mortem and Post-Mortem Judgement of Slaughter Animals and Meat (CAC/RCP 41 – 1993). It shall have been passed by an inspector as fit for human consumption. Meat shall not, subsequent to being examined by an inspector, have been exposed to contamination or processed or handled or subjected to the addition of any harmful substance, which renders it unfit for human consumption.

6.3 Raw or semi-processed meat and corned beef shall be handled, stored or transported in an establishment in a manner that will protect the meat and the corned beef from contamination and deterioration.

6.4 Corned beef shall be packed in hermetically sealed containers in compliance with Sub-section 7.4 of the Recommended International Code of Hygienic Practice for Low-Acid and Acidified Low-Acid Canned Foods.

6.5 Corned beef shall be thermally processed in compliance with Sub-sections 7.5 and 7.6.1 to 7.6.7 inclusive, of the Recommended International Code of Hygienic Practice for Low-Acid and Acidified Low-Acid Canned Foods.

6.6 The cooling of the thermally processed filled and sealed containers shall be carried out in compliance with Sub-section 4.6.8 of the Recommended International Code of Hygienic Practice for Low-Acid and Acidified Low-Acid Canned Foods.

6.7 After thermal processing the fitted, sealed containers shall be handled in compliance with Sub-section 7.7 of the Recommended International Code of Hygienic Practice for Low-Acid and Acidified Low-Acid Canned Foods.

7 LABELLING

The provisions of the Codex General Standard for the Labelling of Prepackaged Foods (CODEX STAN 1 – 1985), excepting Section 5.2 (Irradiated Foods) which is not relevant, shall apply:

7.1 The Name of the Food

The name of the food to be declared on the label shall be "Corned Beef".

7.2 Date Marking and Storage Instructions

For canned corned beef which is a shelf-stable product the date of minimum durability shall be indicated by the year.

7.3 Labelling of Non-Retail Containers

Information, as appropriate needed for labelling of retail containers is given either on the non-retail container or in accompanying documents except that the name of the food, date marking and storage instructions, lot identification and the name and address of the manufacturer or packer shall appear on the non-retail container.

However, lot identification, and the name and address of the manufacturer or packer may be replaced by an identification mark provided that such a mark is clearly identifiable with the accompanying documents.

8 METHODS OF ANALYSIS

See Codex Alimentarius Volume 13

8.1 Nitrite

Recommended method: ISO/DIS 2918

8.2 Lead

According to the AOAC (1990, 15th Edition), Lead in Food by General Dithizone Method, 934.07.

8.3 Tin

According to AOAC (1990, 15th Edition), Tin in Canned Foods by Atomic Absorption Spectrophotometric Method, 985.16.

午餐肉标准

CODEX STANDARD FOR LUNCHEON MEAT

(*CODEX STAN 89 – 1981 Rev. 1 – 1991*)

1 范围

本标准适用于用适当的包装材料包装的“午餐肉（Luncheon Meat[1]）”产品。

2 描述

本产品应是经过捣碎、腌制以及烟熏过的肉类或禽肉类，以及上述肉类、禽肉类的混合物精制而成的。

本产品可含有黏结剂成分或不含任何黏结剂。

对本产品进行的热处理、腌制和包装等加工处理应严格按照以下 6.4 和 6.5 条款的要求进行，确保产品的贮藏、运输、销售符合卫生要求，不存在公共卫生风险。

附属定义

以下定义适用于本标准：

可食用下水料是指那些经过检查，适合人类消费的下水料，包括肺（但不包括摘除后在热水中浸泡烫洗过的动物肺脏），不包括耳朵、头皮、猪鼻（包括猪嘴和喷嘴）、黏膜、肌肉、生殖器、乳房、肠和膀胱。可食用下水料也包括家禽的皮。

肉是指在屠宰场屠宰的任何哺乳动物的可食用部分，包括可食用下水料。

包装是指产品用某种材料制造的容器进行包装，包装材料在正常条件下不会造成污染。

禽肉是指任何在屠宰场屠宰的家禽的可食用部分，这些家禽包括鸡、火鸡、鸭、鹅、珍珠鸡和鸽子。

3 基本组成和质量指标

3.1 基本配料

——畜肉、禽肉或者它们的混合物，不包括可食用的下水料；

——水；

——腌制配料，包括食用盐和亚硝酸钠或亚硝酸钾等。

---

[1] 无论文本的语言形式如何，这里只用英语。

3.2 可选配料

——可食用下水料，肉或禽肉来源动物自身的脂肪及其腌制或未腌制的猪肉皮；
—— 碳水化合物和蛋白黏结物，比如：
——谷粉，面粉，马铃薯、甘薯或谷物制成的淀粉；
——面包，饼干或面包制品；
——奶粉，脱脂奶粉，黄油奶粉，酪蛋白酸，乳清粉，鸡蛋蛋白，干血制品，植物蛋白制品；
——蔗糖，转化糖，葡萄糖（右旋糖），乳糖，麦芽糖，葡萄糖浆（包括玉米糖浆）；
——香料，佐料和增味物质；
——水溶性，芳香性水解蛋白。

3.3 成分

	含黏结剂的产品	不含黏结剂和可食用下水料（但包括哺乳动物的心、舌和加热过的肉）的产品（但可包括哺乳动物的心、舌和加热过的肉）
添加肉的最小含量	80%❶	90%
脂肪最大含量	35%	30%

3.4 基本质量指标

3.4.1 原料

本产品的原料成分应该达到人类食用的质量要求，并且没有令人不适的气味和滋味。

3.4.2 成品

产品应干净，并且没有染色，没有来自于容器的污染。肉和禽肉应该是均匀一致、腌制透彻，并且可以切片。

4 食品添加剂

	最大添加量
4.1 防腐剂	
4.1.1 亚硝酸盐，钾盐和（或）钠盐	亚硝酸盐 200mg/kg（以亚硝酸钠计） 按成品净含量计算的最大值
4.1.2 亚硝酸盐，钾盐和（或）钠盐	亚硝酸盐 125mg/kg（以亚硝酸钠计）
4.1.3 氯化钾	按照良好操作规范
4.2 抗氧化剂	
4.2.1 抗坏血酸及其钠盐	500mg/kg（以抗坏血酸单体或复合物表示）
4.2.2 同抗坏血酸及其钠盐	500mg/kg（以抗坏血酸单体或复合物表示）

❶ 肉的含量包括畜肉、可食用内脏以及禽肉。

4.3 香料

按照食品法典中确定的天然和等同于天然的香料	**按照良好操作规范**

4.4 增味剂

4.4.1 5′-鸟苷酸二钠	**按照良好操作规范**
4.4.2 5′-肌苷酸二钠	**按照良好操作规范**
4.4.3 谷氨酸钠	**按照良好操作规范**

4.5 酸度调节剂

4.5.1 葡萄糖酸 δ 内脂	3 000mg/kg
4.5.2 柠檬酸钠	**按照良好操作规范**

4.6 水分保持剂

4.6.1 磷酸盐（天然含有的或添加的❶）	8 000mg/kg（以 P_2O_5 计）
4.6.2 添加的磷酸盐（一元，二元和多元）钠盐和钾盐❷	3 000mg/kg（以 P_2O_5 计），单体或者复合物

4.7 颜色

赤藓红（Cl 45430）替代颜色损耗（仅适于含有黏合剂的产品）	15mg/kg

4.8 残留

按食品法典第 1 卷 5.2 所列示的添加剂，采用法则第三部分中关于食品添加剂的残留标准。

5 污染物

	最大限量
5.1 铅（Pb）	0.5mg/kg❸
5.2 锡（Sn）	
5.2.1 锡（Sn）：马口铁罐装产品	200mg/kg❸
5.2.2 锡（Sn）：其他容器包装的产品	50mg/kg❸

6 卫生

6.1 推荐采用《国际推荐肉禽产品加工卫生操作规程》［Ref. No. CAC/RCP 13 - 1976（Rev. 1，

❶ 天然的磷酸盐（以 P_2O_5 计，mg/kg），按蛋白质（%）的 250 倍计算。

❷ Having INS Nos. 339，340，450，451 和 452。

❸ 暂定标准。

1985)]和《国际推荐禽类加工卫生操作规程》(Ref. No. CAC/RCP14 - 1976)中的可适用部分，以及采用《食品卫生通则国际推荐标准》[Ref. No. CAC/RCP 1 - 1969 (Rev. 2, 1985)],《国际推荐鲜肉加工卫生操作规程》(CAC/RCP 11 - 1976)和《国际推荐低酸和酸化低酸罐头食品卫生操作规程》[Ref. No. CAC/RCP 23 - 1979 (Rev. 1, 1989)] 中的可适用部分。

6.2 制造午餐肉的原料肉[1]都应该按照《国际推荐鲜肉加工卫生操作规程》和《国际推荐禽类加工卫生操作规程》的可适用部分进行检查。源自哺乳动物的肉应该按照《国际推荐动物宰前宰后检验及鉴定的操作规程》(CAC/RCP 41 - 1993)进行检验。应该由检查员判断其是否适合人们消费。不应该在检查后又接触污染物，或者在加工、处理的过程中有不适合人类食用的有害物质的加入。

6.3 未加工或半成品的肉和午餐肉应该在一定的设备中，按照一定的方式进行处理、分类和运输，以保护肉和午餐肉不被污染和变质。

6.4 午餐肉应该依照《国际推荐低酸和酸化低酸罐头食品卫生操作规程》第7.4节中的规定用密封容器包装。

6.5 午餐肉包装之前进行热力杀菌处理，并且应该采取把污染减少到最小的方式进行包装，因此，只要本产品按照标签指示的方式贮存、运输和销售，该产品就能防止变质，而不会造成公众卫生风险。在通常的情况下，容器自身也应不造成任何的卫生风险或者带有污染。容器应干净，并能证明是真空包装。

6.6 午餐肉应该按照《国际推荐低酸和酸化低酸罐头食品卫生操作规程》中的第7.5条、第7.6.1款至第7.6.7款(包含第7.6.7款)进行热处理。

6.7 灌制、密封的罐头热处理后冷却应该按照《国际推荐低酸和酸化低酸罐头食品卫生操作规程》的第4.6.8款执行。

6.8 热处理之后，灌制的、密封容器应该按照《国际推荐低酸和酸化低酸罐头食品卫生操作规程》的第7.7条处理。

7 标签

除《预包装食品标签通用标准》(Ref. No. CODEX STAN 1 - 1985)的规定外，还应标注：

7.1 食品名称

标签上标明食品的名称“午餐肉”。

为避免误导消费者，产品名称应与该产品中使用的各种黏结剂和可食用下水料，以及肉、禽肉及其混合物的来源动物的种类等说明有关联。

7.2 成分表

成分表应该标明肉、禽肉及其混合物来源动物的种类。

7.3 生产日期和贮存说明

7.3.1 对于有稳定货架期的产品，最短的保质期应该标注到年。

7.3.2 对于非稳定货架期的产品，比如在通常的贮存和销售条件下，保质期不超过18个月的，那

[1] 在本节中所用的词“肉”包括鲜肉、可食用下水料和禽肉。

么在提供给消费者或者供餐饮的包装上，最短保质期应按年月日标明。

7.3.3 如果不是直接销售给消费者或供餐饮的非耐贮存包装产品，应该标注适当的贮存和销售说明。

7.4 非零售罐头的标识

非零售罐头按照零售产品需要的标注内容，将食品名称、生产日期、贮存说明，以及批次证明、制造商、批发商名称、地址必须标注在罐头上，或者标注在随产品所附的说明书上。

批次证明和生产商或批发商的名称、地址可由一个识别标志所替代，此识别标识能在附随的文件中被明确地辨别认可。

8 分析方法

见食品法典第13卷。

8.1 脂肪

推荐方法：肉与肉制品中总脂肪的测定（ISO Recommendation R 1443）。

8.2 亚硝酸盐

推荐方法：ISO/DIS 2918。

8.3 铅

按照AOAC（1990，15th Edition，934.07），食品中铅的测定（双硫腙比色法）。

8.4 锡

按照AOAC（1990，15th Edition，985.16），马口铁罐头食品中锡的测定（原子吸收分光光度法）。

CODEX STANDARD FOR LUNCHEON MEAT

(CODEX STAN 89 - 1981 Rev. 1 - 1991)

1 SCOPE

This standard applies to products designated as "Luncheon Meat"[1] which have been packed in any suitable packing material.

2 DESCRIPTION

The product shall be prepared from meat or poultry meat or a combination of these as defined below which has been comminuted and cured and which may have been smoked.

The product may or may not contain binders.

The heat treatment to which the product has been subjected and the type of cure and packaging shall be sufficient to ensure that the product presents no public health hazard and remains wholesome under the conditions of storage, transport and sale as indicated in Sub-sections 6. 4 and 6. 5.

Subsidiary Definitions

For the purpose of this standard:

Edible offal means such offals as have been passed as fit for human consumption including lungs (but not if the animal from which the lungs have been taken has been scalded by immersion in hot water) but not including ears, scalp, snouts (including lips and muzzle), mucous membrane, sinews, genital system, udders, intestines and urinary bladder. Edible offal also includes poultry skin.

Meat means the edible part including edible offal from any mammal slaughtered in an abattoir.

Packaged means packed in a container manufactured of materials which do not permit contamination under normal conditions of handling.

Poultry meat means the edible part of any domesticated birds including chickens, turkeys, ducks, geese, guinea-fowls or pigeons slaughtered in an abattoir.

3 ESSENTIAL COMPOSITION AND QUALITY FACTORS

3. 1 Essential Ingredients

- meat or poultry meat or a combination of these excluding edible offal;

---

[1] Only the English language shall be used whatever the language of the text.

- water;
- curing ingredients consisting of food-grade salt and sodium or potassium nitrite.

3.2 Optional Ingredients

- edible offal, fat per se, cured and uncured pork rind per se;
- carbohydrate and protein binders such as:
- meal, flour or starch prepared from grain, or potato or sweet potato;
- bread, biscuit or bakery products;
- milk powder, skim milk powder, butter milk powder, caseinate, whey powder, egg protein, dried blood products, vegetable protein products;
- sucrose, invert sugar, dextrose (glucose), lactose, maltose, glucose syrup (including corn syrup);
- spices, seasonings and condiments;
- water soluble, aromatic hydrolysed protein.

3.3 Composition

	Product with binder	Product without binder with and edible offal (but binder may include heart, tongue or heat meat from mammals)
Minimum ingoing meat content	80% ❶	90%
Maximum fat content	35%	30%

3.4 Essential Quality Factors

3.4.1 Raw Material

The ingredients from which the product is prepared shall be of a quality suitable for human consumption and free from objectionable odours and flavours.

3.4.2 Final Product

The product shall be clean and substantially free from staining and contamination from the container. The meat and poultry meat shall be uniformly and thoroughly cured and the product shall be capable of being sliced.

4 FOOD ADDITIVES

	Maximum Ingoing Amount
4.1 Preservatives	
4.1.1 Nitrite, potassium and (or) sodium salts	200mg/kg total nitrite expressed as sodium nitrite Maximum Level Calculated on the Total Net Content of the Final Product
4.1.2 Nitrite, potassium and (or) sodium salts	125mg/kg total nitrite expressed as sodium nitrite
4.1.3 Potassium chloride	Limited by Good Manufacturing Practice

❶ The meat content includes meat, edible offal and poultry meat.

4.2 Antioxidants

4.2.1	Ascorbic acid and its sodium salt	500mg/kg (expressed as ascorbic acid singly or in combination)
4.2.2	Iso-ascorbic acid and its sodium salt	500mg/kg (expressed as ascorbic acid singly or in combination)

4.3 Flavours

Natural flavouring substances and nature-identical flavouring Limited by Good Manufacturing Practice substances defined in the Codex Alimentarius.

4.4 Flavour Enhancers

4.4.1	5′-Guanylate, disodium	Limited by Good Manufacturing Practice
4.4.2	5′-Inosinate, disodium	Limited by Good Manufacturing Practice
4.4.3	Monosodium glutamate	Limited by Good Manufacturing Practice

4.5 Acidity Regulators

4.5.1	Glucono-delta-lactone	3 000mg/kg
4.5.2	Sodium citrate	**Limited by Good Manufacturing Practice**

4.6 Water Retention Agents

4.6.1	Phosphates (naturally present plus added)❶	8 000mg/kg (expressed as P_2O_5)
4.6.2	Added phosphates (mono-, di-andpoly-), sodium and potassium salts❷	3 000mg/kg (expressed as P_2O_5), singly or in combination

4.7 Colours

Erythrosine (CI 45430) to replace loss of colour (for the product with binder only)	15mg/kg

4.8 Carry-Over

Section 3 of the Principle relating to the Carry-Over of Additives into Food, as set forth in Section 5.2, Volume 1 of the Codex Alimentarius shall apply.

5 CONTAMINANTS Maximum Level

5.1 Lead (Pb) 0.5mg/kg❸

5.2 Tin (Sn)

5.2.1 Tin(Sn): For products in tinplate containers 200mg/kg❸

---

❶ Natural phosphate (mg/kg P_2O_5) calculated as 250 × % protein.

❷ Having INS Nos. 339, 340, 450, 451 and 452.

❸ Temporarily endorsed.

5.2.2 Tin(Sn): For products in other containers 50mg/kg[3]

6 HYGIENE

6.1 It is recommended that the Recommended International Code of Hygienic Practice for Processed Meat and Poultry Products [Ref. No. CAC/RCP 13 – 1976 (Rev. 1, 1985)], where applicable the Recommended International Code of Hygienic Practice for Poultry Processing (Ref. No. CAC/RCP 14 – 1976), the Recommended International Code of Practice-General Principles of Food Hygiene [Ref. No. CAC/RCP 1 – 1969 (Rev. 2, 1985)], the Recommended International Code of Hygienic Practice for Fresh Meat (CAC/RCP 11 – 1976) and, where applicable, the Recommended International Code of Hygienic Practice for Low-Acid and Acidified Low-Acid Canned Foods [Ref. No. CAC/RCP 23 – 1979 (Rev. 1, 1989)] should apply.

6.2 All meat[1] used in the manufacture of luncheon meat shall have been subjected to the inspection processes prescribed in the Code of Hygienic Practice for Fresh Meat and, where applicable, the Code of Hygienic Practice for Poultry Processing. Meat from mammals shall have been inspected according to the Code for Ante-Mortem and Post-Mortem Inspection of Slaughter Animals and for Ante-Mortem and Post/Mortem Judgement of Slaughter Animals and Meat (CAC/RCP 41 – 1993). It shall have been passed by an inspector as fit for human consumption. Meat shall not, subsequent to being examined by an inspector, have been exposed to contamination or processed or handled or subjected to the addition of any harmful substance, which renders it unfit for human consumption.

6.3 Raw or semi-processed meat and luncheon meat shall be handled, sorted or transported in an establishment in a manner that will protect the meat and the luncheon meat from contamination and deterioration.

6.4 Luncheon Meat shall be packed in hermetically sealed containers in compliance with Subsection 7.4 of the Recommended International Code of Hygienic Practice for Low-Acid and Acidified Low-Acid Canned Foods.

6.5 Luncheon Meat is heat treated before packaging it shall be packaged in such a way that contamination is kept to a minimum so that the product will withstand spoilage and present no public health hazard under the conditions of handling storage, transport and sale indicated on the label. The containers themselves shall not present any health hazard or permit contamination under normal conditions of handling. They shall be clean, and where applicable, show evidence of vacuum.

6.6 Luncheon Meat shall be thermally processed in compliance with Sub-sections 7.5 and 7.6.1 to 7.6.7 inclusive, of the Recommended International Code of Hygienic Practice for Low-Acid and Acidified Low-Acid Canned Foods.

6.7 The cooling of the thermally processed filled and sealed containers shall be carried out in compliance with Sub – section 4.6.8 of the Recommended International Code of Hygienic Practice for Low-Acid and Acidified Low-Acid Canned Foods.

6.8 After thermal processing the fitted, sealed containers shall be handled in compliance with Subsection 7.7 of the Recommended International Code of Hygienic Practice for Low-Acid and Acidified Low-Acid Canned Foods.

---

[1] Wherever the word "meat" is used in this section, it includes meat, edible offal and poultry meat.

7 LABELLING

The provisions of the Codex General Standard for the Labelling of Prepackaged Foods (Ref. No. CODEX STAN 1 - 1985), shall apply:

7.1 The Name of the Food

The name of the food to be declared on the label shall be "Luncheon Meat".

A declaration of the presence of binders and of edible offal and a declaration indicating the species of animal from which the meat, poultry meat or a combination of these is derived shall be given in connection with the name of the product if their omission would mislead the consumer.

7.2 List of Ingredients

The list of ingredients shall indicate the species of animals from which the meat, poultry meat or a combination of these is derived.

7.3 Date Marking and Storage Instructions

7.3.1 For shelf-stable products the date of minimum durability shall be declared by the year.

7.3.2 For products which are not shelf-stable i.e. which may be expected not to keep for at least 18 months in normal conditions of storage and sale, and which are packaged in a container ready for offer to the consumer or for catering purposes, the date of minimum durability shall be declared by day, month and year.

7.3.3 For products which are not shelf-stable and which are packaged in containers not sold directly to the consumer or for catering purposes, adequate storage and distribution instructions shall be declared.

7.4 Labelling of Non-Retail Containers

Information, as appropriate needed for the labelling of retail containers is given either on the non-retail containers or in accompanying documents except that the name of the food, date marking and storage instructions, lot identification and the name and address of the manufacturer or packer shall appear on the non-retail container.

However, lot identification, and the name and address of the manufacturer or packer may be replaced by an identification mark provided that such mark is clearly identifiable with the accompanying documents.

8 METHODS OF ANALYSIS

See Codex Alimentarius Volume 13.

8.1 Fat

Recommended method: Determination of Total Fat Content of Meat and Meat Products, ISO Recommendation R 1443.

8.2 Nitrite

Recommended method: ISO/DIS 2918.

8.3 Lead

According to the AOAC (1990, 15th Edition), Lead in Food by General Dithizone Method, 934.07.

8.4 Tin

According to the AOAC (1990, 15th Edition), Tin in Canned Food by Atomic Absorption Spectrophotometric Method, 985.16.

熟制腌火腿（后腿）标准

CODEX STANDARD FOR COOKED CURED HAM

(CODEX STAN 96 - 1981 Rev. 1 - 1991)

1　范围

本标准适用于命名为“熟制腌火腿”，以本标准第6.4和第6.5条款中定义的以任何适当的包装材料包装的产品。

本标准不适用于那些具有复杂特性的熟火腿产品。这些产品的性状应该给予真实的描述，从而避免误导消费者，也不会与采用本标准的产品产生混淆。

2　描述

本产品中的肉应该采用猪后腿肉，它是从不超过髋骨末端的侧边的剩余部分横切下来的。所有的骨头、分离的软骨、肌腱和韧带都应该剔除。皮和脂肪去除或不去除均可。

肉应该腌制，并且可以烟熏，添加调料和香料。

对本产品进行的热处理、腌制和包装等加工应按照本标准中第6.4和第6.5条款的要求进行，确保产品在贮藏、运输、销售过程中保持卫生，不会造成公众卫生风险。

3　基本成分和质量指标

3.1　基本配料

——未腌制的后腿；

——由水、食用盐和亚硝酸钠或亚硝酸钾组成的盐卤。

3.2　可选配料

——蔗糖，转化糖，葡萄糖（右旋糖），乳糖，麦芽糖，葡萄糖浆（包括玉米糖浆），蜂蜜；

——香料，佐料和调味品；

——水溶性、芳香性水解蛋白；

——食用明胶。

3.3　基本质量指标

3.3.1　原料——本产品所用的原料应该达到适合人们消费的质量要求，并且没有令人不适的气味和滋味。

3.3.2 成品——产品应该是干净的，并且没有染色、没有源自容器的污染。肉质应该是均匀一致、腌制透彻，并且产品应该可以被切片。

3.4 肉的含量

不含脂肪的肉中蛋白质含量平均百分率 >18.0%

不含脂肪的肉中蛋白质含量最小百分率 =16.5%（绝对最小值）

（对于罐装产品肉蛋白质的含量按罐头的总容量计算，如果添加了胶质，则要进行校正，参见第8.4条款）。

4 食品添加剂

	最大添加量
4.1 防腐剂	
4.1.1 亚硝酸盐，钠盐和（或）钾盐	200mg/kg（以亚硝酸钠计）
	按成品净含量计算的最大限值
4.1.2 亚硝酸盐，钠盐和（或）钾盐	125mg/kg（以亚硝酸钠计）
4.1.3 氯化钾	按照良好操作规范
4.2 抗氧化剂	
4.2.1 抗坏血酸及其钠盐	500mg/kg(以抗坏血酸单体或复合物表示)
4.2.2 异抗坏血酸及其钠盐	500mg/kg(以抗坏血酸单体或复合物表示)
4.3 香料	
4.3.1 按照食品法典中确定的天然和等同于天然的香料	按照良好操作规范
4.3.2 按JECFA规范评价的熏制调味料	按照良好操作规范
4.4 增味剂	
4.4.1 5′-鸟苷酸二钠	按照良好操作规范
4.4.2 5′-肌苷酸二钠	按照良好操作规范
4.4.3 谷氨酸钠	按照良好操作规范
4.5 酸度调节剂	
柠檬酸盐，钠盐	按照良好操作规范
4.6 水分保持剂	
4.6.1 磷酸盐（包括天然含有的及添加的）❶	8 000mg/kg（以 P_2O_5 计）
4.6.2 添加的磷酸盐（一价盐，二价盐和多价盐）钠盐和钾盐❷	3 000mg/kg（以 P_2O_5 计），单体或者复合物

❶ 原有的磷酸盐（以 P_2O_5 计，mg/kg），按蛋白质（%）的250倍计算。

❷ 包括 INS Nos. 339，340，450，451 和 452.

4.7 增稠剂

4.7.1 琼脂	**按照良好操作规范**
4.7.2 角叉（菜）胶	**按照良好操作规范**
4.7.3 藻酸盐，钾盐和（或）钠盐	10mg/kg

4.8 残留

按食品法典第1卷5.2所列示的添加剂，采用法则第三部分中关于食品添加剂的残留标准。

5 污染物

	最大限量
5.1 铅（Pb）	0.5mg/kg❶
5.2 锡（Sn）	
5.2.1 锡（Sn）：马口铁罐装产品	200mg/kg❷
5.2.2 锡（Sn）：其他容器包装的产品	50mg/kg❷

6 卫生

6.1 熟制腌火腿生产的卫生标准推荐采用《国际推荐肉禽产品加工卫生操作规程》[Ref. No. CAC/RCP 13-1976（Rev. 1，1985）]，《国际推荐鲜肉加工卫生操作规程》（CAC/RCP 11-1976），《食品卫生通则国际推荐标准》[Ref. No. CAC/RCP 1-1969（Rev. 2，1985）]，以及采用《国际推荐低酸和酸化低酸罐头食品卫生操作规程》[Ref. No. CAC/RCP 23-1979（Rev. 1，1989）] 中的可适用部分。

6.2 熟制腌火腿生产中所使用的肉应该按照《国际推荐鲜肉加工卫生操作规程》和《国际推荐动物宰前宰后检验及鉴定的操作规程》（CAC/RCP 41-1993）进行检验。应该通过质检人员的检查，认定其是适合人类食用的。通过检查后的肉类不应该放置在有污染源的地方，不能在其后的加工、操作等处理过程中混入任何有害物质，导致其不适合食用。

6.3 未加工或半成品的肉和熟制腌火腿的处理、贮存或运输应该在一定的设备中，并按照能够保护肉和熟火腿不被污染和变质的方式进行。

6.4 熟制腌火腿应该依照《国际推荐低酸和酸化低酸罐头食品卫生操作规程》第7.4条款中的规定用密封容器包装。

6.5 如果熟制腌火腿包装之前进行加热杀菌处理，应该采取能把污染减少到最小的方式进行包装，从而使本产品在按照标签指示的方式操作、贮存、运输和销售过程中不变质，不会造成公众卫生风险。在通常的情况下，容器自身也不应该造成任何的卫生风险或者带有污染。容器应该是干净的，并在需要时，用真空包装，并予以标示。

6.6 熟制腌火腿应该按照《国际推荐低酸和酸化低酸罐头食品卫生操作规程》中的第7.5条款、第7.6.1条款至第7.6.7条款（包含第7.6.7条款）规定进行热处理。

---

❶ 暂定标准。

❷ 包括 INS Nos. 339，340，450，451 和 452.

6.7 灌制了熟制腌火腿并密封的罐头加热处理后的冷却应该按照《国际推荐低酸和酸化低酸罐头食品卫生操作规程》的第4.6.8条款的规定进行。

6.8 热处理之后，已灌制密封罐头应该按照《国际推荐低酸和酸化低酸罐头食品卫生操作规程》的第7.7条款的规定进行处理。

7 标签

标签上除按《预包装食品标签通用标准》（Ref. No. CODEX STAN 1 - 1985）的规定标识外，还应标注如下内容：

7.1 食品名称

7.1.1 标签上标明食品的名称“熟制腌火腿”。

7.1.2 本产品的名称应该包括适当的说明，如：

——“带皮”；

——“带原汁”；

——“添加了XX”，适用于添加白明胶，琼脂，藻酸盐或角叉（菜）胶时；

——“熏制”；

——“添加了烟熏剂”。

7.1.3 如果产品名称将误导消费者，则应该随同产品名称一起对产品的制备、加工方法或规格加以正确的说明。

7.2 生产日期和贮存说明

7.2.1 对于有稳定货架期的产品，最短的保质期应该标注到年份。

7.2.2 对于非稳定货架期的产品，比如在通常的贮存和销售条件下，保质期不超过18个月的，那么提供给消费者或者供餐饮的预包装产品，最短保质期应该标注年月日。

7.2.3 如果不是直接销售给消费者或供餐饮的非稳定货架期包装产品，应该提供适当的贮存和销售说明。

7.3 非零售罐头产品的标签

非零售罐头按照零售产品需要的标注内容，将食品名称、生产日期、贮存说明，以及批次证明、生产商或包装商名称、地址等标注在非零售罐头上，或者标注在随产品所附的说明书上。

然而，批次证明、生产商或包装商的名称、地址可以被一个识别标志所替代，此识别标志可在所附的文件中被明确地辨别认可。

8 分析方法

见食品法典第13卷。

8.1 蛋白质

推荐方法：肉与肉制品中总蛋白含量的测定，（ISO Recommendation R 937）（氮的换算系数：6.25）。

8.2 脂肪

推荐方法：肉与肉制品中总脂肪的测定，（ISO Recommendation R 1443）。

8.3 亚硝酸盐

推荐方法：ISO/DIS 2 918。

8.4 添加了胶质的产品中蛋白质含量的校正

对于胶质添加量不明的熟制腌火腿产品，蛋白质含量应该从不含脂肪的肉中蛋白质的百分率中扣除0.5%。

8.5 铅

按照方法：AOAC（1990，15th Edition，934.07），食品中铅的测定（双硫腙比色法）。

8.6 锡

按照方法：AOAC（1990，15th Edition，985.16），马口铁罐头食品中锡的测定（原子吸收分光光度法）。

CODEX STANDARD FOR COOKED CURED HAM

(*CODEX STAN 96 - 1981 Rev. 1 - 1991*)

1 SCOPE

This standard applies to products designated as "Cooked Ham" packaged in any suitable packaging material as defined in sub-sections 6. 4 and 6. 5 below.

It does not apply to cooked ham products with compositional characteristics different from those specified. These products shall be designated with a qualifying statement which describes the true nature in such a way that it does not misled the consumer and that it does not lead to confusion with products covered by this Standard.

2 DESCRIPTION

The product shall be made of meat from the hind leg of a pig-divided transversely from the remainder of the side at a point not further anteriorly than the end of the hip bone. All bones and detached cartilage, tendons and ligaments shall be removed. Skin and fat may or may not be removed.

The meat shall be cured and may be smoked, spiced and (or) flavoured.

The heat treatment to which the product has been subjected and the type of cure and packaging shall be sufficient to ensure that the product presents no public health hazard and remains wholesome under the conditions of storage, transport and sale as indicated in Sub-sections 6. 4 and 6. 5.

3 ESSENTIAL COMPOSITION AND QUALITY FACTORS

3. 1 Essential Ingredients

- Uncured ham;
- Brine consisting of water and food-grade salt and sodium or potassium nitrite.

3. 2 Optional Ingredients

- Sucrose, invert sugar, dextrose (glucose), lactose, maltose, glucose syrup (including corn syrup), honey;
- Spices, seasonings and condiments;
- Water soluble, aromatic hydrolyzed protein;
- Food grade gelatine.

3.3 Essential Quality Factors

3.3.1 Raw material-The ingredients from which the product is prepared shall be of a quality suitable for human consumption and free from objectionable odours and flavours.

3.3.2 Final product-The product shall be clean and substantially free from staining and contamination from the container. The meat shall be uniformly and thoroughly cured and the product shall be capable of being sliced.

3.4 Meat Content

- Average percentage meat-protein on fat-free basis ≥18.0%
- Minimum percentage meat-protein on fat-free basis =16.5% (absolute minimum)

(For canned products the percentage of meat-protein is calculated on the total content of the can and corrected for gelatine, if added-see Sub-section 8.4).

4 FOOD ADDITIVES

	Maximum Ingoing Amount
4.1 Preservatives	
4.1.1 Nitrite, potassium and (or) sodium salts expressed as sodium nitrite	200mg/kg total nitrite
	Maximum Level Calculated on the Total Net Content of the Final Product
4.1.2 Nitrite, potassium and (or) sodium salts expressed as sodium nitrite	125mg/kg total nitrite
4.1.3 Potassium chloride	Limited by Good Manufacturing Practice
4.2 Antioxidants	
4.2.1 Ascorbic acid and its sodium salt combination	500mg/kg (expressed as ascorbic acid singly or in)
4.2.2 Iso-ascorbic acid and its sodium salt combination	500mg/kg (expressed as ascorbic acid singly or in)
4.3 Flavours	
4.3.1 Natural flavouring substances and nature-identical flavouring substances defined in the Codex Alimentarius	Limited by Good Manufacturing Practice
4.3.2 Smoke flavourings as evaluated by Practice JECFA	Limited by Good Manufacturing
4.4 Flavour Enhancers	
4.4.1 5′-Guanylate, disodium	Limited by Good Manufacturing Practice

4. 4. 2	5′-Inosinate, disodium	Limited by Good Manufacturing Practice
4. 4. 3	Monosodium glutamate	Limited by Good Manufacturing Practice

4. 5 Acidity Regulators

Citrate, sodium salt Limited by Good Manufacturing Practice.

4. 6 Water Retention Agents

4. 6. 1	Phosphates (naturally present plus added)❶	8 000mg/kg (expressed as P_2O_5)
4. 6. 2	Added phosphates (mono-, di- and as poly-), sodium and potassium salts❷	3 000mg/kg (expressed P_2O_5), singly or in combination

4. 7 Thickeners

4. 7. 1	Agar	Limited by Good Manufacturing Practice
4. 7. 2	Carrageenan	Limited by Good Manufacturing Practice
4. 7. 3	Alginates, potassium and (or) sodium salts	10mg/kg

4. 8 Carry-Over

Section 3 of the Principle relating to the Carry-Over of Additives into Food, as set forth in Section 5. 2, Volume 1 of the Codex Alimentarius shall apply.

5 CONTAMINANTSp

		Maximum Level
5. 1	**Lead (Pb)**	0. 5mg/kg❸
5. 2	**Tin (Sn)**	
5. 2. 1	Tin (Sn): For products in tinplate containers	200mg/kg❸
5. 2. 2	Tin (Sn): For products in other containers	50mg/kg❸

6 HYGIENE

6. 1 It is recommended that the Recommended International Code of Hygienic Practice for Processed Meat and Poultry Products [Ref. No. CAC/RCP 13 – 1976 (Rev. 1, 1985)], the Recommended International Code of Hygienic Practice for Fresh Meat (CAC/RCP 11 – 1976), the Recommended International Code of Practice-General Principles of Food Hygiene [Ref. No. CAC/RCP 1 – 1969 (Rev. 2, 1985)] and, where applicable, the Recommended International Code of Hygienic Practice for Low-Acid and Acidified Low-Acid Canned Foods [Ref. No. CAC/RCP 23 – 1979 (Rev. 1, 1989)] should apply.

6. 2 All meat used in the manufacture of cooked cured ham shall have been subjected to the inspection

❶ Natural phosphate (mg/kg P_2O_5) calculated as 250 × % protein.

❷ Having INS Nos. 339, 340, 450, 451 and 452.

❸ Temporarily endorsed.

processes prescribed in the Code of Hygienic Practice for Fresh Meat and the Code for Ante-Mortem and Post-Mortem Inspection of Slaughter Animals and for Ante-Mortem and Post-Mortem Judgement of Slaughter Animals and Meat (CAC/RCP 41 - 1993). It shall have been passed by an inspector as fit for human consumption. Meat shall not, subsequent to being examined by an inspector, have been exposed to contamination or processed or handled or subjected to the addition of any harmful substance, which renders it unfit for human consumption.

6.3 Raw or semi-processed meat and cooked cured ham shall be handled, stored or transported in an establishment in a manner that will protect the meat and the cooked cured ham from contamination and deterioration.

6.4 Cooked cured ham shall be packed in hermetically sealed containers in compliance with Subsection 7.4 of the Recommended International Code of Hygienic Practice for Low-Acid and Acidified Low-Acid Canned Foods.

6.5 If cooked cured ham is heat treated before packaging it shall be packaged in such a way that contamination is kept to a minimum, so that the product will withstand spoilage and present no public health hazard under the conditions of handling, storage, transport and sale indicated on the label. The containers themselves shall not present any health hazard or permit contamination under normal conditions of handling. They shall be clean, and where applicable, show evidence of vacuum.

6.6 Cooked cured ham shall be thermally processed in compliance with Sub-sections 7.5 and 7.6.1 to 7.6.7 inclusive, of the Recommended International Code of Hygienic Practice for Low-Acid and Acidified Low-Acid Canned Foods.

6.7 The cooling of the thermally processed filled and sealed containers shall be carried out in compliance with Sub-section 4.6.8 of the Recommended International Code of Hygienic Practice for Low-Acid and Acidified Low-Acid Canned Foods.

6.8 After thermal processing the fitted, sealed containers shall be handled in compliance with Subsection 7.7 of the Recommended International Code of Hygienic Practice for Low-Acid and Acidified Low-Acid Canned Foods.

7 LABELLING

The provisions of the Codex General Standard for the Labelling of Prepackaged Foods (CODEX STAN 1 - 1985), the following specific provisions apply:

7.1 The Name of the Food

7.1.1 The name of the food to be declared on the label shall be "Cooked Ham".

7.1.2 The name of the product shall include, as appropriate, the designation:

- "with skin";
- "in/with natural juice";
- "X added" applying to gelatine, agar, alginates or carrageenan;
- "smoked";
- "smoking agent added".

7.1.3 A declaration that accurately describes the method of preparation, processing or presentation shall be given so as to appear simultaneously visible with the name of the product if its omission would mislead the consumer.

7. 2 Date Marking and Storage Instructions

7. 2. 1 For shelf-stable products the date of minimum durability shall be declared by the year.

7. 2. 2 For products which are not shelf-stable, i. e. which may be expected not to keep for at least 18 months in normal conditions of storage and sale, and which are packaged in a container ready for offer to the consumer or for catering purposes, the date of minimum durability shall be declared by day, month and year.

7. 2. 3 For products which are not shelf-stable and which are packaged in containers not sold directly to the consumer or for catering purposes, adequate storage and distribution instructions shall be declared.

7. 3 Labelling of Non-Retail Containers

Information, as appropriate needed for labelling of retail containers is given either on the non-retail containers or in accompanying documents except that the name of the food, date marking and storage instructions, lot identification and the name and address of the manufacturer or packer shall appear on the non-retail container.

However, lot identification, and the name and address of the manufacturer or packer, may be replaced by an identification mark provided that such mark is clearly identifiable with the accompanying documents.

8 METHODS OF ANALYSIS

See Codex Alimentarius Volume 13.

8. 1 Protein

Recommended method: Determination of Nitrogen Content of Meat and Meat Products, ISO Recommendation R 1443.

8. 2 Fat

Recommended method: Determination of Total Fat Content of Meat and Meat Products, ISO Recommendation R 1443.

8. 3 Nitrite

Recommended method: ISO/DIS 2918.

8. 4 Correction for Added Gelatine

For products in which the amount of added gelatine is not known, 0. 5% protein should be deducted from the percentage protein expressed on a fat-free basis.

8. 5 Lead

According to AOAC (1990, 15th Edition) Lead in Food by General Dithizone Method, 934. 07.

8.6 Tin

According to AOAC (1990, 15th Edition) Tin in Canned Foods by Atomic Absorption Spectrophotometric Method, 985.16.

熟制腌猪蹄膀（前腿）标准

CODEX STANDARD FOR COOKED CURED PORK SHOULDER

(CODEX STAN 97 - 1981 Rev. 1 1991)

1 范围

本标准适用于命名为“熟制腌猪蹄膀”，以本标准第6.4和第6.5条款中定义的以任何适当的包装材料包装的产品。

本标准不适用于那些由多种特性不同的成分组成的熟制猪蹄膀产品。这些产品的性状应该给予真实的描述，从而避免误导消费者，也不会与采用本标准的产品产生混淆。

2 描述

本产品应该采用猪前腿肉加工。所有的骨头和分离的软骨，肌腱和韧带都应该剔除。皮和脂肪可以去除，也可以不去除。

肉应该被腌制，并且可以烟熏，添加调料和香料。

对产品进行的热处理、腌制和包装等加工应该按本标准中第6.4和第6.5条款的要求进行，确保产品在贮藏、运输、销售的通常情况下保持卫生，不会造成公共卫生风险。

3 基本成分和质量指标

3.1 基本配料

未腌制的猪蹄膀；

由水、食用盐和亚硝酸钠或亚硝酸钾组成的盐卤。

3.2 可选配料

蔗糖，转化糖，葡萄糖（右旋糖），乳糖，麦芽糖，葡萄糖浆（包括玉米糖浆），蜂蜜；

香料，佐料和增味物质；

水溶性、芳香性水解蛋白；

食用明胶。

3.3 基本质量指标

3.3.1 原料——本产品所用的原料质量应该达到适合人们消费的质量要求，并且没有令人不适的气味和滋味。

3.3.2 成品——本产品是干净的，并且没有染色、没有源自容器的污染。肉质应该是均匀一致、腌制透彻，并且本产品应该可以被切片。

3.4 肉的含量

——不含脂肪的肉中蛋白质含量平均百分率 >17.5%
——不含脂肪的肉中蛋白质含量最小百分率 =16.0%（绝对最小值）
（对于罐装产品肉蛋白的百分比按罐子的总容量计算，如果添加了胶质，还要进行校正，参见第8.4条款。）

4 食品添加剂

	最大添加量
4.1 防腐剂	
4.1.1 亚硝酸盐，钾盐和（或）钠盐	200mg/kg（以亚硝酸钠计） 按成品净容量计算的最大限值
4.1.2 亚硝酸盐，钾盐和（或）钠盐	125mg/kg（以亚硝酸钠计）
4.1.3 氯化钾	按照良好操作规范
4.2 抗氧化剂	
4.2.1 抗坏血酸及其钠盐	500mg/kg(以抗坏血酸单体或复合物表示)
4.2.2 异抗坏血酸及其钠盐	500mg/kg(以抗坏血酸单体或复合物表示)
4.3 香料	
4.3.1 按照食品法典中确定的天然和等同于天然的香料	按照良好操作规范
4.3.2 按 JECFA 规范评价的熏制调味剂	按照良好操作规范
4.4 增味剂	
4.4.1 5′-鸟苷酸二钠	按照良好操作规范
4.4.2 5′-肌苷酸二钠	按照良好操作规范
4.4.3 谷氨酸钠	按照良好操作规范
4.5 酸度调节剂	
柠檬酸钠	按照良好操作规范
4.6 水分保持剂	
4.6.1 磷酸盐（包括天然含有的或添加的）[1]	8 000mg/kg（以 P_2O_5 计）
4.6.2 添加的磷酸盐（一价盐，二价盐和多价盐），	3 000mg/kg（以 P_2O_5 表示），

[1] 天然的磷酸盐（以 P_2O_5 计 mg/kg），按蛋白质（%）的250倍计算。

钠盐和钾盐❶	单体或者复合物

4.7 增稠剂

4.7.1 琼脂	**按照良好操作规范**
4.7.2 角叉（菜）胶	**按照良好操作规范**
4.7.3 藻酸盐，钾盐和（或）钠盐	**10mg/kg**

4.8 残留

按食品法典第1卷5.2所列示的添加剂，采用法则第三部分中关于食品添加剂的残留标准。

5 污染物

	最大限量
5.1 铅（Pb）	0.5mg/kg❷
5.2 锡（Sn）	
5.2.1 锡（Sn）：马口铁罐装产品	200mg/kg❶
5.2.2 锡（Sn）：其他容器包装的产品	50mg/kg❶

6 卫生

6.1 推荐采用《国际推荐肉禽产品加工卫生操作规程》[Ref. No. CAC/RCP 13－1976（Rev. 1，1985）]，《国际推荐鲜肉加工卫生操作规程》（CAC/RCP 11－1976），《食品卫生通则国际推荐标准》[Ref. No. CAC/RCP 1－1969（Rev. 2，1985）] 以及推荐采用《国际推荐低酸和酸化低酸罐头食品卫生操作规程》[Ref. No. CAC/RCP 23－1979（Rev. 1，1989）] 中的可适用部分。

6.2 熟制腌猪蹄膀加工中所使用的肉应该按照《国际推荐鲜肉加工卫生操作规程》和《国际推荐动物宰前宰后检验及鉴定的操作规程》（CAC/RCP 41－1993）进行检查处理。应该通过质检人员的检查，认定其是适合人类食用的。通过检查后的肉类不应该放置在有污染源的地方，不能在其后的加工、操作等处理过程中混入任何有害物质，导致它不适合食用。

6.3 未加工或半成品的肉和熟制腌猪蹄膀应该在一定的设备中，按照一定的方式进行处理、贮存或运输，以保护肉和熟制腌猪蹄膀不被污染和变质。

6.4 熟制腌猪蹄膀应该依照《国际推荐低酸和酸化低酸罐头食品卫生操作规程》第7.4条款中的规定用密封容器包装。

6.5 如果熟制腌猪蹄膀包装之前进行加热杀菌处理，应该采取能把污染减少到最小的方式进行包装，从而使产品在按照标签指示的方式贮存、运输和销售的过程中不变质，也不会造成公众健康风险。在通常的情况下，容器自身也不应该造成任何的健康风险或者带有污染。容器应该是干净的，并在需要时，进行真空包装，予以标示。

6.6 熟制腌猪蹄膀应该按照《国际推荐低酸和酸化低酸罐头食品卫生操作规程》中的第7.5条

---

❶ Having INS Nos. 339，340，450，451 和 452。

❷ 暂定标准。

款、第7.6.1条款至第7.6.7条款（包含第7.6.7条款）的规定进行热加工处理。

6.7 灌制了熟制腌猪蹄膀的密封罐头热处理后的冷却应该按照《国际推荐低酸和酸化低酸罐头食品卫生操作规程》的第4.6.8条款的规定进行。

6.8 热处理之后，灌制的密封容器应该按照《国际推荐低酸和酸化低酸罐头食品卫生操作规程》的第7.7条款的规定进行处理。

7 标签

标签除按《预包装食品标签通用标准》（Ref. No. CODEX STAN 1－1985）的规定标识外，还应标注如下内容：

7.1 食品名称

7.1.1 标签上食品的名称为“熟制腌猪蹄膀”。

7.1.2 本产品的名称应该包括适当的说明，如：

——“带皮”；

——“带原汁”；

——“添加了X”，适用于添加明胶，琼脂，藻酸盐或角叉（菜）胶等；

——“熏制”；

——“添加了烟熏剂”。

7.1.3 如果产品名称将误导消费者，则应该随同产品名称一起对产品的制备、加工方法或规格加以正确的说明。

7.2 生产日期和贮存说明

7.2.1 对于有稳定货架期的产品，保质期应该标注到年份。

7.2.2 对于非稳定货架期的产品，比如在通常的贮存和销售条件下，保质期不超过18个月的，那么提供给消费者或者供餐饮的预包装产品，最短保质期应该标注年月日。

7.2.3 如果不是直接销售给消费者或供餐饮的非稳定货架期包装产品，应该标注适当的贮存和销售说明。

7.3 非零售罐头产品的标识

非零售罐头按照零售产品需要的标注内容，将食品名称、生产日期、贮存说明以及批次证明、生产商或包装商名称、地址等标注在非零售罐头上，或者标注在随产品所附的说明书上。

然而，批次证明、生产商或包装商的名称、地址可以被一个识别标志所替代，此识别标志可在所附的文件中被明确地辨别认可。

8 分析方法

见食品法典第13卷。

8.1 蛋白质

推荐方法：肉与肉制品中总蛋白含量的测定（ISO Recommendation R 1443）。（氮的换算系数：6.25）

8.2 脂肪

推荐方法：肉与肉制品中总脂肪的测定（ISO Recommendation R 1443）。

8.3 亚硝酸盐

推荐方法：ISO/DIS 2918。

8.4 添加了胶质的产品中蛋白质含量的校正

对于胶质添加量不明的熟制腌猪蹄膀产品，蛋白质含量应该从不含脂肪的肉中蛋白质的百分率中扣除 0.5%。

8.5 铅

按照方法：AOAC（1990，15th Edition，934.07），食品中铅的测定（双硫腙比色法）。

8.6 锡

按照方法：AOAC（1990，15th Edition，985.16），马口铁罐头食品中锡的测定（原子吸收分光光度法）。

CODEX STANDARD FOR COOKED CURED PORK SHOULDER

(CODEX STAN 97 – 1981 Rev. 1 1991)

1 SCOPE

This standard applies to products designated as " Cooked Pork Shoulder" packaged in any suitable packaging material as defined in Sub-sections 6. 4 and 6. 5 below.

It does not apply to cooked pork shoulder products with compositional characteristics different from those specified. These products shall be designated with a qualifying statement which describes the true nature in such a way that it does not misled the consumer and that it does not lead to confusion with products covered by this Standard.

2 DESCRIPTION

The product shall be made of meat from fore-leg of a pig. All bones and detached cartilage, tendons and ligaments shall be removed. Skin and fat may or may not be removed.

The meat shall be cured and may be smoked, spiced and (or) flavoured.

The heat treatment to which the product has been subjected and the type of cure and packaging shall be sufficient to ensure that the product presents no public health hazard and remains wholesome under the conditions of storage, transport and sale as indicated in Sub-sections 6. 4 and 6. 5.

3 ESSENTIAL COMPOSITION AND QUALITY FACTORS

3. 1 Essential Ingredients

- Uncured pork shoulder;
- Brine consisting of water and food-grade salt and sodium or potassium nitrite.

3. 2 Optional Ingredients

- Sucrose, invert sugar, dextrose (glucose), lactose, maltose, glucose syrup (including corn syrup), honey;
- Spices, seasonings and condiments;
- Water soluble, aromatic hydrolyzed protein;
- Food grade gelatine.

3.3 Essential Quality Factors

3.3.1 Raw material-The ingredients from which the product is prepared shall be of a quality suitable for human consumption and free from objectionable odours and flavours.

3.3.2 Final product-The product shall be clean and substantially free from staining and contamination from the container. The meat shall be uniformly and thoroughly cured and the product shall be capable of being sliced.

3.4 Meat Content

- Average percentage meat-protein on fat-free basis ≥17.5%
- Minimum percentage meat-protein on fat-free basis =16.0%

(absolute minimum)

(For canned products the percentage of meat-protein is calculated on the total content of the can and corrected for gelatine, if added-see Sub-section 8.4).

4 FOOD ADDITIVES

	Maximum Ingoing Amount
4.1 Preservatives	
4.1.1 Nitrite, potassium and (or) sodium expressed as sodium nitrite salts	200mg/kg total nitrite
	Maximum Level Calculated on the Total Net Content of the Final Product
4.1.2 Nitrite, potassium and (or) sodium expressed as sodium nitrite salts	125mg/kg total nitrite
4.1.3 Potassium chloride	Limited by Good Manufacturing Practice
4.2 Antioxidants	
4.2.1 Ascorbic acid and its sodium salt	500mg/kg (expressed as ascorbic acid singly or in combination)
4.2.2 Iso-ascorbic acid and its sodium salt	500mg/kg (expressed as ascorbic acid singly or in combination)
4.3 Flavours	
4.3.1 Natural flavouring substances and nature-identical flavouring substances defined in the Codex Alimentarius	Limited by Good Manufacturing Practice
4.3.2 Smoke flavourings as evaluated by JECFA	Limited by Good Manufacturing Practice
4.4 Flavour Enhancers	
4.4.1 5′-Guanylate, disodium	Limited by Good Manufacturing Practice

4.4.2	5′-Inosinate, disodium	Limited by Good Manufacturing Practice
4.4.3	Monosodium glutamate	Limited by Good Manufacturing Practice

4.5 Acidity Regulators

Citrate, sodium salt	Limited by Good Manufacturing Practice

4.6 Water Retention Agents

4.6.1	Phosphates (naturally present plus added[1]	8 000mg/kg (expressed as P_2O_5)
4.6.2	Added phosphates (mono-, di- and poly-), sodium and potassium salts[2]	3 000mg/kg (expressed as P_2O_5), singly or in combination

4.7 Thickeners

4.7.1	Agar	Limited by Good Manufacturing Practice
4.7.2	Carrageenan	Limited by Good Manufacturing Practice
4.7.3	Alginates, potassium and (or) sodium salts	10mg/kg

4.8 Carry-Over

Section 3 of the Principle relating to the Carry-Over of Additives into Food, as set forth in Section 5.2, Volume 1 of the Codex Alimentarius shall apply.

5 CONTAMINANTS

		Maximum Level
5.1	Lead (Pb)	0.5mg/kg[3]
5.2	Tin (Sn)	
5.2.1	Tin (Sn): For products in tinplate containers	200mg/kg[3]
5.2.2	Tin (Sn): For products in other containers	50mg/kg[3]

6 HYGIENE

6.1 It is recommended that the Recommended International Code of Hygienic Practice for Processed Meat and Poultry Products [Ref. No. CAC/RCP 13 - 1976 (Rev. 1, 1985)], the Recommended International Code of Hygienic Practice for Fresh Meat (CAC/RCP 11 - 1976), the Recommended International Code of Practice-General Principles of Food Hygiene [Ref. No. CAC/RCP 1 - 1969 (Rev. 2, 1985)] and, where applicable, the Recommended International Code of Hygienic Practice for Low-Acid and Acidified Low-Acid Canned Foods [Ref. No. CAC/RCP 23 - 1979 (Rev. 1, 1989)] should apply.

---

[1] Natural phosphate (mg/kg P_2O_5) calculated as 250 × % protein.

[2] Having INS Nos. 339, 340, 450, 451 and 452.

[3] Temporarily endorsed.

6.2 All meat used in the manufacture of cooked cured pork shoulder shall have been subjected to the inspection processes prescribed in the Code of Hygienic Practice for Fresh Meat and the Code for Ante-Mortem and Post-Mortem Inspection of Slaughter Animals and for Ante-Mortem and Post-Mortem Judgement of Slaughter Animals and Meat (CAC/RCP 41 – 1993). It shall have been passed by an inspector as fit for human consumption. Meat shall not, subsequent to being examined by an inspector, have been exposed to contamination or processed or handled or subjected to the addition of any harmful substance, which renders it unfit for human consumption.

6.3 Raw or semi-processed meat and cooked cured pork shoulder shall be handled, stored or transported in an establishment in a manner that will protect the meat and the cooked cured pork shoulder from contamination and deterioration.

6.4 Cooked cured pork shoulder shall be packed in hermetically sealed containers in compliance with Sub-section 7.4 of the Recommended International Code of Hygienic Practice for Low-Acid and Acidified Low-Acid Canned Foods.

6.5 If cooked cured pork shoulder is heat treated before packaging it shall be packaged in such a way that contamination is kept to a minimum, so that the product will withstand spoilage and present no public health hazard under the conditions of handling, storage, transport and sale indicated on the label. The containers themselves shall not present any health hazard or permit contamination under normal conditions of handling. They shall be clean, and where applicable, show evidence of vacuum.

6.6 Cooked cured pork shoulder shall be thermally processed in compliance with Sub-sections 7.5 and 7.6.1 to 7.6.7 inclusive, of the Recommended International Code of Hygienic Practice for Low-Acid and Acidified Low-Acid Canned Foods.

6.7 The cooling of the thermally processed filled and sealed containers shall be carried out in compliance with Sub-section 4.6.8 of the Recommended International Code of Hygienic Practice for Low-Acid and Acidified Low-Acid Canned Foods.

6.8 After thermal processing the fitted, sealed containers shall be handled in compliance with Subsection 7.7 of the Recommended International Code of Hygienic Practice for Low-Acid and Acidified Low-Acid Canned Foods.

7 LABELLING

The provisions of the Codex General Standard for the Labelling of Prepackaged Foods (CODEX STAN 1 – 1985), shall apply:

7.1 The Name of the Food

7.1.1 The name of the food to be declared on the label shall be "Cooked Pork Shoulder".

7.1.2 The name of the product shall include, as appropriate, the designation:

- "with skin";
- "in/with natural juice";
- "X added" applying to gelatine, agar, alginates or carrageenan;
- "smoked";
- "smoking agent added".

7.1.3 A declaration that accurately describes the method of preparation, processing or presentation shall be given so as to appear simultaneously visible with the name of the product if its omission would mislead the consumer.

7.2 Date Marking and Storage Instructions

7.2.1 For shelf-stable products the date of minimum durability shall be declared by the year.

7.2.2 For cooked Cured Pork Shoulders which are not shelf-stable, i.e. which may be expected not to keep for at least 18 months in normal conditions of storage and sale, and which are packaged in a container ready for offer to the consumer or for catering purposes, the date of minimum durability shall be declared by day, month and year.

7.2.3 For products which are not shelf-stable and which are packaged in containers not sold directly to the consumer or for catering purposes, adequate storage and distribution instructions shall be declared.

7.3 Labelling of Non-Retail Containers

Information, as appropriate needed for labelling of retail containers is given either on the non-container or in accompanying documents except that the name of the food, date marking and storage instructions, lot identification and the name and address of the manufacturer or packer shall appear on the non-retail container.

However, lot identification, and the name and address of the manufacturer or packer, may be replaced by an identification mark provided that such mark is clearly identifiable with the accompanying documents.

8 METHODS OF ANALYSIS

See Codex Alimentarius Volume 13.

8.1 Protein

Recommended method: Determination of Nitrogen Content of Meat and Meat Products, ISO Recommendation R 1443.

8.2 Fat

Recommended method: Determination of Total Fat Content of Meat and Meat Products, ISO Recommendation R 1443.

8.3 Nitrite

Recommended method: ISO/DIS 2918.

8.4 Correction for Added Gelatine

For products in which the amount of added gelatine is not known, 0.5% protein should be deducted from the percentage protein expressed on a fat-free basis.

8.5 Lead

According to AOAC (1990, 15th Edition) Lead in Food by General Dithizone Method, 934.07.

8.6 Tin

According to AOAC (1990, 15th Edition), Tin in Canned Foods by Atomic Absorption Spectrophotometric Method, 985.16.

熟制腌肉肠标准

CODEX STANDARD FOR COOKED CURED CHOPPED MEAT

(*CODEX STAN 98 - 1981 Rev. 1 1991*)

1 范围

本标准适用于用适当的包装材料包装的命名为“熟制腌肉肠”的产品。

2 描述

本产品是由畜肉、禽肉或者其混合物经腌制或熏制加工而成的产品。所用的肉至少有50%被切成可以通过直径不小于8毫米的磨孔的切块，且从任何一个角度测量，切块的长度不能超过15毫米。

本产品可含有黏结剂成分或不含任何黏结剂。

对本产品进行的热处理、腌制和包装等加工应该按本标准中第6.4和第6.5条款的要求进行，确保产品在贮藏、运输、销售的通常情况下，不会造成公共卫生风险。

附属定义

用于本标准：

可食用下水是指那些通过检查的适合人类消费的下水，但不包括肺、耳朵、头皮、猪鼻（包括猪嘴和喷嘴）、黏膜、肌肉、生殖器、乳房、肠和膀胱。可食用下水也包括家禽的皮。

肉是指在屠宰场屠宰的任何哺乳动物的可食用部分，包括可食用下水。

包装是指产品用某种材料制造的容器进行包装，包装材料在正常条件下不会造成污染。

禽肉是指任何家禽的可食用部分，包括在屠宰场屠宰的鸡，火鸡，鸭、鹅，珍珠鸡和鸽子。

3 基本成分和质量指标

3.1 基本配料

畜肉、禽肉或者它们的混合物，不包括其可食用的下水；

水；

腌制配料，包括食用盐和亚硝酸钠或亚硝酸钾组成等。

3.2 可选配料

——可食用的下水，肉或禽肉来源动物自身的脂肪以及腌制或未腌制的猪肉皮，禽肉；

——碳水化合物和蛋白黏结剂，比如：

——谷粉，面粉或用谷物、马铃薯或者甘薯制成的淀粉；
——面包，饼干或面包制品；
——奶粉，脱脂奶粉，黄油奶粉，酪蛋白酸，乳清粉，鸡蛋蛋白，干血制品，植物蛋白制品；
——蔗糖，转化糖，葡萄糖（右旋糖），乳糖，麦芽糖，葡萄糖浆（包括玉米糖浆）；
——香料，佐料和增味物质；
——水溶性，芳香性水解蛋白。

3.3 成分

	含黏结剂的产品	不含黏合剂和可食用下水（但可含哺乳动物的心脏，舌头和头部的肉）的产品
添加肉的最小含量	80%❶	90%
脂肪最大含量	35%	25%

3.4 基本质量指标

3.4.1 原料——制造本产品的原料应该达到人类食用的的质量要求，并且没有令人不适的臭气和气味。
3.4.2 成品——本产品应该干净，并且没有染色，没有来自于容器的污染。畜肉和禽肉应该是均匀一致、腌制透彻，并且本产品可以被切片。

4 食品添加剂

	最大添加量
4.1 防腐剂	
4.1.1 亚硝酸盐，钾盐和（或）钠盐	亚硝酸盐 200mg/kg（以亚硝酸钠计） 按成品净含量计算的最大值
4.1.2 亚硝酸盐，钾盐和（或）钠盐	总亚硝酸盐 125mg/kg（以亚硝酸钠计）
4.1.3 氯化钾	按照良好操作规范
4.2 抗氧化剂	
4.2.1 抗坏血酸及其钠盐	500mg/kg（以抗坏血酸单体或复合物表示）
4.2.2 异抗坏血酸及其钠盐	500mg/kg（以抗坏血酸单体或复合物表示）
4.3 香料	
4.3.1 按照食品法典中确定的天然和等同于天然的香料	按照良好操作规范
4.4 增味剂	
4.4.1 5′-鸟苷酸二钠	按照良好操作规范

❶ 肉的含量包括哺乳动物的肉、可食用下水以及禽肉。

4.4.2 5′-肌苷酸二钠 按照良好操作规范
4.4.3 谷氨酸钠 按照良好操作规范

4.5 酸度调节剂

4.5.1 葡萄糖酸δ内脂 3 000mg/kg
4.5.2 柠檬酸钠 按照良好操作规范

4.6 水分保持剂

4.6.1 磷酸盐（天然含有的或添加的）❶ 8 000mg/kg（以 P_2O_5 计）
4.6.2 添加的磷酸盐（一元，二元和多元）钠盐和钾盐❷ 3 000mg/kg（以 P_2O_5 计），单体或者复合物

4.7 颜色

赤藓红（Cl 45430）替代 15mg/kg
颜色损耗（仅适于含有黏合剂的产品）

4.8 残留

按食品法典第1卷5.2所列示的添加剂，采用法则第三部分中关于食品添加剂的残留标准。

5 污染物

	最高限量
5.1 铅（Pb）	0.5mg/kg❸
5.2 锡（Sn）	
5.2.1 锡（Sn）：马口铁罐装产品	200mg/kg❸
5.2.2 锡（Sn）：其他容器包装的产品	50mg/kg❸

6 卫生

6.1 推荐采用《国际推荐肉禽产品加工卫生操作规程》[Ref. No. CAC/RCP 13-1976（Rev. 1, 1985）]，《国际推荐鲜肉加工卫生操作规程》（CAC/RCP 11-1976），《食品卫生通则国际推荐标准》[Ref. No. CAC/RCP 1-1969（Rev. 2, 1985）] 以及推荐采用《国际推荐低酸和酸化低酸罐头食品卫生操作规程》[Ref. No. CAC/RCP 23-1979（Rev. 1, 1989）] 中的可适用部分。

6.2 熟制腌肉肠加工中所使用的肉❹应该按照《国际推荐鲜肉加工卫生操作规程》以及《国际推荐动物宰前宰后检验及鉴定的操作规程》（CAC/RCP 41-1993）的可适用部分执行。应该通过检

❶ 原有的磷酸盐（以 P_2O_5 计 mg/kg），按蛋白质（%）的250倍计算。
❷ Having INS Nos. 339, 340, 450, 451 和 452。
❸ 暂定标准。
❹ 在本节中所用的词“肉”包括鲜肉、可食用下水和禽肉。

查员的检查，认定其是适合人类消费的。不应该在检查后又接触污染物，或者在加工、处理的过程中有不适合人类食用的有害物质的加入。

6.3 未加工或半成品的肉和熟制腌肉肠应该在一定的设备中，按照一定的方式进行处理、贮存或运输，以保护肉和熟制腌肉肠不被污染和变质。

6.4 熟制腌肉肠应该依照《国际推荐低酸和酸化低酸罐头食品卫生操作规程》第7.4条款中的规定用密封容器包装。

6.5 熟制的腌肉肠包装之前进行杀菌处理，并且应该采取能把污染减少到最小的方式进行包装，从而使产品按照标签标示的方式贮存、运输和销售，就能防止变质，而不会造成公共卫生风险。在通常的情况下，容器自身也不应该造成任何的卫生风险或者带有污染。容器应该是干净的，并在需要时，进行真空包装，予以标示。

6.6 熟制的腌肉肠应该按照《国际推荐低酸和酸化低酸罐头食品卫生操作规程》中的第7.5条款、第7.6.1条款至第7.6.7条款（包含第7.6.7条款）的规定进行热处理。

6.7 灌制了熟制腌肉肠的密封罐头热处理后的冷却应该按照《国际推荐低酸和酸化低酸罐头食品卫生操作规程》的第4.6.8条款的规定进行。

6.8 热处理之后，灌制的密封罐头应该按照《国际推荐低酸和酸化低酸罐头食品卫生操作规程》的第7.7条款的规定进行处理。

7 标签

标签上除按《预包装食品标签通用标准》（Ref. No. CODEX STAN 1－1985）的规定标识外，还应标注如下内容：

7.1 食品的名称

标签上标明食物的名称为“熟制腌肉肠”。但“肉”可以换作其他的用以描述所使用肉品种的词语，或者描述某几种肉的词语并按序排列，比如“熟制腌猪肉肠”，“熟制腌猪肉和牛肉肠”。

产品中使用的各种黏结剂和可食用下水以及畜肉、禽肉及其混合物的种类等情况说明都应该与产品的名称相关联，以免误导消费者。

7.2 成分表

成分清单应该标明畜肉、禽肉及其混合物来源动物的种类。

7.3 生产日期和贮存说明

7.3.1 对于有稳定货架期的产品，最短的保质期应该标注到年份。

7.3.2 对于非稳定货架期的产品，比如在通常的贮存和销售条件下，保质期不超过18个月的，那么提供给消费者或者供餐饮的预包装产品，最短保质期应该标注年月日。

7.3.3 如果不是直接销售给消费者或供餐饮的非稳定货架期包装产品，应该标注适当的贮存和销售说明。

7.4 非零售罐头的标识

非零售罐头产品应将食品名称、生产日期、贮存说明以及批次证明、生产商、包装商名称、地址必须标注在罐头上，除此之外的内容可以标识在容器上，也可以标明在产品附随的文件上。

然而，批次证明、生产商或包装商的名称、地址可以由一个识别标志所替代，但此识别标识能在附随的文件中被明确地辨别认可。

8 分析方法

见食品法典第13卷。

8.1 脂肪

推荐方法：肉与肉制品中总脂肪的测定（ISO Recommendation R 1443）。

8.2 亚硝酸盐

推荐方法：ISO/DIS 2918。

8.3 铅

按照方法：AOAC（1990，15th Edition，934.07），食品中铅的测定（双硫腙比色法）。

8.4 锡

按照方法：AOAC（1990，15th Edition，985.16），马口铁罐头食品中锡的测定（原子吸收分光光度法）。

CODEX STANDARD FOR COOKED CURED CHOPPED MEAT

(*CODEX STAN 98 - 1981 Rev. 1 1991*)

1 SCOPE

This standard applies to products designated as "Chopped Meat"[1] which have been packed in any suitable packaging material.

2 DESCRIPTION

The product shall be prepared from meat or poultry meat or a combination of these as defined below which has been cured and which may have been smoked. At least 50% of the meat used shall consist of coarsely cut pieces equivalent to meat ground through holes of not less than 8 mm in diameter. No piece shall be greater than 15 mm in any one dimension.

The product may or may not contain binders.

The heat treatment to which the product has been subjected and the type of cure and packaging shall be sufficient to ensure that the product presents no public health hazard and remains wholesome under the conditions of storage, transport and sale as indicated in Sub-sections 6.4 and 6.5.

Subsidiary Definitions

For the purpose of this Standard:

Edible offal means such offals as have been passed as fit for human consumption but not including lungs, ears, scalp, snout (including lips and muzzle), mucous membrane, sinews, genital system, udders, intestines and urinary bladder. Edible offal does not include poultry skin.

Meat means the edible part including edible offal of any mammal slaughtered in an abattoir.

Packaged means packed in a container manufactured of materials which do not permit contamination under normal conditions of handling.

Poultry meat means the edible part of any domesticated birds including chickens, turkeys, ducks, geese, guinea-fowls or pigeons slaughtered in an abattoir.

---

[1] The word "meat" may be replaced by a word describing the kind (s) of meat used.

3 ESSENTIAL COMPOSITION AND QUALITY FACTORS

3.1 Essential Ingredients

- Meat or poultry meat or a combination of these excluding edible offal;
- Water;
- Curing ingredients consisting of food-grade salt and potassium or sodium nitrite.

3.2 Optional Ingredients

- Edible offal, fat per se, cured and uncured pork rind per se, poultry meat;
- Carbohydrate and protein binders such as:
- meal, flour or starch prepared from grain or potato or sweet potato;
- bread, biscuit or bakery products;
- milk powder, skimmed milk powder, butter milk powder, caseinate, whey powder, egg protein, dried blood products, vegetable protein products;
- Sucrose, invert sugar, dextrose (glucose), lactose, maltose, glucose syrup (including corn syrup);
- Spices, seasonings and condiments;
- Water soluble, aromatic hydrolyzed protein.

3.3 Composition

	Product with binder	Product without binder and edible offal (but may include heart, tongue or head meat from mammals)
Minimum ingoing meat content	80% ❶	90%
Maximum fat content	35%	25%

3.4 Essential Quality Factors

3.4.1 Raw material-The ingredients from which the product is prepared shall be of a quality suitable for human consumption and free from objectionable odours and flavours.

3.4.2 Final product-The product shall be clean and substantially free from staining and contamination from the container. The meat and poultry meat shall be uniformly and thoroughly cured and the product shall be capable of being sliced.

❶ The meat content includes meat, edible offal and poultry meat.

4 FOOD ADDITIVES

		Maximum Ingoing Amount
4.1	**Preservatives**	
4.1.1	Nitrite, potassium and (or) sodium salts	200mg/kg total nitrite expressed as sodium nitrite Maximum Level Calculated on the Total Net Content of the Final Product
4.1.2	Nitrite, potassium and (or) sodium salts	125mg/kg total nitrite expressed as sodium nitrite
4.1.3	Potassium chloride Limited by Good Manufacturing Practice	
4.2	**Antioxidants**	
4.2.1	Ascorbic acid and its sodium salt	500mg/kg (expressed as ascorbic acid singly or in combination)
4.2.2	Iso-ascorbic acid and its sodium salt	500mg/kg (expressed as ascorbic acid singly or in combination)
4.3	**Flavours**	
4.3.1	Natural flavouring substances and nature-identical flavouring substances defined in the Codex Alimentarius	Limited by Good Manufacturing Practice
4.4	**Flavour Enhancers**	
4.4.1	5′-Guanylate, disodium	Limited by Good Manufacturing Practice
4.4.2	5′-Inosinate, disodium	Limited by Good Manufacturing Practice
4.4.3	Monosodium glutamate	Limited by Good Manufacturing Practice
4.5	**Acidity Regulators**	
4.5.1	Glucono-delta-lactone	3 000mg/kg
4.5.2	Sodium citrate	Limited by Good Manufacturing Practice
4.6	**Water Retention Agents**	
4.6.1	Phosphates (naturally present plus added)[1]	8 000mg/kg (expressed as P_2O_5)
4.6.2	Added phosphates (mono-, di- and poly-), sodium and potassium salts[2]	3 000mg/kg (expressed as P_2O_5), singly or in combination
4.7	**Colours**	
	Erythrosine (CI 45430) to replace loss of	15mg/kg

[1] Natural phosphate (mg/kg P_2O_5) calculated as 250 × % protein.

[2] Having INS Nos. 339, 340, 450, 451 and 452.

colour (for the product with binder only)

4.8 Carry-Over

Section 3 of the Principle relating to the Carry-Over of Additives into Food, as set forth in Section 5.2, Volume 1 of the Codex Alimentarius shall apply.

5 CONTAMINANTS Maximum Level

5.1 Lead (Pb) 0.5mg/kg❶

5.2 Tin (Sn)

5.2.1 Tin (Sn): For products in tinplate containers 200mg/kg❶

5.2.2 Tin (Sn): For products in other containers 50mg/kg❶

6 HYGIENE

6.1 It is recommended that the Recommended International Code of Hygienic Practice for Processed Meat and Poultry Products [Ref. No. CAC/RCP 13 – 1976 (Rev. 1, 1985)], the Recommended International Code of Hygienic Practice for Fresh Meat (CAC/RCP 11 – 1976), the Recommended International Code of Practice-General Principles of Food Hygiene [Ref. No. CAC/RCP 1 – 1969 (Rev. 2, 1985)] and, where applicable, the Recommended International Code of Hygienic Practice for Low-Acid and Acidified Low-Acid Canned Foods [Ref. No. CAC/RCP 23 – 1979 (Rev. 1, 1989)] should apply.

6.2 All meat❷ used in the manufacture of cooked cured chopped meat shall have been subjected to the inspection processes prescribed in the Code of Hygienic Practice for Fresh Meat and, where applicable, the Code for Ante-Mortem and Post-Mortem Inspection of Slaughter Animals and for Ante-Mortem and Post-Mortem Judgement of Slaughter Animals and Meat (CAC/RCP 41 – 1993). It shall have been passed by an inspector as fit for human consumption. Meat shall not, subsequent to being examined by an inspector, have been exposed to contamination or processed or handled or subjected to the addition of any harmful substance, which renders it unfit for human consumption.

6.3 Raw or semi-processed meat and cooked cured chopped meat shall be handled, stored or transported in an establishment in a manner that will protect the meat and the cooked cured chopped meat from contamination and deterioration.

6.4 Cooked cured chopped meat shall be packed in hermetically sealed containers in compliance with Sub-section 7.4 of the Recommended International Code of Hygienic Practice for Low-Acid and Acidified Low-Acid Canned Foods.

6.5 If cooked cured chopped meat is heat treated before packaging it shall be packaged in such a way that contamination is kept to a minimum, so that the product will withstand spoilage and present no public health hazard under the conditions of handling, storage, transport and sale indicated on the label. The containers themselves shall not present any health hazard or permit contamination under normal conditions of

❶ Temporarily endorsed.

❷ Wherever the word "meat" is used in this section, it includes meat, edible offal and poultry meat.

handling. They shall be clean and, where applicable, show evidence of vacuum.

6. 6 Cooked cured chopped meat shall be thermally processed in compliance with Sub-sections 7. 5 and 7. 6. 1 inclusive, of the Recommended International Code of Hygienic Practice for Low-Acid and Acidified Low-Acid Canned Foods.

6. 7 The cooling of the thermally processed filled and sealed containers shall be carried out in compliance with Sub-section 4. 6. 8 of the Recommended International Code of Hygienic Practice for Low-Acid and A-cidified Low-Acid Canned Foods.

6. 8 After thermal processing the fitted, sealed containers shall be handled in compliance with Subsection 7. 7 of the Recommended International Code of Hygienic Practice for Low-Acid and Acidified Low-Acid Canned Foods.

7 LABELLING

The provisions of the Codex General Standard for the Labelling of Prepackaged Foods (CODEX STAN 1 - 1985), shall apply:

7. 1 The Name of the Food

7. 1. 1 The name of the food to be declared on the label shall be "Chopped Meat" except that the word "Meat" may be replaced by a word describing the kind of meat used, or where more than one kind of meat has been used, by the names in descending order of proportion, e. g. "Chopped Pork", "Chopped Pork and Beef".

A declaration of the presence of binders and of edible offal and a declaration indicating the species of animal from which the meat, poultry meat or a combination of these is derived, shall be given in connection with the name of the product if their omission would mislead the consumer.

7. 2 List of Ingredients

The list of ingredients shall indicate the species of animals from which the meat, poultry meat or a combination of these is derived.

7. 3 Date Marking and Storage Instructions

7. 3. 1 For shelf-stable products the date of minimum durability shall be declared by the year.

7. 3. 2 For products which are not shelf-stable, i. e. which may be expected not to keep for at least 18 months in normal conditions of storage and sale, and which are packaged in a container ready for offer to the consumer or for catering purposes, the date of minimum durability shall be declared by day, month and year.

7. 3. 3 For products which are not shelf-stable and which are packaged in containers not sold directly to the consumer or for catering purposes, adequate storage and distribution instructions shall be declared.

7. 4 Labelling of Non-Retail Containers

Information as appropriate needed for labelling of retail containers is given either on the non-retail container or in accompanying documents except that the name of the food, date marking and storage instructions, lot identification and the name and address of the manufacturer or packer shall appear on the non-retail container.

However, lot identification, and the name and address of the manufacturer or packer, may be replaced by an identification mark provided that such mark is clearly identifiable with the accompanying documents.

8 METHODS OF ANALYSIS

See Codex Alimentarius Volume 13.

8.1 Fat

Recommended method: Determination of Total Fat Content of Meat and Meat Products, ISO Recommendation R 1443.

8.2 Nitrite

Recommended method: ISO/DIS 2918.

8.3 Lead

According to AOAC (1990, 15th Edition) Lead in Food by General Dithizone Method, 934.07.

8.4 Tin

According to AOAC (1990, 15th Edition), Tin in Canned Foods by Atomic Absorption Spectrophotometric Method, 985.16.

加工肉禽制品使用的香料、香草的微生物品质指南

GUIDE FOR THE MICROBIOLOGICAL QUALITY OF SPICES AND HERBS USED IN PROCESSED MEAT AND POULTRY PRODUCTS

(*CAC/GL 14 - 1991*)

1 范围

本指南适用于野生或栽培的，经加工处理，用作肉禽制品加工原料的香料和香草。

本指南列示了香料、香草的加工处理方法及成品标准，从而确保香料、香草适用于肉禽制品的加工，并提高其适用性。

2 定义

2.1 香料和香草是指用于提高食物香味和口感的植物叶子、花或植物的其他部位。

2.2 适用性是指将香料和香草受到微生物污染，引起变质或导致公共卫生问题的可能性降到最低，从而保证香料和香草在肉制品加工中使用的效果。

2.3 净化是指通过物理或化学方法减少活性微生物数量，以降低香料和香草的适用性。

2.4 处理是指对香料和香草进行净化加工。包括筛选，辐照，化学曝光，提取，热加工，挤压和其他类似的物理或化学方法。

3 处理

3.1 处理应该由有资格的技术人员进行指导。

3.2 处理过程中所有步骤包括包装都应该适时完成，处理过程的环境要求尽量降低污染、变质和破坏产品适用性的微生物滋生。

3.3 香料和香草的处理方式应满足本指南的成品标准。

3.4 处理工序应该对产品的质量和成分造成尽可能小的影响，净化达到最佳效果。

3.4.1 尽管热加工和挤压处理具有很好的杀菌效果，即便不影响香味和色泽的情况下也不是所有的香料和香草都可以进行这样的处理。

3.4.2 涉及提取处理时，提取剂应该选择允许在食品中使用的，并按良好操作规范操作。

3.4.3 用于控制微生物和昆虫污染的辐照应该符合良好辐照规范，并且符合《辐照食品的通用法规标准》（CODEX STAN 106 - 1983）和国际推荐的用于食品辐照的设备的操作规程（CAC/RCP 19 - 1979 - Rev. 1）。

3.4.4 如果处理过程包装采用化学曝光控制微生物（比如熏蒸消毒剂），不论是固体，液体还是

气体形式，所使用的化学药品必须经过核准才可以用于该用途。

3.5 过程辨识

如果香料、香草或者其混合物一旦采用上述任一处理方式，应标识在非零售包装物的包装上或者在附属文件上说明。

3.6 抽样和质量控制规程

3.6.1 加工成香料和香草的每一种植物都应该采用质量控制规程，以确保该产品使用的安全性和适宜性。该规程应该与HACCP中针对产品的具体处理过程、产品及其最终使用的规定相一致。该规程应规定不得使用会导致香料、香草适用性减弱的产品。

3.6.2 使用的实验室规程应该采用适当且认可的方法，以便结果能被普遍接受。

4 成品标准

用于采样、分析和其他测定的标准方法应符合以下香料、香草及其混合物（混合物包括香草、香料混合物及包含其他食物成分的香草香料混合物）标准，并且这些香料和香草应该按照本指南进行加工处理：

4.1 按照3.4.2和3.4.4处理的香料和香草含有所使用化学药品或提取剂的量应达到最低残留值。

4.2 处理过的香料和香草的微生物规格参数应该与肉禽制品所使用的防腐参数一致。

GUIDE FOR THE MICROBIOLOGICAL QUALITY OF SPICES AND HERBS USED IN PROCESSED MEAT AND POULTRY PRODUCTS

(*CAC/GL 14 - 1991*)

1 SCOPE

This Guide applies to spices and herbs, harvested wild, or cultivated, which require treatment prior to their use as ingredients in processed meat and poultry products.

It lists methods for the treatment of spices and herbs together with end-product criteria that will improve and assure their suitability for use in processed meat and poultry products.

2 DEFINITIONS

2. 1 Spices and herbs are the aromatic parts of the leaves, flowers or other parts of plants used to impart an aroma or taste to foods.

2. 2 Suitability for use means a condition where the contamination of spices and herbs with microorganisms causing spoilage or public health problems has been reduced to an extent that the spices and herbs are acceptable as ingredients in processed meat and poultry products.

2. 3 Decontamination means the reduction by physical or chemical means of viable microorganisms that would impair the suitability for use of spices and herbs.

2. 4 Treatment means a decontamination process for spices and herbs. This includes sorting, irradiation, exposure to chemicals, extraction, heat processing, extrusion, and other similar physical or chemical methods.

3 TREATMENT

3. 1 Treatment should be supervised by technically competent personnel.

3. 2 All steps in the treatment process, including packaging should be performed without undue delay and under conditions which will minimize contamination, deterioration and development of microorganisms that will impair the suitability for use.

3. 3 Methods of treatment should be so that the treated spices and herbs will meet the end-product criteria of these Guidelines.

3.4 The treatments should be performed in such a way that there is a minimum effect on quality and composition and a maximum decontamination effect.

3.4.1 Although heat processing or extrusion processes can have a strong bactericidal effect, not all spices and herbs can be exposed to such treatments without adversely affecting flavour and colour.

3.4.2 Where the treatment involves an extraction process, the extractant should be approved for use in food and used according to good manufacturing practice.

3.4.3 Where irradiation is used for the control of microbial contamination or insect infestation, this should be done in accordance with good irradiation practice and in conformity with the "Codex General Standard for Irradiated Foods" (CODEX STAN 106 – 1983) and the "Recommended International Code of Practice for the Operation of Irradiation Facilities Used for the Treatment of Foods" (CAC/RCP 19 – 1979 – Rev. 1).

3.4.4 Where the treatment involves exposure to chemicals to control microorganisms (e. g. fumigants) whether in solid, fluid or gaseous form, the chemicals used should be those approved for the purpose.

3.5 Process Identification

If the spices, herbs or mixtures thereof have been exposed to one of the above treatments, labelling of the non-retail containers shall either be given on the container or in accompanying documents.

3.6 Sampling and Quality Control Procedures

3.6.1 Each plant treating spices and herbs should employ a quality control programme to assure the safety and suitability for use of its products. This programme should be developed in accordance with the principles of HACCP for the specific treatment process, product and end-use of the product.

The programme should provide for rejection of products whose suitability for use is impaired.

3.6.2 Laboratory procedures used should follow appropriate and recognized methods in order that the results may be readily interpreted.

4 PRODUCT CRITERIA

Standard methods should be used for sampling, analysis and other determinations to meet the following criteria for spices, herbs and mixtures thereof with or without other food ingredients, and which have been treated according to this Guide:

4.1 Spices and herbs treated as in 3.4.2 and 3.4.4 should contain the lowest attainable amount of residue of the chemical (s) or extractant (s) used.

4.2 The microbiological specification of the treated spices or herbs should be compatible with the preservation parameters of the meat and poultry products in which they are used.

肉羹和肉汤法典标准

REVISED CODEX STANDARD FOR BOUILLONS AND CONSOMMÉS

（*CODEX STAN 117－1981*，*2001* 第二次修订）

1 范围

本标准应用于肉羹，肉汤（畜肉和禽肉）及其他类似的直接用于烹饪的产品，或者间接用于速煮的食品，或者经脱水、提炼、冷冻或经浓缩而成的食品。

2 概述

2.1 产品定义

2.1.1 肉羹和肉汤

肉羹和肉汤是一种稀且清彻的液体，由含有丰富蛋白质的食物或它们的提取物和（或）水解产物加水烹制而成，添加或不添加佐料和（或）调味料、香料、可食用脂肪、食盐、香料和它们的天然提取物或蒸馏物或其他改善口味的食物，并且此类添加剂在第四部分应获得许可，或者是依据使用说明可复原成与脱水前成分相当的混合物。

2.1.2 牛肉

牛肉取自去除了厚韧带和大量脂肪，平均瘦肉含量达 70% 的牛胴体。为了达到牛肉汤中含有 35mg/L 的肌酸，必需要 10～12g 上述生牛肉，牛肉中肌酸含量的变化与生牛肉的使用量有关。

2.1.3 牛肉膏

牛肉膏是生牛肉水溶成分的浓缩物。它由游离的可凝固的白蛋白、胶质和脂肪组成。

3.2.1.1 与 3.2.1.2 所列牛肉膏的需要含量，根据牛肉膏含 60% 的干物质计算，但添加的食用盐除外。

肌酸（按干物质计，添加的食用盐除外）最低含量：8.5%，根据 AIIBP 标准方法。

干物质含量的变化改变了相应的肌酸含量和使用的牛肉膏的数量。

2.1.4 禽肉

禽肉包括家禽的肉、家禽脂肪、去除内脏后的家禽胴体或禽类肉的提取物。

家禽是指鸡、鸭、鹅、火鸡或其他鸟类，比如鹧鸪、鸵鸟、猎禽、雏鸡等。

2.2 成品规格类型

2.2.1 速煮食品肉羹和肉汤是一种加热或不加热即可食用的食品。

2.2.2 提炼的和浓缩的肉羹和肉汤是指一种液体、半流体或类似于糊状的产品，在根据使用说明加入水之后，得到的符合本标准的 2. 1. 1 的定义的食品。

2. 2. 3 脱水的肉羹和肉汤是指干的产品，根据使用说明加水复原后，经过加热或不加热得到的符合本标准的 2. 1. 1 的定义的食品。

3 基本组成及质量指标

3. 1 洁净要求

所有原料必须清洁、质量完好、适合人类消费。所有原料必须符合最新版本的国际法典卫生操作规范。水应该达到可饮用质量，应符合 WHO 最新的饮用水质量标准。

3. 2 成分要求

下列要求适用于当根据使用说明制备成即食的食品。

3. 2. 1 肉羹和肉汤应采用牛肉和（或）牛肉膏制备而成，可使用或者不使用除了牛肉类以外的其他肉类或肉类浸膏。

3. 2. 1. 1 每升肉汤应含：

牛肉，按鲜肉计	最少量 10g
或	
牛肉膏	最少量 0. 67g
食盐	最高量 12. 5g

3. 2. 1. 2 每升肉羹应含：

牛肉，按鲜肉计	最少量 15g
或	
牛肉膏	最少量 1g
食盐	最高量 12. 5g

3. 2. 2 每升家禽的肉汤应含：

总氮	最少量 100mg
食盐	最高量 12. 5g

3. 2. 3 其他的肉汤每升应含：

总氮	最少量 50mg
食盐	最高量 12. 5g

3. 3 特殊限制

本标准覆盖的产品中，不添加肌酸之类的物质。

4 食品添加剂

4. 1 酸度调节剂

任何酸度调节剂已在《食品添加剂通用法典标准》（CODEX STAN 192 – 1995，Rev. 3 – 2001）表格Ⅲ中列出。

号码	食物添加剂	最大量(基于即食水平)
514	硫酸钠	受 GMP 限制
574	(D－)葡萄糖酸	
339	磷酸钠	1 000mg/kg(磷酸盐的总量，以 P_2O_5 计)
340	磷酸氢二钾	
450 i	二磷酸二钠	
450 ii	二磷酸三钠	
450 iii	二磷酸四钠	
450 iv	二磷酸二钾	
450 v	焦磷酸钾	
451 i	三磷酸五钠	
451 ii	三磷酸五钾	
452 i	聚偏磷酸钠	
452 ii	多聚磷酸钾	

4.2 抗结剂(仅用于脱水产品)

任何抗结剂已在《食品添加剂通用法典标准》(CODEX STAN 192－1995，Rev. 3－2001)表格Ⅲ中列出。

341	磷酸钙	3g/kg 基于干物质

4.3 消泡剂

任何消泡剂已在《食品添加剂通用法典标准》(CODEX STAN 192－1995，Rev. 3－2001)表格Ⅲ中列出。

900a	聚二甲基硅氧烷	10mg/kg
570	脂肪酸	受 GMP 限制

4.4 抗氧化剂

任何抗氧化剂已在《食品添加剂通用法典标准》(CODEX STAN 192－1995，Rev. 3－2001)表格Ⅲ中列出。

304	抗坏血酸棕榈酸盐	200mg/kg，单独或混合使用
305	抗坏血酸硬脂酸酯	
306	混合的生育酚浓缩物	50mg/kg，单独或混合使用
307	维生素 E	

（续表）

310	没食子酸丙酯	200mg/kg，单独或混合使用
319	叔丁基对苯二酚（TBHQ）	
320	丁基羟基茴香醚（BHA）	
321	二丁基羟基甲苯（BHT）	

4.5 着色剂

任何着色剂已在《食品添加剂通用法典标准》（CODEX STAN 192－1995，Rev. 3－2001）表格Ⅲ中列出。

100i	姜黄	50mg/kg
101i	核黄素	200mg/kg
141i	叶绿素铜络合物	400mg/kg
102	柠檬黄	50mg/kg
104	喹啉黄	
110	日落黄 FCF	
120	胭脂红	
122	偶氮玉红	
124	大红	
129	阿洛拉红 AC	
132	靛蓝	
133	亮蓝 FCF	
150c	焦糖Ⅲ－加氨生产	受 GMP 限制
150d	焦糖Ⅳ－亚硫酸铵生产	3 000mg/kg
160a（ⅱ）	自然提取物	50mg/kg，单独或混合使用
160e	β－阿朴－胡萝卜素醛	
160f	β－阿朴－胡萝卜醇，甲酯和乙酯	

4.6 乳化剂，稳定剂和增稠剂

任何乳化剂，稳定剂和增稠剂已在《食品添加剂通用法典标准》（CODEX STAN 192－1995，Rev. 3－2001）表格Ⅲ中列出。

432	聚氧乙烯山梨醇甘油－桂酸酯	1g/kg，单独或混合使用
433	聚氧乙烯（20）失水山梨醇单油酸酯，吐温－80	
434	聚氧乙烯（20）失水山梨醇单棕榈酸酯，吐温－40	
435	聚氧乙烯（20）失水山梨醇单硬脂酸酯，吐温－60	
436	聚氧乙烯（20）失水山梨醇三硬脂酸酯，吐温－65	

（续表）

450 ⅵ 452 ⅳ	二磷酸二钙 多磷酸钙	3g/kg（磷酸盐的总量，以 P_2O_5 计）
472d	二酰基甘油酒石酸酯脂肪酸	受 GMP 限制
473 474	蔗糖脂肪酸酯 蔗糖甘油酯	2g/L
1421	由乙酸乙酯酯化的淀粉醋酸盐	受 GMP 限制

4.7 香料和调味料

4.7.1 天然香料和调味物质以及可视为天然的调味物质 受 GMP 限制

4.7.2 人造香料 受 GMP 限制

4.7.3 具有一定香料特性的混合物，由各种成分或不同成分的混合物混合而得的，而这些成分本身是可以在食物中使用的，或者存在于食物中的，通过食物的加工过程而获得。

4.8 佐料

任何佐料已在《食品添加剂通用法典标准》（CODEX STAN 192－1995，Rev. 3－2001）表格Ⅲ中列出。

4.9 水分保持剂

任何水分保持剂已在《食品添加剂通用法典标准》（CODEX STAN 192－1995，Rev. 3－2001）表格Ⅲ中列出。

4.10 防腐剂

任何防腐剂已在《食品添加剂通用法典标准》（CODEX STAN 192－1995，Rev. 3－2001）表格Ⅲ中列出。

200 202 203 210 211 212 213	山梨酸 山梨酸钾 山梨酸钙 苯甲酸 苯甲酸钠 苯甲酸钾 苯甲酸钙	500mg/kg，单独或混合使用

4.11 增甜剂

任何增甜剂已在《食品添加剂通用法典标准》（CODEX STAN 192－1995，Rev. 3－2001）表格Ⅲ中列出。

4.12 填充气体

任何填充气体已在《食品添加剂通用法典标准》（CODEX STAN 192 - 1995，Rev. 3 - 2001）表格Ⅲ中列出。

5 卫生

5.1 被本标准覆盖的产品推荐按照《食品卫生通则国际推荐规程》（CAC/RCP 1 - 1969，3 - 1997）加工和处理，或其他相关法典文本，如卫生操作规范。

5.2 产品应符合根据《食品微生物指标设定及应用原则》（CAC/GL 21 - 1997）而制定的微生物标准。

6 标签

除了满足《预包装食品标签通用标准》（Ref. No. CODEX STAN 1 - 1985，1 - 1991）以外，还应符合以下要求：

6.1 产品名称

产品的名称应该为：

6.1.1 肉汤：如果产品符合3.2.1和3.2.1.1的要求。

6.1.2 牛肉汤：如果产品符合3.2.1和3.2.1.1的要求，并且所有的肌酸来自于牛肉。

6.1.3 肉羹：如果产品符合3.2.1和3.2.1.2的要求。

6.1.4 牛肉羹：如果产品符合3.2.1和3.2.1.2的要求，并且所有的肌酸来自于牛肉。

6.1.5 禽肉汤：如果产品符合3.2.2的要求。

6.1.6 肉汤：如果产品符合3.2.3的要求。适当的修饰形容词或最主要成分的名称可以包含在产品名称中。

6.2 可选择条款

如果每类的参考数量已制定，则应符合下列标准：

盘子	最少量250ml
杯子	最少量150ml
小杯子	最少量100ml
瓶子	最少量40ml

7 样品的分析和采样方法

7.1 采样方法

采样必须根据法典采样一般指导原则执行。

7.2 肌酸的测定

按照AIIBP方法2/5，2000修订版，HPLC法 - AIIBP官方分析方法（2001）。

7.3 总氮的测定

7.3.1 按照 AIIBP 官方分析方法 2/6 执行（1978 年 2 月）。

7.3.2 按照 AOAC 方法 928.08，干制或脱水产品在分析前要进行复原。

7.4 氨基氮的测定

按照 AIIBP 官方分析方法 2/7 执行（1985 年 9 月）。

7.5 食盐含量的测定

7.5.1 按照 AIIBP 官方分析方法 2/4（1998）执行。

7.5.2 根据电位测定，按照 AOAC 方法 971.27（法典的一般方法）执行。

REVISED CODEX STANDARD FOR BOUILLONS AND CONSOMMÉS

(*CODEX STAN 117 – 1981, Rev. 2 – 2001*)

1 SCOPE

This Standard applies to bouillons, consommés (meat and poultry) and similar products named by other corresponding culinary terms intended for direct consumption and presented either in their ready-to-eat or in dehydrated, condensed, frozen or concentrated form.

2 DESCRIPTION

2.1 Product Definitions

2.1.1 Bouillons and Consommés

Bouillons and consommés are thin clear liquids obtained either by cooking of suitable protein-rich substances or their extracts and (or) hydrolysates with water, with or without the addition of seasonings and (or) flavouring substances, edible fats, sodium chloride (salt), spices and their natural extracts or distillates or other foodstuffs to improve their taste, and such additives as are permitted in Section 4, or by reconstitution of an equivalent mixture of dehydrated ingredients according to the directions for use.

2.1.2 Beef

Beef from bovine carcasses from which the thick ligaments and the larger fat tissues have been removed and with an average content of 70% visible lean beef. In order to reach 35 mg creatinine/l in beef bouillon 10 – 12 g of such raw beef meat is necessary. The variation of the creatinine content in beef meat changes the amount of raw beef meat to be used in correlation.

2.1.3 Beef Extract

Beef extract is the concentrate of water-soluble components of raw beef; it is free of coagulable albumin, gelatine and fat.

The beef extract requirements listed in 3.2.1.1 and 3.2.1.2 are calculated on the basis of beef extract containing 60% dry matter, added salt excluded.

Min. creatinine (on dry matter, added salt excluded): 8.5% based on the AIIBP reference method.

The variation of the dry matter content changes the creatinine content in correlation and the amount of beef extract to be used.

2.1.4 Poultry

Poultry may consist of poultry meat, poultry fat, raw eviscerated carcasses of poultry or meat extracts of poultry origin. Poultry may refer to chicken, duck, goose, turkey and other birds, e.g., emu, ostrich, game birds and the chicks thereof.

2.2 Forms of Presentation

2.2.1 Ready-to-eat Bouillons and Consommés are products intended to be consumed as presented with or without heating.

2.2.2 Condensed and Concentrated Bouillons and Consommés means liquid, semi-liquid or paste-like products which, after the addition of water according to the directions for use, yield food preparations which comply with those defined in sub-section 2.1.1 of this Standard.

2.2.3 Dehydrated Bouillons and Consommés means dry products which, after reconstitution with water according to the directions for use and with or without heating, yield food preparations which comply with those defined in sub-section 2.1.1 of this Standard.

3 ESSENTIAL COMPOSITION AND QUALITY FACTORS

3.1 Purity Requirements

All ingredients shall be clean, of sound quality and fit for human consumption. They shall be in accordance with the latest edition of the Codex International Codes of Hygienic Practice for the respective ingredients. Water shall be of potable quality in accordance with the latest edition of the WHO Guidelines for Drinking Water Quality.

3.2 Compositional Requirements

The following requirements apply to the product when prepared ready-for-consumption in accordance with the directions for use.

3.2.1 Meat Bouillon and Meat Consommé shall be prepared by using beef meat and (or) beef extracts with or without the use of other meats or meat extracts than those of bovine origin.

3.2.1.1 Meat Bouillon shall contain per litre:

Beef, expressed as fresh meat	min. 10g
or	
Beef extract	min. 0.67g
Sodium chloride	max. 12.5g

3.2.1.2 Meat Consommé shall contain per litre:

Beef, expressed as fresh meat	min. 15g
or	
Beef extract	min. 1g
Sodium chloride	max. 12.5g

3.2.2 Poultry Bouillon shall contain per litre:

Total Nitrogen	min. 100mg
Sodium chloride	max. 12.5g

3.2.3 Other Bouillons shall contain per litre:

Total Nitrogen	min. 50mg
Sodium chloride	max. 12.5g

3.3 Specific Prohibitions

The addition of creatinine as such to products covered by this Standard shall not be permitted.

4 FOOD ADDITIVES

INS No	Food Additive	Maximum Level (on ready-to-eat-basis)

4.1 Acidity Regulators

Any acidity regulators listed in Table III of the Codex General Standard for Food Additives (CODEX STAN 192 - 1995, Rev. 3 - 2001).

INS No	Food Additive	Maximum Level
514	Sodium sulphates	Limited by GMP
574	Gluconic acid (D-)	
339	Sodium phosphates	1 000mg/kg (sum of phosphates expressed as P_2O_5)
340	Potassium phosphates	
450i	Disodium diphosphate	
450ii	Trisodium diphosphate	
450iii	Tetrasodium diphosphate	
450iv	Dipotassium diphosphate	
450v	Tetrapotassium diphosphate	
451i	Pentasodium triphosphate	
451ii	Pentapotassium triphosphate	
452i	Sodium polyphosphate	
452ii	Potassium polyphosphate	

4.2 Anticaking Agents (in dehydrated products only)

Any anticaking agents listed in Table III of the Codex General Standard for Food Additives (CODEX STAN 192 - 1995, Rev. 3 - 2001).

INS No	Food Additive	Maximum Level
341	Calcium phosphates	3g/kg on dry matter

4.3 Antifoaming Agents

Any antifoaming agents listed in Table III of the Codex General Standard for Food Additives (CODEX STAN 192 - 1995, Rev. 3 - 2001).

INS No	Food Additive	Maximum Level
900a	Polydimethylsiloxane	10mg/kg
570	Fatty acids	Limited by GMP

4.4 Antioxidants

Any antioxidants listed in Table III of the Codex General Standard for Food Additives (CODEX STAN 192 - 1995, Rev. 3 - 2001).

304	Ascorbyl palmitate	200mg/kg, singly or in combination
305	Ascorbyl stearate	
306	Mixed tocopherols concentrate	50mg/kg, singly or in combination
307	Alpha-tocopherol	
310	Propyl gallate	200mg/kg, singly or in combination
319	Tertiary butylhydroquinone (TBHQ)	
320	Butylated hydroxyanisole (BHA)	
321	Butylated hydroxytoluene (BHT)	

4.5 Colours

Any colouring agents listed in Table III of the Codex General Standard for Food Additives (CODEX STAN 192 - 1995, Rev. 3 - 2001).

100i	Curcumin	50mg/kg
101i	Riboflavin	200mg/kg
141i	Chlorophyll copper complex	400mg/kg
102	Tartrazine	50mg/kg
104	Quinoline yellow	
110	Sunset yellow FCF	
120	Carmines	
122	Azorubine	
124	Ponceau 4R	
129	Allura red AC	
132	Indigotine	
133	Brilliant blue FCF	
150c	Caramel III-ammonia process	GMP
150d	Caramel IV - ammonia sulphite process	3 000mg/kg
160a (ii)	Natural extracts	50mg/kg, singly or in combination
160e	Beta-apo-Carotenal	
160f	Beta-apo-8' -Carotenic acid, methyl or ethyl ester	

4.6 Emulsifiers, Stabilizers, Thickeners

Any emulsifiers, stabilizers and thickeners listed in Table III of the Codex General Standard for Food Additives (CODEX STAN 192 - 1995, Rev. 3 - 2001).

432	Polyoxyethylene (20) sorbitan monolaureate	1g/kg singly or in combination
433	Polyoxyethylene (20) sorbitan monooleate	
434	Polyoxyethylene (20) sorbitan monopalmitate	
435	Polyoxyethylene (20) sorbitan monostearate	
436	Polyoxyethylene (20) sorbitan tristearate	
450vi	Dicalcium diphosphate	3g/kg (sum of phosphates expressed as P_2O_5)
452iv	Calcium polyphosphates	
472d	Tartaric acid esters of mono- and diglycerides of fatty acids	Limited by GMP
473	Sucrose esters of fatty acids	2g/l
474	Sucroglycerides	
1421	Starch acetate esterified with vinyl acetate	Limited by GMP

4.7 Flavours and Flavourings

4.7.1 Natural flavours and flavouring substances and nature-identical flavouring substances. Limited by GMP

4.7.2 Artificial flavouring substances. Limited by GMP

4.7.3 Mixture prepared for its flavouring properties and produced from ingredients or mixtures of ingredients which are themselves permitted for use in foodstuffs, or are present naturally in foodstuffs, which is obtained by a process for the preparation of foods for human consumption authorised.

4.8 Flavours Enhancers

Any flavour enhancers listed in Table III of the Codex General Standard for Food Additives (CODEX STAN 192 - 1995, Rev. 3 - 2001).

4.9 Humectants

Any humectants listed in Table III of the Codex General Standard for Food Additives (CODEX STAN 192 - 1995, Rev. 3 - 2001).

4.10 Preservatives

Any preservatives listed in Table III of the Codex General Standard for Food Additives (CODEX STAN 192 - 1995, Rev. 3 - 2001).

200	Sorbic acid	
202	Potassium sorbate	
203	Calcium sorbate	
210	Benzoic acid	500mg/kg, singly or in combination
211	Sodium benzoate	
212	Potassium benzoate	
213	Calcium benzoate	

4.11 Sweeteners

Any sweeteners listed in Table III of the Codex General Standard for Food Additives (CODEX STAN 192-1995, Rev. 3-2001).

4.12 Packing Gas

Any packing gas listed in Table III of the Codex General Standard for Food Additives (CODEX STAN 192-1995, Rev. 3-2001).

5 HYGIENE

5.1 It is recommended that the products covered by the provisions of this Standard be prepared and handled in accordance with the appropriate sections of the Recommended International Code of Practice-General Principles of Food Hygiene (CAC/RCP 1-1969, Rev. 3-1997), and other relevant Codex texts such as Codes of Hygienic Practice and Codes of Practice.

5.2 The products should comply with any microbiological criteria established in accordance with the Principles for the Establishment and Application of Microbiological Criteria for Foods (CAC/GL 21-1997).

6 LABELLING

In addition to the provisions of the Codex General Standard for the Labelling of Pre-packaged Foods (CODEX STAN 1-1985, Rev. 1-1991), the following specific provisions apply:

6.1 The Name of the Product

The name of the product shall be:

6.1.1 Meat bouillon if the product complies with the appropriate requirement as contained in Sections 3.2.1 and 3.2.1.1.

6.1.2 Beef bouillon if the product complies with the appropriate requirement as contained in Section 3.2.1 and 3.2.1.1 and the total creatinine content is derived from beef.

6.1.3 Meat consommé if the product complies with the appropriate requirement as contained in Sections 3.2.1 and 3.2.1.2.

6. 1. 4 Beef consommé if the product complies with the appropriate requirement as contained in Sections 3. 2. 1 and 3. 2. 1. 2 and the total creatinine content is derived from beef.

6. 1. 5 Poultry bouillon if the product complies with the appropriate requirement as contained in Section 3. 2. 2.

6. 1. 6 Bouillon if the product complies with the appropriate requirement as contained in Section 3. 2. 3. An appropriate qualifying adjective or the name of the most significant ingredients may be included in the designation.

6. 2 Optional Provisions

If reference to the number of servings is made, it shall be in accordance with the following standard servings:

Plate	250ml minimum
Cup	150ml minimum
Small Cup	100ml minimum
Bottle	40ml minimum

7 METHODS OF ANALYSIS AND SAMPLING

7. 1 Method of Sampling

Sampling shall be in accordance with the Codex General Guidelines on Sampling (under preparation).

7. 2 Determination of Creatinine

7. 2. 1 According to the AIIBP Method 2/5, Revision 2000, HPLC of the AIIBP Official Collection of Methods of Analysis (2001).

7. 3 Determination of Total Nitrogen

7. 3. 1 According to Method 2/6 of the AIIBP Official Collection of Methods of Analysis (February 1978).

7. 3. 2 According to the AOAC Method 928. 08. Dried or dehydrated products may need to be reconstituted prior to analysis.

7. 4 Determination of Amino Nitrogen

According to Method 2/7 of the AIIBP Official Collection of Methods of Analysis (September 1985).

7. 5 Determination of Sodium Chloride

7. 5. 1 According to Method 2/4 of the AIIBP Official Collection of Methods of Analysis, Revision 1998.

7. 5. 2 According to the AOAC Method 971. 27 (Codex general method) based on potentiometric determination.

肉类卫生操作规程❶

CODE OF HYGIENIC PRACTICE FOR MEAT

(CAC/RCP 58 - 2005)

❶ 本规程取代了下列法典操作规程：《国际推荐的鲜肉卫生操作规程》(CAC/RCP 11 - 1976, Rev. 1 - 1993)；《国际推荐的野味卫生操作规程》(CAC/RCP 29 - 1983, Rev. 1 - 1993)；《国际推荐的屠宰动物宰前宰后的检验检疫及屠宰动物和肉类宰前宰后的评定规范》(CAC/RCP 41 - 1993)；《国际推荐的加工肉和禽肉的卫生操作规程》(CAC/RCP 13 - 1976, Rev. 1 (1985))；《家禽加工卫生操作推荐规程》(CAC/RCP 14 - 1976)；《国际推荐的预深加工机械分离肉的生产、储存和构成的操作规程》(CAC/RCP 32 - 1983)。

1 导言

1. 肉类是人类大部分食源性疾病的重要载体。尽管跟公众健康具有重要意义的肉源性疾病的范围已经随着生产和加工系统的变化而改变，近几年，人类对某些特殊的肉源性病原体如大肠杆菌O157：H7（*Escherichia coli* O157：H7），沙门氏菌（*Salmonella* spp.），弯曲杆菌（*Campylobacter* spp.）和小肠结肠子尔赞氏菌（*Yersinia enterocolitica.*）的监视研究，依旧发现了一些问题的存在。除了现有的生物、化学和物理危害外，发现了一些新的危害，例如，牛海绵状组织脑病（BSE）的发生。此外，消费者期待解决一些对人类健康不是特别重要的相应问题。

2. 现今，用于控制肉类卫生的为基于风险的方法，此方法要求在食物链的重要环节实施卫生措施，这些重要环节实施卫生措施对于减少食源性风险具有最重要的作用。关于这方面，应采用基于科学和风险评估的特定措施，在肉类生产和进一步加工过程中，这些措施更多地强调对污染的预防和控制。风险分析关键控制点系统（HACCP）原则的应用是一项必要的措施。实施当前计划的成功措施应是对消费者所要求的食品危害控制水平的客观进行证实，而不是那些仅注重于对细节详细说明的，但不知其效果的措施。

3. 在国家层面上，对屠宰场拥有管理权限的部门（通常为兽医管理部门[1]），应密切关注动物健康和公众健康。特别是在涉及屠宰前后检验检疫的情况下，在整个动物健康（包括人畜共患病）的监督过程中，屠宰场是关键点。对职责双重性的认识及相关公众健康和动物健康的综合措施实施十分重要。

4. 一些国家政府正在实施相关体系，重新定义了企业和政府主管部门在肉类卫生传递行为中的各自职责。在不考虑传递系统的情况下，主管部门的职责是定义肉类卫生行为所涉及人员的责任，并核实所有的法规要求得以实施。

5. 适当时，应将食品安全风险管理原则[2]与肉类卫生计划的设计和实施相结合。特别应该对联合微生物危险性评估专家组（JEMRA）、联合食品添加剂专家组（JECFA）和FAO/WHO专家咨询委员会的研究结果及所形成的风险管理建议加以考虑。最近发现的食源性风险可能要求除实施通常适用于肉类卫生的措施外，另外实施其他措施。例如，被屠宰牲畜的中枢神经疾病在人畜间的潜在传播，这意味着可能需要实施额外的动物健康监督计划。

2 本规程的范围和使用

6. 本规程的范围覆盖了从活体动物到产品零销点之间的生肉、半加工肉和肉制品的卫生规定。针对这些产品，进一步制定了“推荐性国际操作规程：食品卫生总则”[3]。适当时，制定的规程附录危害分析关键控制点系统（HACCP）及其应用指南和食品微生物标准的设定与应用原则可在肉类卫生方面加以实施。

7. 基于本规程的目的，肉指的是源于家养的有蹄类动物、单蹄动物、禽类、兔类动物、农场养殖的野味动物、野味鸟类（包括平胸类鸟）和野生动物。本操作规程同样适用于相关主管部门所要求需有卫生措施的其他种类动物。除了上述适用于所有动物种类的一般卫生措施外，本规程还

---

[1] OIE目前正致力于在国家层面上提出“肉类生产宰前宰后行为以降低对公众和动物健康的危害影响”的应用指南。

[2] 《食品法典框架风险分析工作原则》（法典程序手册，第14次修订）；《微生物风险管理提议草拟工作原则和指南》（CX/FH 05/37/6）。

[3] CAC/RCP 1-1969，Rev. 4-2003.

规定了适用于不同物种和不同类别的动物（如在野外杀死的野生动物）的特殊措施。

8. 本规程所述的适用于产品的卫生措施应考虑消费者可能使用的任何其他措施和食品处理操作。应注意，本规程所述的某些产品可能在食用前无需进行加热或其他灭菌处理。

9. 肉类卫生是综合行为，本规程参考了食品法典体系中的标准、文本和其他建议，如《食品进口和出口检验和认证的原则》（CAC/GL 20 - 1995），《微生物风险管理提议草拟原则和指南》（CX/FH 01/7 和 ALINORM 03/13 第 99 ~ 128 段），《“清真肉”术语使用的通用指南》（CAC/GL 24 - 1997）和《动物饲料国际政府间特色工作组的建议》（ALINORM 01/38 和 ALINORM 01/38A）。

10. 为了保证所提供的信息的一致性，应该与涉及人畜共患病的 OIE 陆地动物卫生规程中的标准、指南和建议相结合。

11. 总则（第 4 节）后面章节内容在“双线表”中列出。而那些更能说明本质特征的指南性内容列于“单线表”中。这是为了表明它们是基于现有知识和实践的建议。它们具有一定的机动性，并受制于已有的相关规定，只要求其在肉类的安全性和适宜性方面能够达到所要求的结果。

12. 当肉类被生产以用于本地贸易时，传统的操作惯例可能脱离本规程中的某些肉类卫生建议。

3 定义

13. 本规程中，以下定义适用（有关食品卫生的更多一般定义在《国际推荐的操作规程：食品卫生一般原则》[1] 中有述）。

屠宰场：用于指定动物的屠宰和修整以供人类食用的场所，需要由主管部门对其进行批准、注册和（或）备案。

动物：指的是以下类型的动物

- 家养有蹄类动物；
- 家养单蹄动物；
- 家养鸟类，即家禽；
- 兔类动物；
- 农场养殖野味动物；
- 农场养殖的野味鸟类，包括平胸类鸟；
- 野生野味，即所捕获的野生陆地哺乳动物和鸟类（包括生活在类似于野生动物生长的自由空间中的动物）；
- 主管部门另外指定的动物。

宰前检验[2]：为了判断安全性、适宜性和生理特性，由主管人员对活体动物执行的程序或测试。

胴体：修整后的动物躯体。

化学品残留：食品法典[3]的定义中所描述的兽药和农药的残留。

[1] 《国际推荐的操作规程：食品卫生总则》（CAC/RCP 1 - 1969，Rev. 4 - 2003）。

[2] 主管机构规定的这些检验及其他程序和测试也可以基于动物健康的目的而执行。

[3] 食品法典委员会程序手册。

主管部门[1]：由政府主管的官方机构，负责控制食品卫生，包括设定和执行所规定的肉类卫生要求。

管理机构：由主管部门认可和监督的机构，负责执行特定的肉类卫生工作。

主管人员：拥有执行指派任务所需的经培训经验、知识、技能和能力，符合主管部门规定和要求的人员。

判定为不合格：经主管人员或主管部门检查判定，被视为不安全或不适于人类食用并要求作适当的处理。

污染物：非故意添加至食品中的、可能危及食品安全性或适宜性的生物制剂或化学药剂、异物或其他物质[2]。

疾病或缺陷：影响安全性和（或）适宜性的任何异常。

修整：将动物躯体逐步分割为胴体、其他可食用部分和不可食用部分。

等效性：不同的肉类卫生系统实现同一食品卫生和（或）适宜性目标的能力。

加工厂：用于执行肉类卫生加工的建筑或区域，并由主管部门批准、登记和（或）备案。

加工厂负责人：加工厂的管理者，负责确保法定的肉类加工卫生要求得以实施。

食品安全目标（FSO）：通过保护措施，实现食品在食用时存在危害的最大频率和（或）程度控制在某一适当水平为目的（ALOP）。

鲜肉：除冷藏及保护性包装可保持肉类自然特性的处理外，未经其他基于保存目的方式处理的肉类。

野味库房：在转移至加工厂前，临时存放所捕杀的野生野味的建筑，由主管部门批准、登记和（或）备案。（注：在本规程中，野味库房是加工厂的一种特殊类型）。

良好卫生操作规范（GHP）：涉及必要措施和条件的所有实际操作，以确保食物加工链所有阶段中食品的安全性和适宜性[3]。

危害：食品中存在的可能引起不利于健康的生物、化学、物理因素或环境条件[4]。

猎人：对野生野味进行杀死、放血、局部取出内脏和对杀死野生野味进行部分修整的人员。

不适于食用：经主管人员检验判断或主管部门确定为不适于人类食用。

加工肉：对生肉进行加工或进一步深加工所得的产品，当切割该产品时，切割表面已经不具备鲜肉的特征。

肉：预期用于人类食用或经判断为安全的、可适于人类食用的动物的所有部分。

肉类卫生：确保食物加工链所有阶段中肉的安全性和适宜性的所有条件和措施。

肉制品：加有食料、调味品或添加剂的生肉。

机械分离肉（MSM）：使用机械方式，在剔骨后从肉骨头或家禽胴体中分离所得的肉。机械方式会导致肌肉纤维结构的损失或改变。

切碎肉：形成小碎片的无骨的肉。

官方检验员：由主管部门指定、授权或认可的主管人员，在代表主管部门或在其监督下负责执行官方肉类卫生措施。

感官检验：通过观察、触摸、品尝和嗅觉鉴别疾病或缺陷。

---

[1] 主管机构在肉类的国际贸易中提供了官方担保。基于公众健康和公平贸易的目的，食品进出口检验和认证系统法典委员会已经规定了认证要求（ref. CA/GL 26－1997）。基于动物卫生（包括人畜共患病）目的，OIE 陆地动物卫生规程包含了认证要求（ref. Section 1. 2 国际贸易中的义务和道德规范）。当要求认证时，上述两种认证可理解为等效。

[2] 《国际推荐的操作规程：食品卫生总则》（CAC/RCP 1－1969，Rev 4－2003）。

[3] 《WHO 教师手册》，1999。

[4] 《食品法典程序手册》第 14 次修订版的定义。

执行标准：通过实施，用于实现执行目标（PO）或食品安全目标（FSO）的一种或多种控制措施，以达到控制有关食品中危害发生频率或程度的效果。

执行目标：在消费前，食物链指定阶段中，为实现食品安全目标（FSO）或适当水平保护（ALOP）所允许的食品危害的最大频率和（或）程度。

宰后检验[1]：在屠宰/杀死动物后，主管人员为判断安全性、适宜性和生理特性所实施的程序或测试。

初级生产：食物加工链中涉及动物生产、将动物运至屠宰场，或者捕杀野生野味和将野味运至野味库房的所有步骤。

加工控制：在生产过程中，为实现肉类安全和适宜性所必需的所有条件和措施[2]。

加工标准：指定阶段中，用于实现执行目标或执行标准的物理加工控制参数（例如，时间、温度）[3]。

质量保证（QA）：在质量体系中执行的所有计划性和系统化的行动，用于确保企业行为符合质量要求[4]。

质量保证（QA）体系：实施质量保证所必需的组织结构、程序、过程和资源。

生肉：鲜肉、切碎肉或机械分离肉[5]。

即食（RTE）产品：即可食用的无需进一步杀菌处理的产品。

基于风险：根据风险分析原则而制定的包含任何执行目标、执行标准或加工标准[6]。

人类安全食用：人类安全食用的标准如下：

- 在履行与其最终用途相应的所有食品安全要求的情况下生产的；
- 符合针对指定危害的基于风险的执行标准和加工标准；
- 不包含足以对人类健康构成损害的危害。

卫生标准操作程序（SSOPs）：保证人员、设备、设施和器具干净，并保证必要时在操作前或操作过程中进行一定程度消毒的文件系统。

适于人类食用：适于人类消费的标准是：

- 在本规程指定的卫生条件下生产；
- 适于其预期用途[7]；
- 符合主管部门所制定的针对特定疾病或缺陷的参数。

确认：获得证据证实食品卫生控制措施或用于控制食品中危害的措施能够有效并持续地将危害控制在适当水平[8]。

查证：主管部门和（或）管理机构执行的用于确定管理要求符合性的行动。

验证（操作者）：由操作者实施的对加工控制系统的连续审核，包括纠正和预防行为，以确认符合规章和（或）指定的要求。

兽医检查员：由主管部门指定的专业的、有资格作为兽医或执行官方肉类卫生行动[9]的官方检查员。

---

[1] 主管机构规定的这些检验及其他程序和检测也可以基于动物健康的目的而执行。

[2] "加工"包括宰前和宰后检验。

[3] 本规程中，此为临时定义。

[4] ISO 8402。

[5] 不排除基于减少病原体的目的所实施的干涉行为。

[6] 本规程中，此为临时定义。

[7] 参见《"清真肉"术语食用一般指南》的例子（CAC/GL 24－1997）。

[8] 本规程中，此为临时定义。

[9] 可能包括动物健康目标。

4 肉类卫生总则

i. 肉必须安全并适于人类消费，包括政府、企业和消费者在内的所有相关方有责任实现该目标❶。

ii. 主管部门应有法律权力用于制定和执行肉类卫生要求，并最终负责验证肉类卫生要求是否被履行。加工厂操作者的责任是根据肉类卫生要求生产安全、适于人类食用的肉。相关方应承担法定义务，提供主管部门所要求的信息和协助。

iii. 肉类卫生计划的首要目标是保护公众健康，并应以肉类对人类健康的食源性风险科学评估为基础，考虑到由研究、监控和其他相关行动所确定的所有相关的食品安全危害。

iv. 在可能的情况下，适当时，食品安全风险分析原则应与肉类卫生计划的设计和实施相结合❷。

v. 在可能和可行的情况下，主管部门应根据基于风险的方法规划食品安全目标，以客观地表述符合公众健康目标所要求的危害控制水平。

vi. 肉类卫生要求应在整个食物加工链中最大程度地控制危害。应考虑从初级生产获得的信息，以使肉类卫生要求与肉源性危害在群体中的发生范围和流行情况相匹配。

vii. 加工厂操作者应实施 HACCP 原则。整个食物加工链中卫生措施的设计和实施也应最大程度地应用 HACCP 原则。

viii. 主管部门应明确定义肉类卫生行动所涉及的相关人员的职责，适当时定义兽医检查员的特殊职责。

ix. 肉类卫生所涉及的行动应由主管部门确定的具备相关知识、技能、能力和经适当培训的人员执行。

x. 主管部门应核实加工厂操作者具备适当的体系用于肉类食物链的追溯和召回。适当时，应考虑并执行与消费者和其他利益方的沟通。

xi. 在适当情况下，必要时，在肉类卫生要求的后续审议和（或）修改过程中结合考虑对动物和人群的监控和监督的结果。

xii. 适当时，主管部门应承认可选卫生措施的等效性，公布那些可实现肉类安全性、适宜性的卫生措施，以便促进肉类的公平贸易。

5 初级生产

14. 初级生产过程是肉类的危害的重要来源。预屠宰的动物群中存在诸多危害，在初级生产的控制过程中也经常会面临相当大的挑战，如大肠杆菌 O157：H7（*E. coli* O157：H7），沙门氏菌（*Salmonella* spp.）、弯曲杆菌（*Campylobacter* spp）和各种不同的化学和物理危害。基于风险的肉类卫生方法包括对风险管理可选方案的考虑。风险管理可选方案在初级生产阶段的使用，可能对风险缩减有显著影响❸。

15. 有关预屠宰动物的信息规定有利于基于风险的肉类卫生计划的实施，允许检验程序与特殊

---

❶ 特殊肉类卫生要求应解决生物、化学和物理危害；及与人类食用适宜性相关的病理心理学特征及其他特征。

❷ 食品法典框架风险分析工作原则，程序手册，第 14 次修订版；食品卫生法典委员会，《微生物风险管理提议草拟原则和指南》（CX/FH 05/37/6）；FAO/WHO 有关在指定食品安全标准、指南和相关文本中结合微生物风险分析的原则和指南的联合报告；Kiel，德国，2002 年 3 月 18－22。

❸ 食品法典框架风险分析工作原则，程序手册，第 14 次修订版。

动物群体中疾病和缺陷的范围和流行情况相匹配。当常规的感官测试或实验室测试不能检测到某些人畜共患病原体的存在时，信息规定尤为重要，必要时可能需要采取特殊措施，如对可能存在的牛囊尾蚴（*Cysticercus bovis*）的查出。

16. 在查证管理要求的过程中，应适当考虑初级生产阶段所实施的自愿或经官方认可的 QA 体系。

17. 本节所述的原则和指南是对国际推荐的操作规程：食品卫生总则（CAC/RCP 1 - 1969，Rev. 4 - 2003）第Ⅲ部分的目标和指南的补充。

5.1 适用于初级生产的肉类卫生原则

i. 应以减少引入危害的可能性并有助于保证肉类安全和使其适于人类食用的方式运行初级生产。

ii. 在可能和可行的情况下，初级生产部门和主管部门应建立相应系统，收集、比较和获得可能存在于动物群中，并影响肉类安全和适宜性的危害信息和有关条件的信息。

iii. 初级生产应包含官方或官方认可的计划，用于控制和监控动物群和（适当时）环境中的人畜共患病原体，应按要求报告需通报的人畜共患病。

iv. 初级生产的良好卫生操作规范（GHP）应包含动物健康和卫生、治疗记录、饲料和饲料成分及相关环境因子，并应最大程度地使用 HACCP 原则。

v. 动物的识别操作应允许在可行的范围内追溯生产地，必要时应允许进行管理调查。

5.2 屠宰动物的卫生

18. 初级生产者和主管部门应联合工作，在初级生产阶段实施基于风险的肉类卫生计划，以记载屠宰动物的一般性健康状况，同时实施保持或改善健康状况的实际操作，如人畜共患病控制计划。应鼓励在初级生产阶段实施 QA 计划，QA 计划可以采用适于当地情况的 HACCP 原则。主管部门在设计和实施基于风险的肉类卫生计划应考虑此类计划。

为了便于实施基于风险的肉类卫生计划：

- 初级生产商应最大程度地记录动物健康状况的相关信息，这些信息与安全和适于人类食用的肉类生产有关。相关信息应可被屠宰场获得。
- 为了改善农场的卫生状况，应实施相关体系，将屠宰场中有关屠宰动物及肉的安全性和适宜性的信息反馈给初级生产商。在实施以生产商为主的 QA 计划时，此类体系应与这些计划结合，以改善其成效。
- 主管部门应系统化地分析源于初级生产的监控和监督信息，据此在必要时可以对肉类卫生要求作修改。

19. 主管部门应实施控制特定人畜共患病原体、化学危害和污染物的官方计划。应最大程度地与负责公众和动物健康的其他机构协作。

针对特定人畜共患病原体的官方计划或官方认可的计划应包含基于以下目的的措施：

- 控制和根除人畜共患病原体在动物群体或子群体（如特定家禽群体）中的存在；
- 预防新的人畜共患病原体的引入；
- 提供监控和监督体系，设定基准数据并引入基于控制肉中此类危害的基于风险的方法；
- 控制动物在初级生产单位之间的转移。转移至屠宰场的动物需进行严格检疫。

针对化学危害和污染物的官方计划或官方认可的计划应包含基于以下目的的措施：

- 控制兽药和农药的注册登记和使用，以使其在肉中的残留水平不会对人类食用产生不安全因素[1]；

- 提供监控和监督体系，设定基准数据并引入控制肉中此类危害的基于风险的方法。

20. 在可行的范围内，对初级生产阶段实施动物识别体系，以使肉的来源可从屠宰场或加工厂追溯至动物的生产地。

21. 当发生以下情况时，不应装载动物将其运至屠宰场：

- 动物外部表面的污染物浓度可能危及屠宰和修整的卫生情况，而诸如清洗或剪毛的适当干预处理也不可行；
- 获得的信息表明动物可能危及供人类食用的肉生产的安全性和适用性，如特殊疾病的存在或兽药的新近使用。在某些情况下，若已经确定了此类危险动物（如“疑似”）并在特殊监管下被屠宰，则可以进行运输；
- 存在或出现可能导致对肉类安全性和适宜性产生不利影响的情形。

5.3 野生野味的卫生

22. 所获得的有关杀死的野生野味群体健康状况的知识极为有限。但是，主管部门在收集此类信息时，应考虑所有信息来源。在这方面，应鼓励猎人提供相关的信息，如野生野味的地理源及野生野味群体中所观测到的疾病的临床症状。

23. 应以以下方式捕杀野生野味：

- 宰杀方法符合生产安全，并与适于人类食用的肉的要求相一致；
- 其地理源不受有关的官方禁猎令限制，如不在官方正在实施化学有害物质控制计划或动物健康检疫隔离的地域捕猎。

24. 在提供有关杀死的动物的信息方面，猎人尤其重要。猎人应意识到其有责任向加工厂提供可能影响野生野味肉安全性和适宜性的相关信息，如杀死前的疾病症状，在局部修整和（或）取内脏时发现的极为明显的疾病和缺陷的相关信息。主管部门应要求猎人和涉及野生野味捕获的其他人员经过适于野外捕获的肉类卫生的基本培训，如疾病和缺陷的识别，在局部修整和将动物运输至野味库房时应用 GHP 规则。

25. 因野生野味是在野外被杀死，在其死亡后立即采取适当的卫生操作对于降低可食用部位的污染极为重要。在放血、局部修整（如去除头）和（或）局部取内脏[2]（若主管部门允许）时，应在可行的范围内实施 GHP。

在野外对所捕杀的野生野味进行放血和局部修整应包括：

- 在杀死动物后，尽可能快地进行放血和局部取出内脏（除非主管部门对特定种类的野生野味的本项要求作了免除）；
- 应以能最大程度减少可食用部位的污染的方式进行局部脱皮和（或）局部修整；
- 仅移除不需要进行屠宰后检验和判定的部位；
- 若进行局部取出内脏，必须保留肺、肝脏、心脏和肾，使其自然保留于胴体中，或确定后将其包装作为胴体的附件；除非猎人有能力和资格，并已经对其实施了检验，确定未发现可疑的异常情况[3]，则另当别论。

26. 除了接收和存放杀死的野生野味外，不得同时基于其他用途而使用野味库房，除非主管部门指定为其他的用途和情况。

---

[1] 《食品兽药残留控制管理计划设定指南》（CAC/GL 16－1993）（修订中）。

[2] 通常，局部取出内脏仅包括取出胃肠道，这需要冷却。

[3] 当捕杀的野生野味体型较小时，主管机构可以允许取出全部内脏。

27. 结合捕获条件、环境条件和所要求的食品安全性，应在主管部门设定的时限内，将杀死的野生野味转移至野味库房或加工厂。在修整或宰后检验前，不应将屠体和动物的其他部位冷冻，除非由于周围环境温度而不可避免地冷冻。

5.4 饲料和饲料成分的卫生

28. 初级生产过程中动物的饲养应符合良好动物饲养操作规范❶。在生产过程中，应保持有关饲料和饲料成分来源的记录，以便于查证。

29. 涉及生产、加工和使用饲料和饲料成分的相关方有必要进行协作，以此确定所识别的危害和对消费者产生的风险水平之间的关联。此风险可能导致其在食物加工链中传播❷。

当饲料和饲料成分出现以下情况时，不得喂食动物：

- 被视为可能对屠宰动物群引入人畜共患病原体（包括传染性海绵状脑病－TSEs）；
- 含有化学物质（例如兽药，农药）或污染物，它们在肉中的残留达到一定水平可能使得人类食用该产品不安全。

30. 当可能发生人畜共患病原体传播时，主管部门应执行相关的法律法规和控制手段，对向动物喂养动物蛋白饲料进行控制管理，其中可以包括有关此饲料喂养的禁令，前提是风险管理证明其为正当。饲料和饲料成分根据特定的采样计划和测试方案及霉菌毒素的最大限量，应符合适当的微生物和其他参数标准。

5.5 初级生产环境的卫生

31. 当环境中存在的危害可导致肉类存在不可接受的危害水平时，该区域不应进行动物的初级生产。

主管部门应设计并执行适于环境的监控和监督计划，以解决以下问题：

- 源于动植物的危害，该危害可能危及安全并适于人类食用的肉的生产；
- 环境污染物，该污染物可能在肉中残留达到一定程度而使得人类食用该产品不安全；
- 确保潜在的媒介（如水）不会构成危害的传播。

应运行相关的设备和程序，以确保：

- 可能积聚人畜共患病原体和其他危害物质的住房和饲养平台应有效清洁，使其保持良好卫生状态（参考第10节）；
- 死亡动物和废物的有效处理和（或）处置系统不应成为人类和动物健康的食源性危害的来源；
- 基于技术原因而必需的化学危害物质应以不污染环境或饲料、饲料成分的方式贮藏，从而不对人类健康造成风险。

5.6 运输

5.6.1 屠宰动物的运输

32. 应以不会对肉类安全性和适宜性造成不利影响的方式运输屠宰动物❸。

屠宰动物运输设备应符合以下要求：

- 最大程度降低排泄物造成的污染和交叉污染；

---

❶ 良好动物饲料法典操作规程（CAC/RCP 54－2004）。

❷ OIE 国际动物卫生规程（有关人畜共患病的章节）；杀菌剂抗性 OIE 指南。

❸ OIE 国际动物卫生规程（有关运输的章节）；OIE 工作组有关动物福利的报告，2002 年 10 月。

- 在运输过程中不会引入新的危害；
- 保持有关源产地的动物识别标记；
- 避免对动物造成不适当的压力，该压力可能对肉的安全性造成负面影响（如应缴引发的病原体的扩散）。

应根据以下要求设计并维修运输车辆：

- 可以轻易装载和卸载动物，且所伴随的对动物的伤害程度最小；
- 在运输过程中，可以将可能发生彼此伤害的不同种类动物或同种动物分开；
- 使用地板栅栏、板条箱或类似设施限制车辆被排泄物弄脏或交叉污染；
- 当车辆有多个甲板时，避免动物受交叉污染；
- 保证适当的通风；
- 符合一定的洁净和卫生条件（参见第 10 节）。

33. 运输车辆和板条箱应洁净，必要时，在动物卸载之后尽快对其实施消毒杀菌。

5.6.2 屠宰野生野味的运输

34. 在野外对野生野味进行捕杀和局部修整之后，应立即将胴体和其他部位运输至加工厂或野味库房，运输方式应使对可食用部位的污染最小化。基于该目的的车辆的使用应符合良好卫生操作规范和所规定的法规要求。

35. 在完成野外局部修整和运输后，应尽快降低胴体的温度，除非周围环境的温度较低而无需对其进行冷却。

6 适于屠宰的动物的递交

36. 仅健康的、干净的和经适当鉴别的动物可以递交适于屠宰。

37. 在到达屠宰场时，应对所有动物进行筛选。当个别动物或该批动物的外观或行为出现异常，显示需被隔离时，应进行动物筛选，并向负责宰前检验的主管人员通报。

38. 宰前检验是重要的屠宰前行为，在肉类卫生系统中应利用预送至屠宰的动物的所有相关信息。

6.1 适用于屠宰动物的肉类卫生原则

i. 供屠宰的动物应足够干净，保证不会危及屠宰和修整的卫生。

ii. 供屠宰的动物的关押环境应使食源性病原体对其的交叉污染降至最低，并便于有效地屠宰和修整。

iii. 屠宰动物应受制于宰前检验，并由主管部门确定其检验程序和检测方法，实施检验需由经过培训、具备必要知识、技能和能力的人员参加。

iv. 宰前检验应基于适时情况的科学和风险分析，并应考虑源于初级生产的所有相关信息。

v. 在加工控制中，应利用源于初级生产的相关信息和宰前检验的结果。

vi. 应分析宰前检验的相关信息，并在适当时将信息反馈至初级生产商。

6.2 围栏环境

39. 供屠宰的动物的关押对屠宰、修整、生产安全并适于人类消费的肉类的诸多方面有重要影响。动物的清洁对屠宰和修整过程中胴体和其他可食用部位的微生物交叉污染程度有重要影响。可以采用适于特定动物物种的清洁措施，确保足够洁净的动物被屠宰，并保证减少微生物交叉污染。

40. 加工厂操作者所实施的质量保证（QA）体系应改善围栏的适当条件。

加工厂操作者应确保围栏的环境条件符合以下要求：

- 以最大程度降低带食源性病原体的动物的交叉污染和感染的方式运行设施；
- 动物的关押应保证不危及其生理条件的安全，并保证宰前检验可以有效执行，如动物应有足够的休息，必要时避免过度拥挤并保护免受恶劣天气影响；
- 适当时，将不同种类和类型的屠宰动物相分离，如将需要进行特殊修整的动物隔离，将有特定食源性病原体潜在转移给其他动物的“嫌疑动物”隔离（参考6.3）；
- 确保只有足够干净的动物可被屠宰的体系；
- 确保在屠宰前有适当饲养暂停期的体系；
- 在屠宰和修整前保持动物识别（个体或群体，如家禽）；
- 传递有关个体动物或动物群体的相关信息，以便于实施宰前和宰后检验。

41. 主管部门或管理机构在设定用于确定围栏条件与法规要求符合性的核查行为的频率和强度时，应考虑加工厂操作者是否正确实施的QA体系。

6.3 宰前检验

42. 所有供屠宰的动物应由主管人员针对动物个体和动物批次实施宰前检验。检验包括动物的正确识别，以此使得在宰前检验过程中考虑其初级生产地的特殊条件，包括相关的公众和动物健康检验控制。

43. 宰前检验通过采用一系列特殊的程序和（或）测试，结合观察活体动物的行为、举止和外表及疾病征兆。

在以下情况下，下述动物应受制于由主管部门强加的特殊控制、程序和操作（可能包括拒绝进入屠宰场）：

- 不够干净的动物；
- 在运输过程中已经死亡的动物；
- 存在或怀疑可能存在对动物或人类造成直接威胁的人畜共患病；
- 存在或怀疑可能存在受制于检疫限制的动物疾病；
- 不符合动物识别要求；
- 当主管部门要求（包括是否符合动物用药的良好操作规范）时，缺少初级生产商的声明或该声明不充分。

6.3.1 宰前检验体系的设计

44. 宰前检验和结合适当要素的加工控制体系（参见第9节）应作为肉类生产基于风险的体系的完整要素。在设计和实施宰前检验体系的过程中，应利用有关屠宰群体的相关信息，例如，动物种类、健康状况、来源地。

45. 主管部门应根据基于风险和科学的方法设定宰前检验，包括其程序和检测。在缺少基于风险体系的情况下，程序必须以现有的科学知识和实践为依据。

46. 为了实现公众健康和动物健康目标，应整合并联合实施宰前检验程序和测试。在这种情况下，宰前检验的所有方面应以科学为依据，并应与相关的风险相匹配。

47. 当确定引起公众健康关注时，可能要求实施除常规宰前检验外的其他措施。

基于风险的宰前检验计划的特征是：

- 根据国家法规，有适当的动物识别确认的程序；
- 结合疾病的临床症状和极为明显的异常状态，设计和应用与肉源性风险相关的感官测试程序和试验；
- 结合动物类型、来源地和初级生产系统，将程序与可能存在于屠宰群体中的疾病和缺陷的范围和流行情况相匹配；

- 尽可能结合基于 HACCP 的过程控制，如应用确保预屠宰动物洁净程度的目标性标准；
- 适当时，将程序与源于初级生产单位的信息相匹配；
- 当存在可疑的危害物质（如化学残留物和污染物）而不能由感官检验确定时，使用实验室检测；
- 将信息反馈给初级生产商，以持续改善提供屠宰的动物的安全性和适宜性（参见6.4）。

6.3.2 宰前检验的实施

48. 主管部门应确定如何实施宰前检验，包括可能应用于初级生产而不是屠宰场的要素的鉴别，如在集中饲养家禽的情况下[1]。主管部门应设定涉及的所有人员的培训、知识、技能和能力的要求，并规定官方检验员和兽医检验员的职责（参见9.2）。由主管部门或管理机构执行对检验行为的查证和判决。主管部门负责核实所有法规要求的遵守情况。

加工厂操作者在宰前检验方面的职责是：

- 提供主管部门要求的有关初级生产阶段实施的宰前检验的相关信息；
- 在适当情况下将动物分离，如在运输或围栏中出生的动物或流产或仍带胎儿膜的动物；
- 应用针对个体动物或批次动物的识别系统，记载宰前检验的结果，并记载“嫌疑”动物宰后的检验结果；
- 将足够干净的动物送至屠宰；
- 促使移除因代谢疾病、应缴、窒息等原因而死于围栏中的动物，允许主管人员实施宰前检验。

49. 在屠宰动物到达屠宰场后，尽快进行宰前检验。只有得到充分休息的动物可以进行屠宰，但是停留时间不能超过其休息的必要时间。若已经实施了宰前检验，且在屠宰前延迟超过24小时，则应重复宰前检验。

主管部门所要求的宰前检验应包括以下内容：

- 源于初级生产的所有相关信息应作为基础加以考虑，如初级生产者有关兽药使用的声明、官方危害物质控制计划的信息；
- 应对被疑为不安全或不适于人类食用的动物进行鉴别，并将其与正常动物分开处理（参见6.2和8.2）；
- 当动物进入宰后检验前，实施宰后检验的主管人员应可获得宰前检验的结果，以利于做出最终的判决。这对于那些由宰前检验的主管人员做出嫌疑动物是否可以在特定的卫生条件下继续进行屠宰的最终决定，尤为重要；
- 在更为可疑的情况下，执行宰前检验的主管人员可以用特殊的设备关押动物或动物群，以进行进一步的详细检验、诊断测试和（或）治疗；
- 被判定为不安全或不适于人类食用的动物，应立即加以区别，并以食源性危害不会在其他动物中形成交叉污染的方式进行处理（参见8.2）；
- 记录判定不合格的理由。若确实需要执行实验室测试加以证实，则还应同时附上实验室测试记录。将该信息反馈给初级生产商。

50. 受控于官方或官方认可的基于根除或控制特定人畜共患病（如沙门氏菌病）的计划中的动物屠宰，应在主管部门规定的卫生条件下执行。

---

[1] 在某些情况下，主管机构允许在农场屠宰特定种类的动物，如农场养殖的野味，在这种情况，屠宰动物应受制于主管机构所确定的宰前检验和其他卫生控制措施。

6.3.3 宰前检验判断分类

宰前检验判断分类包括：

- 审查通过，适于屠宰；
- 当动物休息不够或临时受生理或代谢条件影响时，在附加的一段时间的关押后，需要进行再一次宰前检验；
- 在特殊条件下进行屠宰，即：被宰前检验的主管人员视为“嫌疑动物”，若延迟屠宰，可能导致宰后检验中被局部或整体判定为不合格；
- 有害于公众健康，被判定为不合格不可屠宰。可归因于：肉源性危害、职业健康危害、可能污染屠宰环境和屠宰后修整环境[1]；
- 肉类不适合人类消费，被判定为不合格，不可屠宰；
- 对于出现紧急情况的动物，审查通过需在特殊条件下则施行紧急屠宰，若延迟屠宰将使其发生恶化；
- 基于动物健康理由被判定为不合格，如相关国家法规所规定的，不可屠宰。

6.4 待屠宰的动物的信息

51. 所提供的有关待屠宰的动物的信息是确定最佳屠宰和修整程序的重要因素，是加工厂操作者有效设计和实施加工控制的先决条件。主管部门应分析相关信息，并在规定贯穿整个食物加工链的基于风险的卫生体系的相关卫生要求时加以考虑（参见9.2）。

52. 主管部门可以要求提供待屠宰的动物的监控资料以获得有关危害在屠宰群体中流行的基本信息，如指定的肉源性病原体、超过最大残留限量的化学残留。主管部门应根据国家公众健康目标，设计并实施此类监控行为。主管部门负责进行科学分析，并将分析结果分发给相关方。

为了推动整个食物加工链中基于科学和风险的肉类卫生，应实施相关的体系，提供：

- 有关待屠宰的动物的现行信息，作为实施 HACCP 计划和（或）质量保证（QA）计划过程控制的一部分；
- 反馈给初级生产商的有关提供屠宰的动物的安全性和适宜性状况；
- 提交给主管部门的便于进行现行审议的信息。

7 待修整的已杀死的野生野味

53. 送至加工厂的已杀死的野生野味，其有关捕获、处理和运输的安排与送至屠宰的活体动物不相同。在修整和宰后全面检验开始之前，应对杀死的野生野味进行适当的检验，以防止受修整环境和废物的污染。

7.1 适用于检验待修整的被捕杀野生野味肉类的卫生原则

在修整前实施的对被捕杀野生野味的安全性和适宜性的检验，应尽可能以风险为基础，并应考虑有关野外环境的相关信息。

7.2 待修整的被捕杀野生野味的检验

54. 在可行的范围内，检验应确定是否适当应用了针对野外捕获动物的卫生操作，包括对实施卫生修整所必需的洁净程度的评估。此时应确认主管部门为了便利宰后检验所要求的特殊措施是否

[1] 在宰后检验实施后，主管人员可以判决动物的可食用部位可以基于特殊用途而回收，如宠物食品。

已采取，如正确的识别标识及与动物胴体相分离的内脏附件。

55. 检验应涉及源于野外捕获的所有信息，如死亡时存在的异常情况、地理位置。可行时，将检验结果告知猎人或涉及野生野味捕获行为的其他人员，从而提高他们的知识水平，继而改善肉类卫生。

56. 如被捕杀的大型野生野味的胃肠道极可能在野外就被丢弃，可能不是完整的动物体送至修整，在这种情况下，在修整前实施的被捕杀野生野味的安全性和适宜性的检验应基于可行的风险。在修整和宰后检验前实施的检验将受实际情况的限制。此类检验应着重于探测野生野味捕获过程中的异常特性，如自然死亡或濒临死亡的动物的征兆、子弹误射的影响、腐烂、受毒药或环境污染物中毒的迹象。检验程序和判决的实施系统应以用于其他种类动物的宰前检验的系统为基础（参见6.3）。

57. 要求进行宰后检验的动物躯体及其相关部位的识别应予以保持，直至得出最终的宰后判决。

8 加工厂：设计、设施和设备

58. 本节所述的原则和指南是国际推荐的操作规程：食品卫生总则（CAC/RCP 1－1969，Rev 4 2003）第Ⅳ部分中目标和指南的补充。

59. 主管部门应允许在野味库房和处理被捕杀野生野味的加工厂的设计和结构、及其设施上有所变动，只要其暂时是必要的且不会危及肉类卫生。

8.1 适用于加工厂、设施和设备的肉类卫生原则

i. 应以最大程度降低肉类污染的方式对加工厂进行选址、设计和构建。

ii. 应以最大程度降低肉类污染的方式设计、构建和保养设备和设施。

iii. 加工厂、设备和设施的设计应允许人员以卫生的方式进行其相关行为。

iv. 与动物的可食用部位和肉直接接触的设施、设备的设计和构建，应能对其进行有效的清洁，并能对其卫生状况进行监控。

v. 适当的设备应可对肉类的特殊加工系统过程中的温度、湿度和其他因子进行控制。

vi. 水应可以饮用，若使用不同标准的水应不会对肉造成污染。

60. 每个加工厂应配备适当的设施和设备，以使主管人员能正当地实施其肉类卫生行为。

61. 用于支持肉类卫生行为所必需的实验室设备可以置于加工厂中或在其他单独的地方提供。

8.2 围栏的设计和构建

62. 围栏的设计和结构不应对动物造成不当的污染，不会使动物产生不当的压力，或者不会对源于该围栏中的动物的肉的安全性和适宜性产生不利影响。

围栏的设计和构建应使：

- 所关押的动物不会过度拥挤或受伤害，不会暴露于恶劣的气候条件中❶；
- 具有适于对动物进行清洁和干燥的适当布局和设备；
- 便于实施宰前检验；
- 地板是铺设的或装有板条，具有良好排水功能；

❶ 当涉及家禽和农场养殖野生鸟类时，设施应可用于在区域内停放运输车辆，有良好通风，并可避免暴露于直接光照、恶劣天气和极端温度中。

- 供应足够的饮用水和清洁用水，必要时配备输送设备；
- 当屠宰场存有可食用材料时，将围栏和屠宰场进行物理隔离；
- 隔离“嫌疑”动物，在单独的区域里对该动物进行检验[1]。这些区域应装备适当的设施，能够安全关押处于监管下的待屠宰的“嫌疑”动物，并可排除其对其他动物的污染；
- 附近应有配备适当设施的单独区域，用于对运输车辆和板条箱进行清洁和卫生处理，否则，在加工厂近距离内应有主管部门批准的相应设施。

63. 要求配备特殊设施，处理判定为不合格的动物。

要求这些设施：

- 其构造应能使判定为不合格的动物的所有部位、内脏内容物和排泄物得以安全存放；
- 其构造和装备应便于进行有效的清洁和卫生处理（参见第10节）。

8.3 屠宰区域的设计和构建

64. 击晕和放血区域应与修整区域相分离（通过物理方式或增大距离的方式），以使最大程度降低动物的交叉污染。

65. 用于烫洗、去毛、脱羽毛、敲碎和燎毛（或类似操作）的区域应与修整区域适当分离。

66. 当实施屠宰时，加工作业线的设计应保证动物之间有固定的距离，以避免交叉污染。

67. 屠宰“嫌疑”动物或受伤动物和对其进行修整可能要求特殊的设施。

要求这些设施应：

- 可轻易进入关押“嫌疑”或受伤动物的围栏；
- 配备适当的设施，用于卫生贮藏源于“嫌疑”动物或受伤动物的部位；
- 以便于进行有效清洁和卫生处理的方式构建和装备（参见第10节）。

8.4 用于动物胴体修整或肉呈递的区域的设计和构建

68. 用于动物胴体修整或肉呈递的所有区域和设施应以推动GHP[2]的实施和最大程度降低肉类污染的方式进行设计和构建。

用于动物胴体修整或肉呈递的房间和其他区域应基于以下目的进行设计并构建：

- 在操作过程中，可最大程度地降低交叉污染；
- 在操作过程中或间隔期间，可执行有效的清洁、卫生和维护（参见第10节）；
- 当有水存在时，区域的地板应足够倾斜并带有漏格，或应保证出口通畅，以确保持续排水；
- 外部的门不能直接面对本区域；
- 用于分开输送动物不同部位的斜槽应装有便于实施检验和清洁的开口，这是进行卫生措施的必要条件；
- 当同时对猪与其他动物进行修整时，用隔离的房间或区域对猪或其他动物进行皮毛修整操作；
- 隔离的房间用于：

－倒空和清理消化道，及有关消化道清理的进一步准备工作，除非确实不需要施行此类隔离的例外；

－经认定后，对动物的肉和不可食用部位进行处理，否则，应采用时间间隔或距离间隔的方式

[1] 当涉及家禽和农场养殖野生鸟类时，“嫌疑”鸟根据特定的卫生规定，通常在屠宰线上屠宰。

[2] 国际推荐的操作规程：食品卫生一般原则（CAC/RCP 1－1969，Rev. 4－2003）。

对这些产品进行隔离；

–不可食用部位的贮藏，如皮、角、蹄、羽毛和不可食用脂肪；

- 具备用于卫生加工控制的足够自然光照或人工光照；
- 具备适用于制备和贮藏可食用脂肪的设施；
- 有效防止害虫的进入和栖息的设施；
- 具备用于安全贮藏化学品（例如，清洗材料、润滑剂、标记墨水）和其他有害物质的足够设施，防止肉类的意外污染。

69. 经适当设计的隔热房间应可对肉类进行必要的冷却和冷冻。

剔骨或切割肉的加工厂应具备如下要求的相应设施：

- 保持固定的操作进度或确保不同生产批次间相分离的设施；
- 可进行温度控制的一个或多个房间；
- 将剔骨、切割和初级包装的区域与打包区域相分离，除非实施了卫生措施确保打包时不会对肉产生污染。

70. 基于技术原因，可以在实施肉和肉制品加工的料理、烟熏、熟制、腌制、贮藏和派送的房间里使用木材，只要其不对肉类卫生产生影响。

71. 排水和废物处理系统不应成为肉、饮用水供应或加工环境的污染源。所有这些排泄管线不得漏水，应具备足够的截流和排水功能，配备截流井、存水湾和污水坑，并且这些设施均应与用于动物修整或肉呈递的区域相隔离。

72. 加工厂应有适当的区间，足以保护待配送的肉免受环境污染，并可抵御不利的温度变化。

8.5 用于动物胴体修整或肉呈递的设备的设计和构建

73. 用于动物胴体修整或肉呈递的区域所使用的所有设备应有利于良好卫生操作（GHP）的实施。房间和其他区域中的设备和容器的设计和构建应最大程度地降低污染。肉不应与地面和墙壁相接触，其他固定构造的设计应避免此类接触。

74. 当屠宰线运行时，屠宰线的设计应保证动物胴体和其他部位的固定进度，防止屠宰线上的不同部位之间和不同的屠宰线之间发生交叉污染。肉的生产和加工流水线的布局和设备的设计应防止不同点位的产品和不同生产阶段的产品间产生交叉污染。

75. 用于动物修整或存放肉的所有房间和其他区域应装备足够的洗手设施，必要时，配备用于工具清洁和卫生处理的设施（参见第10节）。

对设备进行清洁和卫生处理的设施应：

- 其设计应可对特殊设备进行有效清洁和卫生处理；
- 其选址应在工作场所附近；
- 可使废水排至排水沟。

76. 用于处理动物不可食用部位或判定为不合格部位的设备和器具应予以区分。

77. 加工厂应有足够的自然通风或机械通风，以避免过热、过湿和冷凝成水珠，确保空气不被臭味、灰尘或烟雾污染。

通风系统的设计和构建应：

- 最大程度降低气溶胶和冷凝水珠产生的空气源性污染；
- 周围温度、湿度和气味得以控制；
- 尽量减少污染区域（例如，屠宰和修整区域）至洁净区域（例如，胴体的冷却区域）之间的空气流通。

78. 用于对加工肉和肉制品进行加热处理的设备应装备必要的控制设施，确保适当加热处理的进行。

8.6 水供应[1]

79. 应提供用于监控和维护水的饮用性、水的贮存、水温度的控制、水分流和废水处理等的足够设施。

应安装相应的设备，以使：

- 在任何时间供应足够的冷、热饮用水；
- 供应热水对设备进行有效的清洁，或者提供等效的卫生清洁供水系统；
- 供应适当温度的洗手用温水；
- 根据制造商的规范提供相应的卫生清洁液。

80. 当基于不同用途（例如，灭火、生成蒸汽、制冷）供应非饮用水时，应设计成网状系统并可明显区别，以防止与饮用水供应的交叉污染。

8.7 温度控制

81. 在缺少适宜的温度、湿度和其他环境控制的情况下，肉对于残存和增殖的病原体和腐败微生物特别敏感。

82. 设施和设备应足以：

- 根据标准规范，对肉进行冷却和冷冻；
- 在适宜温度下贮藏肉，该温度能使肉达到安全性和适宜性要求；
- 对温度、湿度、气流和其他环境因子进行监控，以保证过程控制制度得以实施。

83. 当烹饪肉的过程中产生蒸汽时，应尽快将蒸汽散发，以减少其冷凝成水的可能性，防止渗入隔壁房间。

8.8 人员的卫生设施和设备

84. 动物的屠宰和修整、肉品和肉制品的进一步加工都可能通过食品操作者而对肉产生交叉污染（参见第11节）。需要配备适当的人员卫生设施，使人员对肉产生的交叉污染减至最小程度。

85. 所提供的设施和设备的设计和选址不应对肉类安全造成威胁。必要时，提供用于人员处理活体动物和判定为不合格产品的单独环境（参见第11节）。

人员卫生设施应包括：

- 在适当位置设置更衣室、淋浴、冲洗厕所、洗手和烘手设施，隔离得就餐区域；
- 可有效清洁的防护衣，并可最大程度降低污染物的积聚。

放置裸露肉的所有区域应装备足够的洗手设施，该设施应：

- 置于工作地点附近；
- 装有非用手操作的水龙头；
- 供应适当温度的温水，并装有液体皂或其他洗手液的自动挤压器；
- 必要时配备烘手设备及收集丢弃手巾纸的容器；
- 将废水排至排水沟的设施。

8.9 肉的运输工具

运载裸露肉的车辆或船舶容器应：

---

[1] 国际推荐的操作规程：食品卫生一般原则，第5.5节（CAC/RCP 1－1969，Rev 4－2003）。

- 以不使肉与地板相接触的方式加以设计和装备；
- 将接合处和门缝密封，防止所有污染源的进入；
- 必要时，配备适当的装置，对温度控制和湿度保持情况进行监控。

9 过程控制

86. 有许多因子与肉类风险有关，例如，肉品本身的沙门氏菌和兽药残留；加工环境中的李斯特菌；食品操作者的金黄色葡萄球菌和庚型肝炎病毒等。实施包含有 GHP 和 HACCP 的有效过程控制，对于生产适合人类消费的安全的肉类产品是非常必要的。

87. 本节提供的原理和指南应符合国际推荐操作规程食品卫生总则第 V 部分的基本目标和指南；（CAC/RCP 1 - 1969，REV 4 - 2003）。它们在肉类风险部分被改进，但是对于合适的情况同样适用。

88. 屠宰和修整过程中的很多方面可能会给肉类带来污染的风险，例如，皮/毛的去除、取出内脏、胴体清洗、屠宰前检查、修整、以及在低温生产线中进一步的加工。控制程序系统应当限制微生物在这些过程中的交叉污染，将其降低到尽可能低的水平，并相应反映这些控制在降低肉源性对人类健康的风险的作用。

89. 即食的产品（RTE）可以要求特殊的微生物测试制度以合并微生物标准[1]。

9.1 肉类卫生过程控制原理

i. 适合人类消费的安全的肉类产品要求对控制程序的设计、实施、监测和审议特别关注。

ii. 加工厂的负责人对过程控制实施系统负有主要的责任。如果这些系统实施的话，主管部门应当确认其可以满足所有的肉类卫生要求。

iii. 按照基于风险的方法，过程控制应将微生物污染控制在最低的水平。

iv. HACCP 应当在可行的地方作为过程控制予以实施，并应当以包含了卫生操作标准规程（SSOPs）的 GHP 为基础支持。

v. 过程控制应当反映贯穿食物加工链的风险控制的综合策略，并在可能和可行的情况下包括初级生产和屠宰前可以获得的信息。

vi. 所有的动物应当进行以科学和风险为基础的屠宰后检验，并按照风险和（或）可能会在用于检查的动物身体中可能出现的缺陷[2]进行调整。

vii. 主管部门应当确定屠宰前检验中采用的程序，然而检验应当由经过培训，具有相关的知识，技术和必要的能力的人员实施（包括官方兽医，以及加工厂操作者雇用的人员）。

viii. 屠宰后检验应当考虑到从初级生产、屠宰前检验的所有相关信息，这些信息源自官方或者官方认可的风险控制程序。

iv. 屠宰后检验判定应当建立在以下基础上：肉源性疾病对人类健康的风险，其他的人类健康风险，例如，国内肉类处理的职业有害性接触，相关的国家法规和符合特征的特定的食物源性动物健康风险。

x. 过程控制和屠宰后检验活动的实施目标和实施标准应由主管部门根据可行的情况建立，并由主管部门确认。

xi. 在可行的情况下，用于确认目的的微生物检测应当包含在肉类制备和肉类生产的 HACCP

---

[1] 机构的原理和食品微生物标准的实施（CAC/GL 21 - 1997）。

[2] 如果不能进行风险评估，根据目前的科学知识和实践进行的屠宰前检查应当能够满足要求的消费者保护水平。

计划中。此类检测应当与产品的类型和对消费者可能的风险相关，并包括敏感人群。

xii. 管理机构或管理人员在加工厂负责人的允许下可以承担相关的过程控制活动[1]，包括主管部门认可的屠宰前和屠宰后检验。

xiii. 直到销售给消费者之前的即食（RTE）产品的处理应当确保没有接触到非即食（RTE）产品，并尽可能将会造成微生物污染风险的暴露降低到最小水平。

xiv. 自愿的或者官方认可的质量保证（QA）体系可以由加工厂负责人实施，以加强肉类卫生活动，并可以考虑根据主管部门的管理要求进行认证。

9.2 过程控制系统

90. 有效的过程控制要求设计和实施相应的系统。加工厂对实施和监督过程控制系统以保证肉类的安全和适用性负有首要责任，并应与基本要求的 GHP 及 HACCP 的实施计划适当结合。

91. 一份过程控制系统的文件应当表述实施的肉类卫生活动（包括任何取样程序），实施目的或者实施标准（如果有），确认行动，以及纠正和预防的行为。

92. 主管部门认可的管理机构或者管理人员可以在加工厂负责人同意下参与承担前述的过程控制行为，包括屠宰后检验。这些行为在适当的情况下可以作为 HACCP 或者 QA 体系的一部分。

93. 关于食品安全的过程控制体系应结合风险为基础的方法。HACCP 原则在过程控制系统的设计和实施中的具体应用应根据风险分析和 HACCP 体系及其实施指南（CAC/RCP 1 – 1969，REV. 4 – 2003）而定。食品进出口检查和确认系统（CAC/GL 26 – 1997）的设计、评估和鉴定指南提供了关于国际贸易操作控制的基本要求。

9.2.1 卫生标准操作程序（SSOPs）

94. 预处理和卫生操作标准程序（SSOPs）应尽可能将肉类直接和间接的污染降到最低。正确实施的 SSOP 系统应确保设备和设施清洁，适合进行操作，并且在操作过程中保持相应的卫生。SSOP 指南可以由主管部门提供，可以包括一般卫生的最基本操作要求。

卫生标准操作程序（SSOPs）包括：

- 由加工厂制定书面的 SSOPs 系统文件，描述包含的程序和实施的频率；
- 确定实施和监督 SSOPs 的人员；
- 记录有关监控、纠正和（或）预防活动的结果，形成记录文件可供主管部门查证；
- 包括产品适当处理的各种正确的措施；
- 加工厂负责人对程序系统有效性的阶段性评估。

95. SSOPs 中微生物的确诊可以利用一定的直接或间接的方法。加工厂负责人应采用统计过程控制法或者其他方法以监测卫生趋势。

96. 对于即食（RTE）产品，食品接触面和非食品接触面的 SSOPs 微生物确诊频率可能会比其他类型产品的高。

9.2.2 HACCP

97. 肉类生产的 HACCP 系统的应用对于食品安全来说是一种主动的过程控制措施[2]。肉类 HACCP 计划的审核应确保在满足实施目标或者实施标准方面的有效性（Ref 9.2.3），同时考虑到在加工中不同种类的动物呈现的风险的区别程度。

98. 审核的频率可因过程控制的操作因素、加工厂实施 HACCP 计划的历史以及实施的结果而有所变化。

---

[1] 过程控制活动应包括“官方认可的监视系统”（CAC/GL 20 – 1995）。

[2] 危害分析和关键控制点（HACCP）系统和实施指南（CAC/RCP 1 – 1969，Rev. 4 – 2003）。

99. 微生物测试法对实施 HACCP 系统的确认，例如，对限量标准和统计过程控制，是检验许多产品实施 HACCP 系统的重要特征。

100. 由主管当局规定的获得预定程序标准的 HACCP 系统发展的指南应提供给加工厂操作者用以指导操作和 HACCP 计划的发展。指南应当参照工业和其他的利害相关组织进行改进，并区别于各种加工类型，例如：

- 原料加工或者切割，例如：猪肉香肠；
- 采用二级稳定剂的肉类/自身不稳定，例如：谷类腌制的牛肉；
- 热处理过的/未完全烹饪，非自身稳定的肉类，例如：半烹饪的馅饼；
- 完全烹饪的/非自身稳定的，例如：烹饪过的火腿；
- 非热处理的/自身稳定的，例如：干意大利腊肠；
- 热处理的/非自身稳定的，例如：牛肉干；
- 热处理的/经过商业消毒的，例如：罐装肉类；
- 特定风俗加工方法，例如：泥炉烹调法。

101. 在改进对于热处理过的肉类以及加工肉类的 HACCP 计划时，加工厂负责人应建立过程操作、热处理参数、热处理后操作以及附加的保存处理的完整文件，并与预计的过程结果相对应，例如：巴氏杀菌。热处理产品的冷却过程参数应与产品的快速冷冻、慢速冷冻或者间断冷冻的具体过程相结合。预先热处理过的产品不应在高于起码温度（例如4℃）下包装，除非能够证明包装后的冷却产品在安全方面没有受到影响。

102. 为原料肉和熟肉制品制定的 HACCP 计划应包括参数的监测和记录，以保证肉品中心达到适当的温度。肉品中心的温度应当作为确认肉品是否充分煮制的必要参数。

9.2.3 过程控制结果的参数

103. 以风险为基础的肉类卫生系统，某种过程控制是通过实施的目标是否达到或者实施标准的结果如何而得到验证的。在大多数情况下，这将由主管部门建立。如果实施目标或者实施标准已经建立，加工厂可以应用，以确认是否实施了肉类安全参数足够的过程控制。

104. 加工厂应当具有实施正确操作过程控制系统的文件，以持续指导达到过程控制目标或标准的正确操作。过程审议和其他针对不符合行为目标或者行为标准而采取纠正的以及预防性的措施要求都应记录在案。主管部门应实施一套能最大程度上从所有的加工厂收集和分析结果的系统，并对与国家肉类卫生目的相关的过程控制进行阶段性审议。

105. 如果可行的话，实施目标或者实施标准应客观反映风险分析原理的实施水平。如果缺乏对人类健康风险的知识，实施目标或者实施标准应可以通过对当前实施现状的调查为基础而建立，并随后逐渐修改完善直至真实反映公众健康风险目标。如果以结果参数为依据而建立了适合人类消费的肉类特征的目标，过程控制的结果应客观上可以获得，并能反映消费者的预期。

106. 应建立感官参数

过程控制系统结果的感官参数应符合：

- 便于过程控制系统的确认；
- 便于制定食品生产系统的不同阶段的过程参数；
- 允许加工厂负责人在获得需要的参数进行规定水平操作的同时，有最大的灵活性和技术创新的空间；
- 在实施方面促进加工厂的一致性；
- 为规范指南和标准提供客观的基础，例如，统计过程控制要求，沙门氏菌致病率的要求；
- 逐渐改善风险控制以提高消费者的保护水平；
- 促进卫生措施一致性的确定。

107. 即食（RTE）产品的微生物实施目标、实施标准、过程标准和微生物标准应建立在产品分类的风险分析基础上，例如，非热处理自身稳定的食品、热处理自身稳定的食品、完全烹饪的非自身稳定的食品。微生物确认试验应由加工厂承担，并根据环境定期实施。主管部门可以实施测试以确认加工厂实施了相应的控制。加工厂实施的 HACCP 计划应有文件记录，在病原菌或者有毒物质测试阳性的情况下采取纠正的和预防性的措施。

108. 如果按照法定要求建立了实施目的或者实施标准，例如，大肠杆菌允许水平的指南，不得检出大肠杆菌 O157：H7（*E. coli* O157：H7）的标准，急性毒性化学品的最大残留限量，与消费者保护相关水平的有关联的解释等，应向所有利害相关方提供。

109. 在某些情况下，实施标准可以建立微生物标准，规定其在产品批次中的可接受程度，例如规定某种微生物的存在与否、数量多少、其毒性物质或其代谢物的数量等需根据特定的采样计划而定❶。

110. 主管当局应当在可行的情况下，在其职能范围内确认风险基础的肉类卫生行动，并满足同等风险基础上的肉类风险基础上的卫生结果。

9.2.4 管理系统

111. 主管部门应有合法的权利设定和促进肉类卫生要求的管理，并对确认满足所有的要求负有最终的责任。主管部门应：

i. 建立管理体系（例如，恰当的召回、追溯、产品追踪等）以及要求，例如，培训、知识、技能和人员能力（一般为国家水平）。

ii. 采取特定的肉类卫生控制，限制主管部门的活动，例如，官方采样程序，主管部门或者官方确认的屠宰前和屠宰后检查活动。

iii. 确认加工厂操作者实施的过程控制系统满足官方控制的要求，例如，GHP，SSOPs，HACCP。

iv. 确认主管部门履行了要求的功能。

v. 实施了必要的执行措施。

主管部门应当确认符合：

- GHP 的要求：屠宰的动物（以及宰杀后修整的动物），加工厂、设施和设备、控制程序、运输和卫生控制；
- SSOPs；
- HACCP 计划；
- 所有关于屠宰后和屠宰前检查的措施；
- 微生物实施目标或者实施标准，管理要求的过程标准或者微生物标准；
- 低于在相关的法规和国家采样计划中描述的最大限量的化学残留和污染物水平；
- 官方或者“官方认可”的人畜共患病控制程序，例如，大肠埃希氏菌（*E. coli* O157：H7）；
- 主管部门认可的附加官方控制措施。

112. 确认活动可以包括加工厂人员、文件检查、可食部分的感官检查以及实验室采样检测和病原、指示生物、残留的检测的过程行为。加工厂的批准/注册/名单可能便于主管部门确认符合管理要求的能力。

113. 主管部门应对加工厂负责人的确认行为进行相应的监督，监督的性质和密度应建立在风险和具体确认的基础上。其产品的批发和零售应包含在这项监控活动中，以达到能减轻消费者风险

❶ 《食品微生物标准建立和实施指南》（CAC/GL 21 - 1997）。

的程度。

114. 官方检验员（包括兽医检验员）应对照规定的要求对加工厂管理的符合性进行确认，并在确认过程中可使用附属的能够达到此目的的文件检查、程序和测试。屠宰前和屠宰后检验，以及在肉类加工、切割、贮藏过程中官方检验员的检验规则，应由官方根据其他相关管理人员的改进意见和基于肉类和动物种类相关的对人类健康的潜在风险而制定。

115. 国家肉类卫生计划应由主管部门确认：

如果加工厂负责人管理不符合卫生要求，主管部门应采取以下强制措施：

- 在负责人恢复过程控制期间减缓生产；
- 停止生产，并撤销对其预期目的不合适或者不安全的产品认证；
- 撤回官方监督，或者主管部门委派或授权的人员；
- 必要情况下，安排特定的处理、收回或者销毁该加工厂生产的肉类；
- 如果过程控制系统无效或者反复不符合的话，撤回或者延缓加工厂全部或部分的批件/注册/列表。

9.2.5 质量保证（QA）体系

116. 一旦加工厂具有确认的质量保证体系（QA）的话，主管部门应将其纳入自己的管理体系中❶。

9.3 质量控制一般卫生要求

117. 质量控制应满足国际标准推荐法典操作规程的一般卫生要求：食品卫生总则❷。

过程控制的一般卫生要求应包括：

- 清洁和卫生用水的标准应符合特定的目的，并采用不会对肉类产生直接或间接污染的方式使用；
- 设备和设施的清洁，必要的情况下包括拆解，清除碎片、残渣，部件清洗，合格清洁剂的使用，重复清洗、组装和进一步的卫生处理和清洗等；
- 容器和设备的处理和贮存应采用对肉类的污染最小化的方式进行；
- 贮放肉品的容器或者板箱在贮存房间或区域内应采用使污染最小化的方式组织安排；
- 加工区域内人员出入口的控制措施。

118. 主管部门和加工厂在确认过程控制和实施其他肉类卫生行为时，应采用合适的认证或者认可的实验室。样品的操作应采用有效的分析方法❸。

实验室测试应要求：

- 过程控制的确认；
- 实施目标或实施标准的结果的检测；
- 化学品残留的监测；
- 动物致病环境条件的诊断检测；
- 人畜共患病的监测。

9.4 屠宰和修整的卫生要求

119. 只有用于屠宰的鲜活动物才能进入屠宰场，但在屠宰厂外进行紧急屠宰和具有相应的兽

---

❶ 食品进出口检查的设计、操作、评价和促进指南。

❷ 注意到推荐的国际标准：进料的控制、水的使用、包装、文件和记录已经在食品卫生一般要求（CAC/RCP 1 – 1969，Rev 4 – 2003）中有所描述。

❸ 检测实验室的评价指南包含在食品进出口控制中（CAC/GL 27 – 1997）。

医文件的除外。

120. 只有用于屠宰的动物才能进入屠宰场，但停留在屠宰场区域内计划用于批处理的动物除外。

121. 动物只有在管理人员能够进行屠宰前和屠宰后检查的情况下才能进行屠宰或修整。对于管理人员没有在场的紧急屠宰，主管部门应建立特殊的规定，以保证肉类安全适合人类消费。

122. 所有带入屠宰房的动物应立即进行屠宰，动物的击晕、戳刺和放血不能超过动物可以接受的修整的水平。

在最初的修整操作中，应考虑减少以下污染：

- 烫、烙或者经过类似处理的屠宰动物应立即剥除所有的鬃毛、毛发、皮屑、羽毛、外皮和污垢；
- 气管和食管在放血后应保存完整，祭祀屠宰的情况例外；
- 放血应尽量完全，如果得到的血计划用作食物的话，应采用卫生方式收集和处理；
- 舌头的暴露应保证采用扁桃体没有被切除的方式；
- 头部修整对某些种类的动物不做要求，例如，山羊、小牛、绵羊，并保证头部采用不会对肉类产生污染的方式处理；
- 在用于人类消费的头部任何部分去除之前，应将头清洁，经过烫烙的动物除外，修整的程度应保证能够进行检验以及特殊部分的卫生去除；
- 乳腺或者具有明显病症的乳房应尽早从动物体上切除；
- 乳房的切除应保证内容物不会污染动物的身体；
- 气体去皮或去毛（将空气或气体充入皮和组织之间以促进修整），只有在满足加工控制的条件下才能进行；
- 皮/毛不应在用于屠宰或者修整的屠宰场或者建筑物内清洗、剥离或者堆放。

123. 家禽和野味鸟类，在去除羽毛之后，应采用饮用水去除污垢、羽毛和其他污染物。在修整过程中采取多个步骤清洁动物的躯体，并在每一次污染后尽快进行清洁，减少细菌在皮肤的黏着可以减少整个胴体的污染。（考虑到技术因素，取出内脏和屠宰后检验后的清洗非常有必要，因为这是在进入冷冻之前唯一可以进行清洁胴体的通常办法）。清洁可以采取几种方法，例如，喷淋、浸泡清洗。

124. 牧场养殖的鸟类羽毛中可能会有过多的污垢和泥土，可能会在去毛区域的去毛过程中带来污染的潜在危险，除非具有足够的隔离区域、物理障碍或者其他措施，例如，主动通风。

125. 如果开始修整或者脱毛，或者已经去除毛发，动物躯体应彼此分离，以避免接触，并持续至胴体被承担屠宰后检验的主管人员检查和确认后（注：如果胴体的分离对于家禽和野味鸟类比较困难的话，此类接触应使其最小化）。

在修整过程中，应考虑减少污染的措施：

- 如果动物需要剥皮的话，该程序应在去除内脏之前完成；
- 烫洗箱中的水应保证没有过度污染；
- 取内脏应立即进行，不要延误；
- 应当避免食管、嗉囊、胃、泄殖腔或者直肠的破坏或者物质的溢出，胆囊、膀胱、子宫或者乳房的破坏或者物质的溢出也应当避免；
- 在取出内脏的过程中连接胃的肠子不应被切断，也不能打开，除非肠子已预先紧紧结牢。家禽和野味鸟类的情况除外；
- 从屠宰或者修整的动物中取出的胃和肠子以及其他可食的材料应从修整区域尽快移开，并采用不会对肉类产生交叉污染的方式处理；

- 应证明用于去除可见的污染和微生物污染的方法是有效的，并满足主管部门的其他要求；
- 动物胴体内的排泄物和其他废料应予修整处理或者采用不会引起进一步污染的方式移开，并达到过程控制相关的实施目标或者实施标准。

126. 动物躯体和胴体不应接触地面或者设备，除非实际上不可以避免。如果设备在设计中包含了接触，例如自动取出内脏的机器，应保持设备的卫生并监督。

127. 当主管人员进行屠宰后检验时，认为当前动物屠宰或者修整的方式或者肉类进一步处理的方式，对肉类安全性或者适合性有负面影响时，主管人员有权要求降低生产速度，或者中止生产，或者其他任何必要的适当措施（参照9.2.4）。

128. 加工厂负责人应满足主管部门对动物屠宰后检验的可食部分的要求。从屠宰后检验移开的屠宰后的动物部分应保持可以鉴别，如属于某单个胴体的（或者胴体群体的），如果需要屠宰后鉴定的话。

129. 屠宰和（或）修整的设备和设施可以用于其他用途，例如，动物健康紧急情况下的屠宰，如果能够满足相关的清洁和卫生要求的话。

130. 主管部门应促进和采纳能够减少交叉污染和促进食品安全的技术和程序的革新和发展，例如，在袋内圈起肠环并去除。

9.5 屠宰后检验

131. 所有的胴体和相关的部分应进行屠宰后检验，这将成为基于风险的肉类生产整个框架体系的一部分。

132. 胴体和其他相关部分的屠宰后检验应利用初级生产和屠宰前检验的信息，以及头部、胴体和内脏的感官检验结果，以便做出用于人类消费部分的安全性和适应性的判定。如果感官检验不能做出胴体和其他部分适合人类消费的判断的话，相关的部分应留出并进行确认检验程序。

9.5.1 屠宰后检验体系的设计

133. 屠宰后检验和测试应由主管部门根据科学和风险为基础的方法建立。主管部门具有建立判断标准和确认屠宰后检验体系的责任。如果缺乏风险基础的体系，程序应建立在目前的科学知识和实践的基础上。

134. 屠宰后检验程序和检测可以结合，同步进行，以便同时获得公共健康和动物健康的目标，在这些情况下，所有的屠宰后检验应建立在科学的基础上，并适用相关的风险。

135. 动物种群的相关信息，例如，动物类型，健康状况，源产地的地理区域，应在屠宰后检验的设计和实施过程中充分利用。

136. 如果具有公众健康的关注热点问题，可以要求进行除了用常规筛选的感官检验方法之外的其他方法对胴体和其他相关部分进行的可疑风险的检验，例如，旋毛虫。

基于风险分析基础上屠宰后检验的特征：

- 感官检验和测试的设计和实施适用那些与明显可以观察的肉品异常相应的风险；
- 疾病的范围和流行以及合理的影响程序的调整应反映特殊的屠宰数量，同时考虑到种类（年龄），地理区域和屠宰动物的初级生产，例如，应对来自具有猪肉绦虫区域的所有猪肉进行多重切开；
- 将处理过程中减少交叉污染降低到可行的最大水平的程序，可包括胴体肉眼观察的程序以及其他风险评估判定的首次场合；
- 如果动物非食用部分的检验可以作为在食用部分检验的指示；
- 如果科学调研已经表明无效，或者对于其自身来说，对事物具有风险的情况下，对于常规程序的改进，例如，对于幼小动物淋巴腺的常规检验检测肉芽肿病的异常；

- 如果某种疾病或者一般分配的条件发现存在于某种单一的胴体部分和其他相关部分，在常规检验的基础上应进行更加详细的感官程序的实施，例如，牛肉绦虫和黄皮症；
- 如果活体动物对于疾病诊断呈现阳性，常规检验基础上的附加风险检验程序，例如，牛结核菌素的测试和马鼻疽菌素的测试；
- 除了感官检验，风险实验室测试的应用，例如，旋毛形线虫，化学残留和污染物；
- 反映风险基础上测试方法的感官检测结果的实施；
- 与其他程序控制行为的 HACCP 计划的组合；
- 来自初级生产者逐批检验基础上可以考虑的信息，对于程序的持续改进；
- 将信息反馈给初级生产者，以便于寻求对于屠宰动物的安全和适应状态方面的持续改进。

9.5.2 屠宰后检验的实施

137. 屠宰后检验应当在动物屠宰后，或者野味动物送达后，尽可能快地进行。同时应考虑到来自初级生产层面和屠宰前检验的所有相关信息，例如，来自官方或者官方认可的风险控制计划的信息，作为“可疑”的屠宰动物的信息。

138. 主管部门应确定：屠宰后检验如何实施，对相关人员的培训、知识和技能方面的要求（包括官方检验员、兽医检验员和非主管部门雇用的任何人员的角色），以及确认行为的频率和密度等（参照9.2.4）。所有的屠宰后检验确认的最终责任和判断要求应由主管部门列出。

139. 经过屠宰后检验，管理人员判定胴体和其他相关部分不适合人类消费的应作相应确认并采用不会对其他胴体和相关部分产生交叉污染的方式处理。判定的原因应当记录，以及如果必要的情况下，应进行实验室测试确认。

加工厂负责人在屠宰后检验方面的责任包括：

- 保持胴体和其他相关部分（适当情况下包括血）能够可被确认直到检验完成；
- 将头部适当剥皮或修整，以便于实施检验，例如，部分剥皮以利于淋巴腺的检验，将舌根分开以利于检验咽后淋巴结；
- 头部适当剥皮修整以利于可食用部分的卫生去除，如果这是一项操作方案的话；
- 根据主管部门的要求，提供胴体和其他相关部分以备检验；
- 在屠宰后检验之前，禁止加工厂内人员试图去除或者修饰某种疾病或者缺陷，以及动物的确认标志；
- 协助从取内脏的区域取走胎儿，或者进行其他主管部门允许的程序，例如收集脐血；
- 在检验区域对所有的胴体和要求进行检验部分的护理，直到检验和判定完成；
- 提供用于鉴定的设备，保留所有需要进行详细检验的胴体和其他相关部分，直到为作出关于安全性和适应性判定的详细检验和诊断测试全部结束，并应采取预防肉类与其他胴体或者相关部分产生交叉污染的方式进行；
- 指定从创伤区域整理的胴体的部分；
- 如果主管部门已经确定重金属污染累积超过不可接受的水平，提供大龄动物的肾脏或者肝脏；
- 使用传达已通过屠宰后检验的健康标志（由主管部门特制的）；
- 与主管人员合作进行屠宰后检验，在所有的其他必要方法中，促进有效的屠宰后检验，例如，过程记录，以及获得所有胴体和其他相关部分的途径。

屠宰后检验系统应包括：

- 制定以风险为基础的可能及可行的程序和测试；
- 适当的击晕和放血的确认；
- 尽快对修整完成后的对象实施可行的检验；

- 由主管部门确定的，对胴体和相关部分，包括不可食部分的进行肉眼检验；
- 对胴体和其他相关部分，包括不可食部分，进行触诊和（或）切开检验，根据主管部门根据风险基础作出的决定；
- 为了对某一单独的胴体或相关部分作出判断，必要的附加的触诊和（或）切开检验，并在相应的卫生控制下；
- 对人类可食部分进行更加详细的检验，不仅仅限于对那些带有指示性部分的检验，只要情况合适即可；
- 在有必要进行切开检验的情况下，同时对淋巴结进行系统的多部位的切开检验；
- 其他感官检验程序，例如，闻、触摸；
- 必要的情况下，主管部门或者由加工厂负责人在指导下实施的实验室诊断或其他测试；
- 如果可行的话，制定感官检测的实施目的或实施标准；
- 可减缓或者中断加工生产，以允许在所有的时间进行充分的屠宰后检验；
- 如果主管部门要求的话，除去特定的部分，例如，BSE 特殊风险材料；
- 正确使用和安全保存健康标志的标制设备。

140. 主管部门和加工厂应正确记录和传递屠宰后检验的结果。值得关注的人的或者动物的疾病以及不符合的残留或者污染物应向国家主管部门及动物的所有者汇报。屠宰后检验结果的分析是主管部门的责任，而且此类结果应提供给所有的利害相关方。

9.6 屠宰后判定

141. 可食部分安全以及适合消费的屠宰后判定应首先建立在对人类健康的肉源性疾病的基础上。其他的对人类健康的风险，例如，职业接触或者家庭的肉类处理，也应当重点考虑。关于肉类适合性的判定应反映预期的最终用途的接受的要求❶。

142. 除了法典的要求之外，应利用屠宰后检验程序，根据对动物健康的风险，以及相关国家法规的规定，确定和判定胴体和其他相关部分。

可食部分的安全和适合的判定应考虑来自以下的信息：

- 初级生产的信息（参考第 6 段）；
- 动物在围栏中作的观察；
- 屠宰前检验；
- 屠宰后检验，如果要求的话，包括诊断检测。

143. 判定应最大程度地建立在人类健康科学和风险的基础上，并根据主管部门提供的指南。判定只能由主管人员做出。如果可食部分表现出某些特定异常即可判定为不适合人类消费的话，培训、知识和技能水平以及判定要求的能力可以减少。

144. 如果屠宰后检验的最初结果不足以作出可食部分是否适合人类消费的判定的话，应作出临时判定，并随后作更加详细的检验或者测试。在等待获得详细检验和（或）诊断测试的结果期间，动物的所有要求作进一步检验的部分应在实施此类活动的主管人员的控制下暂存。

可食部分的判定类别可包括：

- 安全和适合人类消费；
- 按照描述的加工操作程序，例如，烹饪或者冷冻，适合人类消费❷；

---

❶ 主管机构应考虑不同人群需求的变化以适应不会歪曲食品供应的经济学。

❷ 如果制定某些特定的程序，例如烹饪或冷冻，管理人员可以指导以下屠宰后检查，按照相应的控制程序的可食部分，确认为安全和适合消费。

- 暂停，怀疑有不安全或者不适合人类消费的可能性，等待获得进一步检验和（或）测试的结果；
- 对于人类健康不安全，但可以用于其他目的，例如，宠物食品，饲料和饲料成分，非食物用途的工业类原料，并保证具有足够的卫生控制措施阻止风险的所有传播，或者非法进入人类食物链；
- 对人类消费不安全，并要求废弃或者破坏；
- 不适合人类消费，但可以用于其他用途，例如，宠物食品，饲料和饲料成分，工业类非食物用途，并保证具有足够的卫生控制措施阻止风险的所有传播，或者非法进入人类食物链；
- 不适合人类消费，并要求废弃或者销毁；
- 按照国家法规，对动物健康不安全，并作相应处置❶。

145. 当可食部分按照规定加工处理时，判定为安全和适合人类消费。这一加工规范应由主管部门确认，可足以减轻/减少或者完全去除某种风险或相关的状况例如，干馏，高温处理和冷冻。

9.7 屠宰检验后过程控制的卫生要求

146. 屠宰检验后的操作包括所有的程序，直至销售点，例如，胴体的冷冻，去骨和切割，进一步的修整、加工、包装、冷冻、贮存和向零售店的分配。应特别关注温度控制，使新屠宰的、修整的胴体和其他可食部分的温度尽快降低，使微生物的生长和有毒物质的形成不会达到对人类健康产生危害的程度。

147. 对于家禽和农场养殖的野味鸟类，内脏或者部分内脏，除了肾脏，应尽快去除，除非主管部门允许的情况除外。

经过检验认定安全和适合人类消费的禽肉应：

- 从修整的区域尽快移走；
- 处理、贮存和运输应采用保护肉类不会被污染以及变质的方式进行；
- 尽快置于降低温度和（或）水活度的条件下存放，除非是为了立即进行切割或剔骨操作；
- 保存的温度应确保禽肉能够达到安全和适合人类消费的目的。

对于经过冷浸处理的家禽或农场养殖野味鸟类的情况：

- 紧急冷浸程序应满足主管部门列出的卫生标准；
- 胴体温度的降低应尽可能快；
- 经过冷浸处理的胴体应具有比刚进入冷浸的胴体有更加低的微生物和病原体的计量数值；
- 卫生要求应包括相应彻底的容器的清空、清洗和消毒。

148. 用于肉类、包装或者打包肉品的官方健康标志应提供产品已经按照规定的程序操作的鉴别，并满足溯源到加工厂原产商的要求。如果作为官方肉类卫生程序的一部分，健康标志应包括加工厂的申请/注册/列表的序号，并采用不能够被重复利用的，以及清晰易读的方式。其他的标志可以表明符合商业分类，或者不适合人类消费，例如，宠物食品的特色商标。

149. 官方健康标志应直接用于产品、包装或者打包产品，或者直接印刷在黏附于产品、包装或打包产品的标签上。在成批运输到另外的加工厂作进一步的处理、加工或者包装的时候，健康标志应应用于包装容器的外包装上。

对于保存在房间中的胴体，胴体的部分或者其他肉类应：

- 所有操作的卫生控制要求必须附有指示：制冷负荷率，货物轮换周期、温度和相对湿度的要求；

---

❶ 在某些情况下，可食部分可以判断为适合人类消费，由于动物健康检疫方面的原因，来自某些地理区域的应作限制分配。

- 胴体和胴体的部分，无论是否悬挂或者排列在架子或者盘上，应确保充分的空气流通；
- 应当预防通过液体滴落引起的交叉污染；
- 从顶部的设备或者结露的滴落应控制在可行的范围内，以避免肉和食品接触表面的污染。

150. 用于切割、碎肉、机械分离、肉类分离和肉类生产的房间和设备的设计应能够满足这些操作活动单独进行，或者不会引起交叉污染。

151. 用于切割或去骨的新鲜肉类应按照需要的进程进入操作车间，且不应在工作台上累积。如果新鲜肉类在达到适合贮存和运输的温度之前进行切割或者去骨，应立即降低到所述的温度。

如果新鲜肉类在达到适合贮存和运输的温度之前进行切割或者去骨：

- 应直接从修整的区域转移到切割或者去骨的房间；
- 切割或者去骨的房间应具有温度控制并直接连接到修整的区域，除非主管部门批准了其他可以提供同等的卫生水平的方法；
- 切割、去骨和包装应立即进行，并满足全部的卫生程序控制要求。

如果原料肉切碎：

- 肉只能从主管部门批准的动物部分获得，例如，有纹理的肌肉和依附的脂肪组织[1]；
- 不应含有骨头碎片或者皮肤；
- 任何粗大的异常的组织和（或）修整后的污染物应在切碎之前去除；
- 符合主管部门指定的成分标准。

如果原料肉机械分离的情况，主管部门应：

- 限制可以使用的动物体部位，例如，不可以使用头骨；
- 对产品中最大的钙含量制定成分标准；
- 对最终产品作特殊标签要求。

如果原料肉被切碎、机械分离或者在肉制品中使用：

- 主管部门可以在生产的每个阶段设定控制程序的最大时间/温度表，例如，原料从冷冻或冷藏到制备阶段的最大时间和温度，生产过程中的最高温度，冷冻或冷藏之前的最长时间；
- 除非直接用于肉类制品的某一成分或者生产肉类，应立即包装和（或）打包，并立即冷藏；
- 主管部门可以对原料和成品指定微生物实施目的、实施标准、加工标准或者微生物标准；
- 加工厂应具有在线的电磁或者其他测试金属碎片污染物的方法；
- 肉类溶化后不应再冷冻。

在处理原料肉或者加工的肉时：

- 等待加工或者加工过程中原料肉的流程应确保堆砌产品的一致周转，并避免交叉污染，例如，在原料肉和即食产品之间的交叉污染；
- 非肉类成分的供应和添加应按照良好卫生操作规范和切实可行的HACCP方法进行，并包括净化的处理，例如，香草和香料；
- 含有非肉类蛋白成分的产品（按照法典的定义或标准）应正确标识标签；
- 非商业无菌产品的过程控制应在所有的加工活动中避免细菌生长和有毒物质的产生，例如，在发酵、部分加热处理、干燥、熟制和腌制加工过程中。过程标准可以包括取样、发酵后调节pH值，加热或者烟熏后调节时间/温度表，干燥后调节水分/蛋白比例，调节亚硝酸盐作为加工成分的组成和实施；
- 如果加热和（或）其他加工处理不足以保证产品的稳定性，产品应冷却到相应的贮藏温

[1] 相关的动物种类的有纹理的肉应经过主管机构确认的旋毛形线虫病的检查。

度，并保证产品的安全，不会引起细菌的生长；

- 产品的成分，例如，在加工腊肠乳液中抑制细菌成分，添加培养基、调节 pH 值，应达到可以控制细菌的水平；
- 用于生产发酵产品的原料肉的微生物污染应尽可能低，类似的，机械分离的肉类只能按照合适的时间/温度进程表操作，以满足主管部门对产品安全的要求；
- 加工生产自身稳定的密封坚固容器罐装的产品应根据法典指南51；
- 烹饪的产品应满足能够使病原菌减少的时间/内部温度的控制参数，包括满足特定的操作目的，实施标准和微生物标准；
- 巴氏杀菌或者其他热处理过程应对所有密封罐内的热处理的冷冻产品有效，以确保产品的安全能够维持到自身的使用寿命，并考虑所有可能的保存因素；
- 除非能够通过测试或者其他方法确定不存在旋毛虫病，从各种受旋毛虫感染的动物躯体获得的含有条纹的肌肉的加工处理，无论采用单独或者结合方法处理，应足以消灭旋毛虫；
- 李斯特氏菌污染的热处理的/非自身稳定的，和非热处理的/自身稳定的产品应通过采用 SSOPs 和 GHPs 程序预防，例行进行微生物确认；
- 应防止干燥的产品受环境污染，并防潮；
- 加工碎肉、肉粉、或机械分离的肉类产品应具有在线的电磁的或者其他方式的金属碎片探测检出器。

如果对肉类包装或者打包：

- 包装材料应适合使用和贮存，并采用卫生方式；
- 箱体或者纸板箱应具有合适的内衬或其他保护肉类的材料，除非对于成片的肉，例如，切割的在打包之前单独包装的肉，不需要内衬或者其他的保护。

如果肉类置于某房间中冷藏：

- 没有装在箱子内部的肉应悬挂在架子或者置于盘子中，并保证充分通气；
- 没有装在箱子里的裸露肉的保存方式应避免因滴落的液体引起的交叉污染；
- 装有肉的箱体应堆叠整齐，并保证充分的空气流通；
- 存放于盘子中的肉应避免接触上方盘子的底部。

如果肉类置于一个冷冻房间或其他冷冻设备内：

- 在放置之前肉类的温度应降低到可以接受的水平；
- 暴露的肉的贮存方式应保证其卫生不会被包装的肉或者打包的材料影响；
- 无论是胴体肉还是在箱内的肉，不应直接堆放在地板上，并应保证充分的空气流通；
- 冷冻仓库应在保证肉类的安全性和适应性的条件下运行和维护；
- 应对温度进行连续记录和监测；
- 应保持足够的详细控制记录。

152. 如果原料肉解冻进行进一步的加工，卫生控制应保证解冻不会引起微生物的生长或者有毒物质的形成不会造成对人类健康的风险。卫生控制应包括化冻的液体充分流出。

153. 加工厂负责人应建立和实施确定和验证肉和肉类制品的贮藏寿命的程序。

154. 在某些情况下，没有满足微生物目标、实施标准、过程标准或微生物标准的即食产品（RTE），可以进行重新加工、判定为不合格或者不可食用的。在相应的情况下，应进行跟踪抽样以确保即食产品（RTE）的再加工满足控制的微生物标准。如果即食产品（RTE）已经在随烹饪和（或）其他的保存处理之后受到细菌污染，可能会对公共健康产生危害，产品必须重新制作或者废弃。

155. 如果加工厂被批准、注册或者登记为各种动物的产品加工，所有的操作必须按照时间或者空间分类控制，以避免不同种原屠宰动物的肉类产生混淆事故，并保证包装时不会误识。

9.8 判定为不安全或者不适合人类消费的动物产品部分的卫生要求

156. 对于判定为不安全或者不适合人类消费的动物产品部分应实施特殊的卫生措施。这些措施应避免其与其他可食部分和肉的交叉污染，以及避免任何错换的可能。

判定为不安全或者不适合人类消费的动物的部分应：

- 立即放入指定的槽、容器、手推车或者其他处理设备中；
- 按照相应的类型和最终用途标识确认；
- 对于判定为不合格的材料，应在特定保留的房间内操作，并安全转移到处理的区域。

9.9 对于进入流通环节的产品的撤回体系

157. 加工厂应具有有效的体系能够将进入流通的产品撤回。主管部门应确认该体系的有效性。如果某一加工厂由于公众健康原因进行了产品撤回，主管部门应被告知。消费者和利害相关方在这种情况下也应能够恰当的获得通知。

158. 要求产品撤回体系应具有下列能力：

- 撤销，加工厂负责人实施撤销措施，避免不安全或者不适合人类消费的产品的配送、陈列或者供货；
- 召回，由加工厂采取措施，召回已提供的或加工好准备提供的不安全或者不适合人类消费的产品；
- 扣留，由主管部门对产品实施扣留处置，以保证产品不会在等待做出处理决定之前被移动或者损害；也包括加工厂负责人根据主管部门的指示的产品留存。

159. 根据特定情形或有可能产生公众健康风险情况时采用的特殊撤回系统。

160. 如果有必要进行产品撤回的话，相关的产品数量应大于单一产品或者样品批次的数量。主管部门应在最大程度上确保加工厂已经采取了所有必要的步骤确保所有受到影响或潜在受到影响的产品包含在撤回的产品中。

加工厂负责人设计的撤回体系应包括：

- 有利于快速和完全撤回所涉及批次产品的确认、管理和操作程序；
- 提供能够对问题来源进行追溯的记录；
- 提供可能会促进任何相关的调查和加工投入的记录；
- 定期审议和检测；
- 提供包含对主管部门、消费者和其他利害相关方适用的联系方式。如果涉及公众健康问题，这一点尤其重要。

10 加工厂：维护和卫生

161. 本节提供的原则和指南是对国际推荐操作规程法典标准：食品卫生总则（CAC/RCP 1－1969，Rev 4－2003）的第Ⅵ部分的原则和指南的补充。

10.1 加工厂、设备和设施的维护和卫生计划中的肉类卫生原则的实施

i. 构建、设备和设施的维护和卫生应采用使肉类污染最小化的方法；

ii. 应具有有效和正确的维护和卫生文件程序（参见9.2.1）；

iii. 维护和卫生的有效监测应作为肉类卫生程序的基本要素；

iv. 应对判定为“可疑”的动物的屠宰和修整采取特殊的卫生要求。

10.2 维护和卫生

162. 加工厂、设备和设施应处于正常状态，维修良好，便于卫生检查和防止肉品污染，例如，金属碎片、破碎的石膏和化学品的污染。

163. 卫生标准操作程序（SSOPs）应包含指定清洁计划的范围、清洁的指标、责任人员以及检查和记录等。

清洁程序和计划应：

- 根据相关的实际情况制定适用的SSOPs程序；
- 提供废物和切除物的贮存设施；
- 除非条件允许而使用清洁剂，但应保证对肉类没有由于清洁剂或者卫生因素随之发生的污染；
- 应对清洁程序的效力进行监测，例如，进行感官检验和对肉类接触表面的微生物取样检验，并在必要时进行重新设计清洁程序。

164. 屠宰和修整胴体使用设备的特殊清洁程序，例如，刀、锯、切割设备和冲洗喷头。

此类设备应：

- 在每阶段的工作之前进行清洁和卫生处理；
- 应在工作期间和（或）间隙对其进行适当次数的浸入热水或其他方法的清洁、卫生处理；
- 在接触到可能会具有食源性疾病的非正常或者病体组织的情况，应立即清洁和卫生处理；
- 应在指定的区域保存，并保证不会产生污染。

165. 容器和设备在清洁和卫生处理之前不能从“不可食用”的区域进入“可以食用”的区域。

166. 害虫控制是维护和卫生中的关键步骤，并应遵循GHP程序，按照国际推荐操作规程法典标准：食品卫生总则52的规定。

特别是：

- 程序应正确书面表述并由加工厂负责人确认；
- 使用杀虫剂处理的区域、房间、设施和设备应按照使用说明实施；
- 农药和其他的害虫控制化学品应安全保存，并限制由获得授权的人保管操作。

11 人员卫生

167. 动物的屠宰和修整，以及肉类的处理和检验，都有很多交叉污染的可能。人员卫生操作应避免无谓的一般污染，并避免可能会产生食物源性疾病的人类病原体的交叉污染。本节提供的指南是对国际推荐操作规程法典标准：食品卫生总则（CAC/RCP 1－1969，Rev 4－2003）的第Ⅶ部分的原则和指南的补充。

168. 从含有原料肉的房间或区域出来的人员进入肉成品和肉制品（尤其是熟制产品）的房间或区域时，应彻底清洗、更换和（或）消毒他们的防护服，或者将交叉污染的可能性降到最低限度。

11.1 人员清洁

169. 直接或间接接触动物可食部分或者肉类的人员在他们的工作期间应保持适当的个人清洁和卫生行为，并不应患有可能会向肉类转移传染的临床疾病。

直接或间接接触动物可食部分或肉类的人员应：

- 保持适当的人员清洁标准；
- 穿着与工作环境相应的防护服装，以保证非一次性的防护服装在工作之前和工作中的清洁状态；
- 如果在屠宰和修整以及肉类的处理过程中戴手套，保证其类型适合相应操作行为，例如，不锈钢锁子甲，编织纤维、乳胶，并根据规范使用，例如，在使用之前洗手，如果被污染了更换或者卫生处理；
- 如果接触了可能会具有食物源性细菌的非正常动物部分，手和防护服装应立即清洁和卫生处理；
- 采用防水材料覆盖切口和伤口；
- 防护服装和人员用品应贮存在与肉类贮存区域分开的地方。

11.2 人员健康状态

170. 加工厂应维持相关的人员健康记录。

与动物的可食部分或者肉类直接或间接接触的人员在工作期间应：

- 必要的情况下，在雇用之前和雇用期间应进行体检；
- 如果有人被临床感染，或者怀疑携带了可能会通过肉类传播的传染性病菌，应停止工作；
- 对于传染性病菌，了解和遵守向加工厂负责人的报告要求。

12 运输

171. 本节提供的指南是对国际推荐操作规程法典标准：食品卫生总则（CAC/RCP 1－1969，Rev 4－2003）的第Ⅷ部分的原则和指南的补充。

172. 根据在没有足够的温度控制条件下致病菌和致腐烂微生物繁殖的可能性，肉类应在能够获得安全和合适目的的温度控制条件下运输。温度的持续监控和记录设备应与相应的运输车辆和批次容器匹配。此外，运输条件应提供对外来污染和破坏的足够保护，并尽量减少致病菌和致腐烂微生物的生长。

173. 如果肉类不经意暴露于不当的温度条件下或者污染源时，可能会影响安全和适用性，主管人员在进一步的运输或者发送之前应进行检验。

13 产品信息和消费者意识

174. 相应的产品信息和足够的食品卫生知识对于预防食物加工链后期的错误处理是非常必要的。预包装食品应采用清楚的说明以利食物加工链中的下一人员安全处理、分配、贮藏和使用产品。对于肉类安全和适用性的产品信息和消费者需知的原则和指南在国际推荐操作规程法典标准：食品卫生总则（CAC/RCP 1－1969，Rev 4－2003）的第Ⅸ部分中有详述。

175. 肉类成品和肉制品的贮藏条件应清楚的标识在包装上。

176. 肉类成品和加工品应当给予适当标注，以对消费者提供安全的处理、冷冻和贮藏指导。没有接受足够的微生物杀灭处理的肉类产品（例如，含有新鲜肉、部分烹饪的肉，或者采用了次级抑制剂的产品）需标注应采用有效生物杀灭的处理、冷藏、贮存、烹饪和制备的声明。

14 培训

177. 对于安全和适合人类消费的肉类，对加工厂主管人员充分的培训是非常重要的。本节的指南和原则是对国际推荐操作规程法典标准：食品卫生总则（CAC/RCP 1 - 1969，Rev 4 - 2003）的第X部分的原则和指南的补充。

14.1 肉类卫生培训原则

从事肉类卫生行为的人员应经过培训和（或）指导，达到培训、知识和技能的要求的水平。主管部门指定或认可的培训，应：

i. 与肉类卫生行为或操作相符合；

ii. 使特殊肉类卫生行为的潜力与影响人类健康的食物源性的风险性相适应；

iii. 正确的文件记录，包括培训程序的记录；

iv. 适当的校验；

v. 由第三方递交的经主管部门的认可（证书）。

14.2 培训程序

培训程序应：

- 向人员提供实施指定的肉类卫生任务的培训、知识、技能和能力，例如，屠宰后检验，统计程序控制的确认，HACCP；
- 最大程度上提供符合要求的实际培训；
- 在必要情况下，安排人员的正式测试；
- 确保监管人员具有相应的技能；
- 进行专业资格的识别和建设；
- 提供管理人员的继续教育。

附件

附件 1 肉类屠宰后感官检验程序的风险评估

1 介绍

1. 屠宰后检验是肉类生产特有的食品卫生措施的系列程序。此类程序被认为是总体控制程序的主要组成部分，定义为："在生产过程中所有的条件和措施对获得安全的和适合性肉类是必要的。"

2. 食品卫生的通则表明"在确定某种（食品控制）要求是否必要或者合适时，最好在 HACCP 的框架内做出风险评估，"❶。许多持续时间较长的屠宰后检验程序比较复杂，劳动强度比较大，对于不同的屠宰动物也无所区别，并很少考虑到他们对降低食物源性公共健康风险的影响。考虑到这些原因，一些国家的主管部门目前正在实施科学程序的调查❷。

3. 本附件一般适用于例行在线感官检验程序的评估。其他的检验技术的实施，例如，感官检验的组织透视，也将纳入考虑。

4. 对于屠宰后感官检验风险基础上的评估，应建立在相关的危害风险分析基础上，并获得实施目标。目前很少有这类风险评估。如果缺乏的话，其他的食物源性风险对人类健康的科学知识的资源，例如，人类监视数据，风险等级程序，可以用于开发风险基础上的屠宰后检验程序。

5. 本节的原则和指南应适用于屠宰后感官检验的评估程序，以确定肉类的适应性。

2 基于风险的肉类屠宰后检验的目的

6. 基于风险的肉类屠宰后检验应达到以下目的：

- 确定特定的屠宰后检验程序的消费者保护水平；
- 屠宰后检验的相关措施，以达到肉类的全面风险控制水平（以及对消费者的风险），由此允许风险管理定位与最大程度上减少肉源性暴露风险的卫生资源成比例；
- 适用于同样的目的和内容的不同检验程序的有效性的比较，例如，阳性预期值；
- 提供对不同的风险管理方法进行评估的信息，例如，监控计划的区域划分，可行性和不同屠宰后检验程序的比较投资，交叉污染的潜力；
- 屠宰后检验程序进入"用于消费的生产"的肉类卫生体系的综合方法。

3 风险分析

3.1 风险管理框架

7. 基于风险基础的屠宰后检验程序的制定和实施应利用风险管理框架 55。4 项内容包括：初级风险管理行为，风险管理方案评估，风险管理决议的实施，采取的决议的监控和审议。所有的内

---

❶ 推荐国际操作规范：食品卫生一般原理（CAC/RCP 1－1969，Rev4－2003）。

❷ 主管机构在工业界和主管机构在确定肉类卫生行为的操作的分别的角色方面具有不同的方法，本附件没有涉及这个问题。

容要求在风险评估风险管理和其他利害相关方进行有效的风险交流。风险管理框架的采用是法典系统内持续工作的主题，在有些法典文件中有所描述。

3.2 风险评估

8. 在要求的情况下，风险评估应在初步的风险管理活动中委托进行。风险评估包括4个步骤：危害确认、危害特征，暴露评估，风险识别。该程序的结果应定性，并与所有的关于屠宰后肉类检验的因素结合，以做出关于风险控制相应程序的风险管理决定。

9. 在理想的情况下，风险评估应将对人类健康的风险进行定量，在一定保护水平上的风险管理措施（ALOP）将确定屠宰后检验程序的性质和密度。然而，肉类的微生物风险评价由于定量风险评价模式的缺乏目前受到限制。此外，科学信息和定量风险特征的相关安排以及对人类健康的影响可以提供风险决策的客观基础。在有些情况下，风险管理决议将围绕不同的检验程序带来的危害水平对可能产生的人类健康风险的接受程度。

4 风险基础上的肉类屠宰后检验程序制定的基本原则

i. 风险基础上的检验程序应源于风险分析原则的应用。

ii. 风险基础上屠宰后检验程序的制定应：

- 包括风险管理框架的应用；
- 在适当和可行的情况下，包括量化的风险评价；
- 考虑到源自食物加工链的所有相关信息；
- 考虑到疾病的发展趋势；
- 考虑到动物的初级生产和屠宰后检验的所有相关信息。

iii. 检验程序应在特定的内容中对实施进行评估，例如，屠宰后动物的种类和类别，特定的地理区域，特定的动物养殖体系。

iv. 如果对具有相同的目的和内容进行不同的检验程序的评估：

- 应当建立与这些程序相关的风险控制水平进行比较的客观基础；
- 影响肉类安全的异常和可见的污染的每一种检验程序的效力应纳入考虑；
- 其他的风险管理因素也应相应的纳入考虑中，例如：非疏忽的交叉污染的潜在危险，可能性和可行性。

v. 在必要的情况下，应考虑典型的和充分的现场试验，以确定物种检验程序的实施属性，例如，密度、种群和异常情况的不确定率。

vi. 在适当的情况下，应设计实验室检验以确定可能会影响公共健康的风险的重要程度，这已经在风险确认中有所描述。

vii. 屠宰后检验程序的例行实施不应增加微生物交叉污染的风险。

viii. 除了检验递交体系，主管部门应负责确定屠宰后检验程序相关人员的责任，并确保满足任何风险基础上调整的要求。

ix. 其他的检验程序（例如血清检验）可以用于实施屠宰后检验，也可能会通过肉眼检验即可。

5 风险基础上屠宰后检验程序制定的指南

5.1 肉类卫生因素的确认

10. 风险确定程序应用于确定检验程序评估的目的，类似异常或者明显的污染存在的公共健康迹象的可能范围。在此之后，实地试验应用于验证与风险相关的特定检验程序或者新技术的实施特征。

5.2 实地试验

11. 一旦已经建立了风险的范围，现场试验可以作为确定这些风险在动物种群中流行的一种手段，这些风险对消费者的潜在暴露和不同检验程序对这些暴露的潜在影响。现场试验应在主管部门的监视下和雇用的管理人员的实施下进行。评估中检验的动物数量应对特定的屠宰后检验程序获得的检测速率作出统计有效确认。

12. 采样计划必须对屠宰的群体具有代表性，关顾到生物的变异性，其基本类型和常见的变异形态，例如，动物年龄地理区域、养殖类型和季节的影响。可以考虑不同类型的实验设计，取决于屠宰种群的主要的异常情况，以及详细检验的后勤管理。

13. 如果对不同的检验程序进行比较，所有的程序应适用于相同的动物，每一种检验阶段应设计用于提供独立的结果，测试应包含足够的样品以允许用不同检验程序检验作出的相应结论。靶组织作为测定其他组织和（或）其他处理的组织中可能会包含的异常情况的“指示物”应包含在实地实验设计中。实地检测结果的详细记录是必要的，包括对所有检测到的异常情况的相应病理描述。

14. 实验室调研，例如，微生物和组织学检测，应用于确定潜在的已经在风险确定程序中确认的公共健康重要的风险的范围。应从异常中获得具有代表性的样品的数量和范围，以确定风险评价程序的结果，并提供靶组织的风险流行性（以及积累性）方面尽可能多的信息。实地试验应包括感官正常的靶组织的风险流行性（以及积累性）有代表性的调验，以提供感官上异常的靶组织的风险流行性（以及积累性）的比较。

5.3 灵敏度

15. 采用特殊的检验程序获得的消费者理解的保护水平需要实施过程中获得的风险控制水平的相关知识。应确定屠宰后检验程序的灵敏度，以确定其对全面的公共健康目的的贡献。

16. 屠宰后检验程序的灵敏度是指检定出可能含有相关风险的明显异常的躯体或者部分躯体的概率。

17. 屠宰后检验程序的灵敏度，例如，肉眼检验，触诊和（或）切开检验，应在主管部门确定的统计限度范围内确定。目标组织预期的最终用途对于风险基础上屠宰后检验程序的制定具有重要影响。在选择屠宰后检验程序时，首先应提供这些程序对特定异常的检出与相关风险存在的相关性。

5.4 风险管理决定

18. 对于特定的屠宰后检验程序可接受性的风险管理决定，一般以含有相应的数据统计间隔异常没有检出的最坏的情况为基础。决定应考虑到以下相关的公共健康风险：

- 对于目标组织感官异常的流行性风险（以及积累性）；

- 对于目标组织感官正常的流行性风险（以及积累性）；
- 肉类生产的整个过程中通过所有的途径传播的流行性风险（以及积累性）。

19. 在一般的情况下，新的或者其他的检验程序应提供至少与现有的程序相当的消费者保护水平，除非有可能会影响不同的风险管理选择的强烈因素，例如，新的不可接受风险的引入，以及职业暴露的不恰当的风险。

20. 屠宰后检验要求的调整结果，可以包括对于特定的异常情况未检出比例的限制的实施特征。这些实施特征可以源自风险评价模型的定量化，或者现有实施调研基础上的定性化。

21. 如果关于屠宰后动物健康的详细信息可以通过初级生产获得，风险基础上的屠宰后检验程序可以在以各个批次检验为基础进行调整，同时，主管部门具有调整程序的频率和程度的责任。

22. 主管部门应在加工厂和国家两个层面管理屠宰后检验结果，并向加工厂和其他利害相关方反馈基于风险基础上屠宰后检验程序的检验结果。主管部门应确保体系改进的激励措施，例如，实施的确认，减少农场检验的频率，附加的屠宰程序的变化等。

23. 主管部门可以改变检验的条款要求，以及检验程序的次序，作为不同的屠宰后检验程序的科学评价结果，并允许引入新的检验工具，例如，镜检，检定异常的其他的技术，例如，组织成像，只要确认与目前的程序同等有效即可。

附件2 肉类微生物测试过程控制的确认

1 介绍

1. 对食物加工链中特殊点的微生物检测是验证基于风险的食品安全的一个非常重要的工具。微生物检验结果作为食品安全指标建立了相应的消费者保护水平，同时向加工业界提供了采用的具体的过程控制系统的最大灵活性。

2. 食品卫生的一般原则[1]表明“在确定某项（食品控制）要求是否必要还是适当时，应优先选择HACCP方法框架作风险分析”，同时任何微生物指标“应建立在合理的科学原理和规定的基础上，相应的情况下也应考虑程序、分析方法和措施限制”[2]。程序控制定义为：“生产过程中所有的实施的条件和措施对于获得肉类的安全和适应性是必须的。”

3. 在适当的情况下，微生物实施目的或者实施标准应包含在过程控制的确认中。

4. 如本附件的描述，微生物实施目的或者实施标准不同于微生物标准。后者用于判定产品或者食品批次的接受程度[3]。尽管没有包含在本附件中，肉类的微生物标准同样可用于评价可接受性。

2 微生物测试过程控制的确认

5. 预防性的，HACCP基础的方法应作为确定微生物过程控制最有效的方法。一旦确定了过程控制，微生物测试对于验证食品安全结果满足正在实施的基础要求是非常重要的。过程控制的微生物测试验证应在对消费者保护有意义的情况下实施。

6. 肉类微生物测试的过程控制验证为以下提供了工具：

- 评价加工厂对于排泄物和其他污染的过程控制的充分性和有效性；
- 确保对公共健康有重要意义的特定风险的控制水平；
- 促进程序标准中的特定步骤或者联合步骤的改进，以获得微生物实施目标或实施标准；
- 确定HACCP计划的审议和重新设计的必要性；
- 不同的情况下不同的过程控制系统结果的客观比较；
- 为主管部门制定保证体系提供依据。

3 微生物检测要求建立的原则

i. 微生物检测要求的建立应考虑到食物加工链中的所有相关信息，包括与公共健康相关的活体动物的健康状况。

ii. 微生物检测应要求：指定的风险，指定的产品和指定的过程，可以合理获得的，并只在那些指定的食物加工链中特殊的点上应用。在确定测试要求时，应考虑采样单元中微生物分布的不均匀性和分析程序的内在的变异性。

iii. 微生物检测要求应建立在科学的分析和建议的基础上，以及可以获得足够的源自风险分析

---

[1] 食品卫生推荐国际操作标准（CAC/RCP 1－1969，Rev 4－2003）。

[2] 关于SSOPs的微生物测试分类，不作为过程控制的微生物实施目的或者实施标准。

[3] 工厂原理和食品微生物标准的实施（CAC/GL 21－1997）。

的数据的基础上。如果已经建立了以消费者保护水平为基础的食品安全目标，应确定食品安全目标（FSO）和实施目标（POs）或实施标准（PCs）之间的关系。

iv. 微生物检测要求的严格程度应适合人类健康风险。

v. 如果缺少足够的人类健康风险知识，应以调研目前的加工行业基本实践为基础开始建立微生物检测要求，并在其后根据对人类健康的目标进行调整。基础调研的采样计划应对于屠宰的群体具有代表性，并满足供应的原料样品中由于已知的微生物变异性引起的风险，影响微生物变异的因素，例如，地理区域、养殖类型和季节的变化。

vi. 微生物检测要求应建立在反映特定的食品中对人类健康具有风险指标的微生物或者病原体本身的基础上。

vii. 微生物检测的要求，包括实施目标或实施标准，也可包含实施指南或法定标准，应由主管部门负责，并与相关的利害方协商而制定。

viii. 主管部门应确认微生物检测要求与特定规则的符合性，例如，微生物统计过程控制要求，沙门氏菌的标准等。

4 微生物测试过程控制确认程序的实施

4.1 说明

7. 应建立标准化的随机抽样计划，包括过程步骤的说明，产品、尺寸和样品的类型、抽样的时间和日期，收集和运输方法。食物加工链中多个步骤的抽样和测试应提供更多的关于过程控制的信息，并允许对不符合加工厂和主管部门目标的反映的反馈。

8. 对组织的抽样可以是破坏性的，例如，切除，或者非破坏性的，例如，擦洗或者擦拭。没有一种方法可以恢复样品表面上的所有菌群。由于非破坏性的取样的恢复只破坏性方法恢复的一部分，本方法中描述的微生物检测要求应根据采用的取样类型建立。

9. 考虑到可行性，微生物检测要求不大可能会作为 HACCP 计划的一部分实施基础加以确认。然而，微生物验证应以足够多的频率进行，应以确保作为 HACCP 计划一部分的程序标准的有效性。这些标准可以真实的时间计算，可能会组成 HACCP 的关键控制点中的关键限量，并在相应的情况下服从于微生物验证。

10. 作为微生物的指标，例如，大肠杆菌、肠道细菌和菌落总数（总生菌数），这些指示微生物的存在和（或）浓度应反映过程控制的状态或条件，或者过程控制的缺乏。在特定的风险情况下（例如，胴体中的沙门氏菌或即食产品中的李斯特菌）[1]，其流行性一般是预屠宰风险的反映（例如，沙门氏菌隐藏进入动物的表皮中），以及在生产加工中的特殊步骤风险的反映。

11. 主管部门应提供管理的灵活性，以便于在加工厂水平建立最有效的验证系统，例如，其他的胴体采样点，只要加工厂可以确认他们在确认胴体污染方面同样有效的情况下即可。类似的，主管部门应提供与其他指示微生物相关的样品或测试相关的对比单元和数量，以及能够提供同样保证的程序。

12. 其他的适当的微生物检测方法应建立在能够提供较现行方法优越的基础上。

4.2 采样的频率

13. 对于确定采样的频率没有单一的方法，对于屠宰和修整的加工厂，采样的频率应根据特定

[1] 关于食物源性细菌的 CCFH 和 JEMRA 的进行的工作应纳入考虑。

的程序或者根据动物的量来确定。除了保证随机采样外，应考虑在加工厂层面的变化因素，包括：原料的来源、肉类加工的类型和特性，以及生产的数量。

14. 抽样的频率应根据实施情况增加或者减少。一旦 HACCP 基础上的程序表明，该程序提供了 HACCP 基础上的可接受操作上的一致性水平，随后的微生物测试必须足以保证过程控制的运行。

4.3 实验室分析

15. 测试和计数的方法应具有可行性、精确性、重现性、灵敏性和选择性。只有可靠的和可以重现的方法可以使用。实验室间的测试应作为微生物确认程序的一部分。在有争议的情况下，应采用认可的参考方法。

16. 为进行有意义的分析，并允许进行不同控制体系的比较，应指定结果的计算方法，包括整体的/单个的结果的处理，来自同样的胴体或不同的胴体有意义的结果的计算（例如，对数方法）。

4.4 管理措施

17. 关于微生物检测的管理要求可以用几种方法描述。对于指示微生物，可以采用 2 种或 3 种特征样品数量（M 或 m），在其他的情况下，可以改变采样计划。对于细菌标准应采用两种方案。如果根据目前的工业操作，应采用百分比，例如：m 的 80 个百分点，M 的 98 个百分点，可以采用一定的统计方法。

18. 应有有效的体系用于加工厂和相关利益方信息的分发和共享，相应的，应有有效的体系用于保持和提高肉类的过程控制。

19. 主管部门应在加工厂和国家两个层面调整分析结果，并向加工厂和其他利害相关方的反馈。

20. 除了过程控制的确认之外，应采用微生物检测的结果于养殖场的控制，例如，强制采取措施降低肥胖猪中沙门氏菌的流行。

21. 对于出现不符合微生物要求的情况，应采取确认措施。主管部门和（或）加工厂应对测试结果以及影响公共健康的特定病原菌采取相应的对策。对于与公共健康状态相关的详细信息，对来源于屠宰的动物的，可以从初级生产中获得信息，例如，对于沙门氏菌，在某些生产系统中的肥胖猪和烤鸡，应于加工厂层面的过程控制方面给予反映，并可考虑包含在预屠宰的风险水平中。

22. 主管部门在采取管理措施的时候，应确定与公共健康或其他相关信息相关的微生物检测结果。如果有效的控制不能正确实施的话，有必要调整干预或卫生措施。

23. 对于重复的不符合情况，除了其他措施，主管部门应要求加工厂负责人审议或评价 HACCP 计划，并可以指定增加采样频率以判定要求的过程控制水平是否恢复。

CODE OF HYGIENIC PRACTICE FOR MEAT[1]

(*CAC/RCP 58 – 2005*)

---

[1] This Code supersedes the following Codex Codes of Practices: Recommended International Code of Hygienic Practice for Fresh Meat (CAC/RCP 11 – 1976, Rev. 1 – 1993); Recommended International Code of Hygienic Practice for Game (CAC/RCP 29 – 1983, Rev. 1 – 1993); Recommended International Code for Ante-Mortem and Post-Mortem Inspection of Slaughter Animals and for Ante-Mortem and Post-Mortem Judgement of Slaughter Animals and Meat (CAC/RCP 41 – 1993); Recommended International Code of Hygienic Practice for Processed Meat and Poultry Products (CAC/RCP 13 – 1976, Rev. 1 (1985); Recommended Code of Hygienic Practice for Poultry Processing (CAC/RCP 14 – 1976); Recommended International Code of Practice for the Production, Storage and Composition of Mechanically Separated Meat Intended for Further Processing (CAC/RCP 32 – 1293).

1 INTRODUCTION

1. Meat has traditionally been viewed as a vehicle for a significant proportion of human food-borne disease. Although the spectrum of meat-borne diseases of public health importance has changed with changing production and processing systems, continuation of the problem has been well illustrated in recent years by human surveillance studies of specific meat-borne pathogens such as *Escherichia coli* O157: H7, *Salmonella* spp., *Campylobacter* spp. and *Yersinia enterocolitica*. In addition to existing biological, chemical and physical hazards, new hazards are also appearing e. g., the agent of bovine spongiform encephalopathy (BSE). Furthermore consumers have expectations about suitability issues which are not necessarily of human health significance.

2. A contemporary risk-based approach to meat hygiene requires that hygiene measures should be applied at those points in the food chain where they will be of greatest value in reducing food-borne risks to consumers. This should be reflected in application of specific measures based on science and risk assessment, with a greater emphasis on prevention and control of contamination during all aspects of production of meat and its further processing. Application of HACCP principles is an essential element. The measure of success of contemporary programmes is an objective demonstration of levels of hazard control in food that are correlated with required levels of consumer protection, rather than by concentrating on detailed and prescriptive measures that give an unknown outcome.

3. At the national level the activities of the Competent Authority having jurisdiction at the slaughterhouse (usually Veterinary Administrations[1]) very often serve animal health as well as public health objectives. This is particularly the case in relation to ante- and post-mortem inspection where the slaughterhouse is a key point in animal health surveillance, including zoonoses. Regardless of jurisdictional arrangements, it is important that this duality of functions is recognized and relevant public health and animal health activities are integrated.

4. A number of national governments are implementing systems that redefine the respective roles of industry and government in delivering meat hygiene activities. Irrespective of the delivery systems the competent authority is responsible for defining the role of personnel involved in meat hygiene activities where appropriate, and verifying that all regulatory requirements are met.

5. The principles of food safety risk management[2] should be incorporated wherever appropriate in the design and implementation of meat hygiene programmes. Specifically, work conducted by JEMRA, JECFA and FAO/WHO Expert Consultations and resulting risk management recommendations should be considered. Further, newly-recognised meat-borne risks to human health may require measures additional to those usually applied in meat hygiene, e. g., the potential for zoonotic transmission of central nervous system disorders of slaughtered livestock means that additional animal health surveillance programmes may need to be undertaken.

---

[1] OIE is currently working on guidelines on application at national level addressing 'ante- and post-mortem activities in the production of meat to reduce hazards of public and animal health significance'.

[2] Working Principles for Risk Analysis for Application in the Framework of the Codex Alimentarius (Codex Procedural Manual, 14th Edition); Proposed Draft Working Principles and Guidelines for the Conduct of Microbiological Risk Management (CX/FH 05/37/6).

2 SCOPE AND USE OF THIS CODE

6. The scope of this code covers hygiene provisions for raw meat, meat preparations and manufactured meat from the time of live animal production up to the point of retail sale. It further develops 'The Recommended International Code of Practice: General Principles of Food Hygiene'[1] in respect of these products. Where appropriate, the Annex to that code (Hazard Analysis and Critical Control Point System and Guidelines for its Application) and the Principles for the Establishment and Application of Microbiological Criteria for Foods[2] are further developed and applied in the specific context of meat hygiene.

7. For the purposes of this code, meat is that derived from domestic ungulates, domestic solipeds, domestic birds, lagomorphs, farmed game, farmed game birds (including ratites) and wild game. This Code of Practice may also be applied to other types of animals from which meat is derived, subject to any special hygienic measures required by the competent authority. Further to general hygiene measures applying to all species of animal as described above, this code also presents specific measures that apply to different species and classes of animals, e. g. wild game killed in the field.

8. The hygiene measures that are applied to the products described in this code, should take into account any further measures and food handling practices that are likely to be applied by the consumer. It should be noted that some of the products described in this code may not be subjected to a heat or other biocidal process before consumption.

9. Meat hygiene is by nature a complex activity, and this code refers to standards, texts and other recommendations developed elsewhere in the Codex system where linkages are appropriate, e. g., Principles for Food Import and Export Inspection and Certification (CAC/GL 20 – 1995), Proposed Draft Principles and Guidelines for the Conduct of Microbiological Risk Management (CX/FH 01/7 and ALINORM 03/13 paras 99 – 128), General Guidelines for Use of the Term "Halal" (CAC/GL 24 – 1997) and recommendations of the *Ad hoc* Intergovernmental Task Force on Animal Feeding (ALINORM 01/38 and ALINORM 01/38A).

10. To provide information that will enhance consistency, linkages should also be made to the standards, guidelines and recommendations contained in the OIE Terrestrial Animal Health Code that relate to zoonoses.

11. Subsets of the general principles (Section 4) are provided in subsequent sections within 'double-line boxes'. Where guidelines are provided at the section level, those that are more prescriptive in nature are presented in 'single-line boxes'. This is to indicate that they are recommendations based on current knowledge and practice. They should be regarded as being flexible in nature and subject to alternative provisions so long as required outcomes in terms of the safety and suitability of meat are met.

12. Traditional practices may result in departures from some of the meat hygiene recommendations presented in this code when meat is produced for local trade.

---

[1] CAC/RCP 1 – 1969, Rev. 4 – 2003.

[2] CAC/GL 21 – 1997.

3 DEFINITIONS

13. For the purposes of this code, the following definitions apply. (Note that more general definitions relating to food hygiene appear in The Recommended International Code of Practice: General Principles of Food Hygiene[1]).

Abattoir Any establishment where specified animals are slaughtered and dressed for human consumption and that is approved, registered and (or) listed by the competent authority for such purposes.

Animal Animals of the following types:

- Domestic ungulates;
- Domestic solipeds;
- Domestic birds i. e. poultry;
- Lagomorphs;
- Farmed game;
- Farmed game birds, including ratites;
- Wild game, i. e. wild land mammals and birds which are hunted (including those living in enclosed territory under conditions of freedom similar to those of wild game);
- Animals as otherwise specified by the competent authority.

Ante-mortem inspection[2] Any procedure or test conducted by a competent person on live animals for the purpose of judgement of safety and suitability and disposition.

Carcass The body of an animal after dressing.

Chemical residues Residues of veterinary drugs and pesticides as described in the Definitions for the Purpose of the Codex Alimentarius[3].

Competent authority[4] The official authority charged by the government with the control of meat hygiene, including setting and enforcing regulatory meat hygiene requirements.

Competent body A body officially recognised and overseen by the competent authority to undertake specified meat hygiene activities.

Competent person A person who has the training, knowledge, skills and ability to perform an assigned task, and who is subject to requirements specified by the competent authority.

Condemned Inspected and judged by a competent person, or otherwise determined by the competent authority, as being unsafe or unsuitable for human consumption and requiring appropriate disposal.

Contaminant Any biological or chemical agent, foreign matter, or other substance not intentionally added to food that may compromise food safety or suitability.[5]

---

[1] Recommended International Code of Practice: General Principles of Food Hygiene (CAC/RCP 1 - 1969, Rev. 4 - 2003).

[2] These and other procedures and tests stipulated by the Competent Authority, may also be conducted, in particular for the purposes of animal health.

[3] Procedural Manual of the Codex Alimentarius Commission.

[4] The Competent Authority provides official assurances in international trade of meat. Requirements for certification for public health and fair trade purposes have been developed by the Codex Committee on Food and Import and Export Inspection and Certification Systems (ref. CAC/GL 26 - 1997). Requirements for certification for animal health (including zoonoses) purposes are contained in the OIE Terrestrial Animal Health Code (ref. Section 1. 2 Obligations and ethics in international trade). Both should be read in parallel where veterinary certification is required.

[5] Recommended International Code of Practice: General Principles of Food Hygiene (CAC/RCP 1 - 1969, Rev 4 - 2003).

Disease or defect Any abnormality affecting safety and (or) suitability.

Dressing The progressive separation of the body of an animal into a carcass and other edible and inedible parts.

Equivalence The capability of different meat hygiene systems to meet the same food safety and (or) suitability objectives.

Establishment A building or area used for performing meat hygiene activities that is approved, registered and (or) listed by the competent authority for such purposes.

Establishment operator The person in control of an establishment who is responsible for ensuring that the regulatory meat hygiene requirements are met.

Food safety objective (FSO) The maximum frequency and (or) concentration of a hazard in a food at the time of consumption that provides or contributes to the appropriate level of protection (ALOP).

Fresh Meat Meat that apart from refrigeration has not been treated for the purpose of preservation other than through protective packaging and which retains its natural characteristics.

Game depot A building in which killed wild game is temporarily held prior to transfer to an establishment, and which is approved, registered and (or) listed by the competent authority for this purpose. (*Note that for the purposes of this code, a game depot is a particular type of establishment*).

Good Hygienic Practice (GHP) All practices regarding the conditions and measures necessary to ensure the safety and suitability of food at all stages of the food chain. [1]

Hazard A biological, chemical or physical agent in, or condition of, food with the potential to cause an adverse health effect. [2]

Hunter A person involved in the killing and (or) bleeding, partial evisceration and partial field dressing of killed wild game.

Inedible Inspected and judged by a competent person, or otherwise determined by the competent authority to be unsuitable for human consumption.

Manufactured Meat Products resulting from the processing of raw meat or from the further processing of such processed products, so that when cut, the cut surface shows that the product no longer has the characteristics of fresh meat.

Meat All parts of an animal that are intended for, or have been judged as safe and suitable for, human consumption.

Meat hygiene All conditions and measures necessary to ensure the safety and suitability of meat at all stages of the food chain.

Meat preparation Raw meat which has had foodstuffs, seasonings or additives added to it.

Mechanically separatedmeat (MSM) Product obtained by removing meat from flesh-bearing bones after boning or from poultry carcasses, using mechanical means that result in the loss or modification of the muscle fibre structure.

Minced meat Boneless meat which has been reduced into fragments.

Official inspector A competent person who is appointed, accredited or otherwise recognised by the competent authority to perform official meat hygiene activities on behalf of, or under the supervision of the competent authority.

---

[1] WHO Teachers Handbook, 1999.

[2] Definitions for the Purpose of the Codex Alimentarius. Procedural Manual, 14th edition.

Organoleptic inspection Using the senses of sight, touch, taste and smell for identification of diseases and defects.

Performance criterion The effect in frequency and (or) concentration of a hazard in a food that must be achieved by the application of one or more control measures to provide or contribute to a performance objective (PO) or a food safety objective (FSO).

Performance objective The maximum frequency and (or) concentration of a hazard in a food at a specified step in the food chain before the time of consumption that provides or contributes to a food safety objective (FSO) or ppropriate level of protection (ALOP), as applicable.

Post-mortem inspection❶ Any procedure or test conducted by a competent person on all relevant parts of slaughtered/killed animals for the purpose of judgement of safety and suitability and disposition.

Primary production All those steps in the food chain constituting animal production and transport of animals to the abattoir, or hunting and transporting wild game to a game depot.

Process control All conditions and measures applied during the production process that are necessary to achieve safety and suitability of meat. ❷

Process criterion The physical process control parameters (e. g. time, temperature) at a specified step that can be applied to achieve a performance objective or performance criterion❸.

***Quality assurance* (*QA*)** All the planned and systematic activities implemented within the quality system and demonstrated as needed, to provide adequate confidence that an entity will fulfil requirements for quality. ❹

Quality assurance* (*QA*) *systemThe organisational structure, procedures, processes and resources needed to implement quality assurance.

Raw meat Fresh meat, minced meat or mechanically separated meat❺.

Ready-to-Eat* (*RTE*) *productsProducts that are intended to be consumed without any further biocidal steps.

Risk-based Containing any performance objective, performance criterion or process criterion developed according to risk analysis principles. ❻

Safe for humanconsumptionSafe for human consumption according to the following criteria:

- has been produced by applying all food safety requirements appropriate to its intended end-use;
- meets risk-based performance and process criteria for specified hazards; and
- does not contain hazards at levels that are harmful to human health.

***Sanitation standardoperating procedures* (*SSOPs*)** A documented system for assuring that personnel, facilities, equipment and utensils are clean and where necessary, sanitised to specified levels prior to and during operations.

Suitable for humanconsumptionSuitable for human consumption according to the following criteria:

- has been produced under hygienic conditions as outlined in this code;

---

❶ These and other procedures and tests stipulated by the Competent Authority, may also be conducted, in particular for the purposes of animal health.

❷ The "process" includes ante- and post-mortem inspection.

❸ This is an interim definition for the purpose of this Code.

❹ ISO 8402.

❺ This does not preclude interventions for the purpose of pathogen reduction.

❻ This is an interim definition for the purpose of this Code.

• is appropriate to its intended use[1]; and

• meets outcome-based parameters for specified diseases or defects as established by the competent authority.

Validation Obtaining evidence that the food hygiene control measure or measures selected to control a hazard in a food is capable of effectively and consistently controlling the hazard to the appropriate level.[2]

Verification Activities performed by the competent authority and (or) competent body to determine compliance with regulatory requirements.

Verification (Operator) The continual review of process control systems by the operator, including corrective and preventative actions to ensure that regulatory and (or) specified requirements are met.

Veterinary Inspector An official inspector who is professionally qualified as a veterinarian and carries out official meat hygiene activities[3] as specified by the competent authority.

4 GENERAL PRINCIPLES OF MEAT HYGIENE

i. Meat must be safe and suitable for human consumption and all interested parties including government, industry and consumers have a role in achieving this outcome.[4]

ii. The competent authority should have the legal power to set and enforce regulatory meat hygiene requirements, and have final responsibility for verifying that regulatory meat hygiene requirements are met. It should be the responsibility of the establishment operator to produce meat that is safe and suitable in accordance with regulatory meat hygiene requirements. There should be a legal obligation on relevant parties to provide any information and assistance as may be required by the competent authority.

iii. Meat hygiene programmes should have as their primary goal the protection of public health and should be based on a scientific evaluation of meat-borne risks to human health and take into account all relevant food safety hazards, as identified by research, monitoring and other relevant activities.

iv. The principles of food safety risk analysis should be incorporated wherever possible and appropriate in the design and implementation of meat hygiene programmes.[5]

v. Wherever possible and practical, competent authorities should formulate food safety objectives (FSOs) according to a risk-based approach so as to objectively express the level of hazard control that is required to meet public health goals.

vi. Meat hygiene requirements should control hazards to the greatest extent practicable throughout the entire food chain. Information available from primary production should be taken into account so as to tailor meat hygiene requirements to the spectrum and prevalence of hazards in

---

[1] See for example the General Guidelines for Use of the Term "Halal" (CAC/GL 24 – 1997).

[2] This is an interim definition for the purpose of this Code.

[3] These may include animal health objectives.

[4] Specific meat hygiene requirements should address biological, chemical and physical hazards; and pathophysiological and other characteristics associated with suitability for human consumption.

[5] Working Principles for Risk Analysis for Application in the Framework of the Codex Alimentarius, Procedural Manual, 14th edition; Codex Committee on Food Hygiene, proposed draft Principles and Guidelines for the Conduct of Microbiological Risk Management (CX/FH 05/37/6); Report of a Joint FAO/WHO Consultation on Principles and Guidelines for Incorporating Microbiological Risk Assessment in the Development of Food Safety Standards, Guidelines and Related Texts; Kiel, Germany, 18 – 22 March 2002.

the animal population from which the meat is sourced.

vii. The establishment operator should apply HACCP principles. To the greatest extent practicable, the HACCP principles should also be applied in the design and implementation of hygiene measures throughout the entire food chain.

viii. The competent authority should define the role of those personnel involved in meat hygiene activities where appropriate, including the specific role of the veterinary inspector.

ix. The range of activities involved in meat hygiene should be carried out by personnel with the appropriate training, knowledge, skills and ability as and where defined by the competent authority.

x. The competent authority should verify that the establishment operator has adequate systems in place to trace and withdraw meat from the food chain. Communication with consumers and other interested parties should be considered and undertaken where appropriate.

xi. As appropriate to the circumstances, the results of monitoring and surveillance of animal and human populations should be considered with subsequent review and (or) modification of meat hygiene requirements whenever necessary.

xii. Competent authorities should recognise the equivalence of alternative hygiene measures where appropriate, and promulgate meat hygiene measures that achieve required outcomes in terms of safety and suitability and facilitate fair practices in the trading of meat.

5 PRIMARY PRODUCTION

14. Primary production is a significant source of hazards associated with meat. A number of hazards are present in animal populations intended for slaughter and their control during primary production, often presents considerable challenges, e. g. , *E. coli* O157: H7, *Salmonella* spp. *Campylobacter* spp and various chemical and physical hazards. A risk-based approach to meat hygiene includes consideration of risk management options that may have a significant impact on risk reduction when applied at the level of primary production.[1]

15. Provision of relevant information on animals intended for slaughter facilitates application of risk-based meat hygiene programmes, and allows inspection procedures to be tailor-made to the spectrum and prevalence of diseases and defects in the particular animal population. This may be particularly important in situations where the presence of certain zoonotic agents is not detectable by routine organoleptic or laboratory tests, and special measures may need to be taken, e. g. possible exposure to cysts of *Cysticercus bovis*.

16. Voluntary or officially recognised QA systems implemented at primary production should be appropriately taken into account during verification of regulatory requirements.

17. The principles and guidelines presented in this section are supplemental to the objectives and guidelines in Section Ⅲ of the Recommended International Code of Practice: General Principles of Food Hygiene (CAC/RCP 1 - 1969, Rev. 4 - 2003).

5.1 PRINCIPLES OF MEAT HYGIENE APPLYING TO PRIMARY PRODUCTION

i. Primary production should be managed in a way that reduces the likelihood of introduction of

[1] Working Principles for Risk Analysis for Application in the Framework of the Codex Alimentarius, Procedural Manual, 14th edition.

hazards and appropriately contributes to meat being safe and suitable for human consumption.

ii. Whenever possible and practicable, systems should be established by the primary production sector and the competent authority, to collect, collate and make available, information on hazards and conditions that may be present in animal populations and that may affect the safety and suitability of meat.

iii. Primary production should include official or officially-recognised programmes for the control and monitoring of zoonotic agents in animal populations and the environment as appropriate to the circumstances, and notifiable zoonotic diseases should be reported as required.

iv. Good hygienic practice (GHP) at the level of primary production should involve for example the health and hygiene of animals, records of treatments, feed and feed ingredients and relevant environmental factors, and should include application of HACCP principles to the greatest extent practicable.

v. Animal identification practices should allow trace-back to the place of origin to the extent practicable, to allow regulatory investigation where necessary.

5.2 HYGIENE OF SLAUGHTER ANIMALS

18. Both primary producers and the competent authority should work together to implement risk-based meat hygiene programmes at the level of primary production that document the general health status of slaughter animals, and implement practices that maintain or improve that status, e. g. , zoonoses control programmes. QA programmes at the level of primary production should be encouraged and may include application of HACCP principles as appropriate to the circumstances. Such programmes should be taken into account by the competent authority in the overall design and implementation of risk-based meat hygiene programmes.

So as to facilitate the application of risk-based meat hygiene programmes:

- Primary producers should record relevant information to the extent possible on the health status of animals as it relates to the production of meat that is safe and suitable for human consumption. This information should be made available to the abattoir as appropriate to the circumstances.
- Systems should be in place for return from the abattoir to the primary producer, of information on the safety and suitability of slaughter animals and meat, in order to improve the hygiene on the farm and, where producer-led QA-programmes are applied, to be incorporated into these programmes to improve their effectiveness.
- The competent authority should systematically analyse monitoring and surveillance information from primary production so that meat hygiene requirements may be modified if necessary.

19. The competent authority should administer an official programme for control of specified zoonotic agents, chemical hazards and contaminants. This should be co-ordinated to the greatest extent possible with other competent authorities that may have responsibilities in public and animal health.

Official or officially-recognised programmes for specified zoonotic agents should include measures to:

- control and eradicate their presence in animal populations, or subsets of populations, e. g. , particular poultry flocks;
- prevent the introduction of new zoonotic agents;

• provide monitoring and surveillance systems that establish baseline data and guide a risk-based approach to control of such hazards in meat;

• control movement of animals between primary production units, and to abattoirs, where populations are under quarantine restrictions.

Official or officially-recognised programmes for chemical hazards and contaminants should include measures to:

• control the registration and use of veterinary drugs and pesticides so that residues do not occur in meat at levels that make the product unsafe[1] for human consumption; and

• provide monitoring and surveillance systems that establish baseline data and guide a risk-based approach to control of such hazards in meat.

20. Animal identification systems, to the extent practicable, should be in place at primary production level so that the origin of meat can be traced back from the abattoir or establishment to the place of production of the animals.

21. Animals should not be loaded for transport to the abattoir when:

• the degree of contamination of the external surfaces of the animal is likely to compromise hygienic slaughter and dressing, and suitable interventions such as washing or shearing are not available;

• information is available to suggest that animals may compromise the production of meat that is safe and suitable for human consumption, e. g. , presence of specific disease conditions or recent administration of veterinary drugs. In some situations, transport may proceed if the animals have been specifically identified (e. g. as "suspects") and are to be slaughtered under special supervision; or

• conditions causing animal stress may exist or arise that are likely to result in an adverse impact on the safety and suitability of meat.

5.3 HYGIENE OF KILLED WILD GAME

22. Only limited knowledge can be gained on the health status of populations of wild game hunted for meat; however, the competent authority should consider all sources when gathering such information. In this respect, hunters should be encouraged to provide relevant information, e. g. , geographical origin of wild game, and any clinical symptoms of disease observed in wild animal populations.

23. Wild game should be harvested in a manner so that:

• killing methods are consistent with the production of meat that is safe and suitable for human consumption; and

• their geographical origin is not subject to relevant official prohibitions on harvest, e. g. , in the case of concurrent chemical pest control programmes or animal health quarantine.

24. Hunters are particularly important in providing information on killed animals. They should be aware of their responsibilities in terms of supplying to the establishment, all relevant information that may impact on the safety and suitability of killed wild game meat, e. g. , symptoms of disease immediately before killing, grossly-apparent diseases and defects detected during partial field dressing and (or) evisceration. The competent authority should require that hunters or other people involved in harvesting of wild game undergo basic training in meat hygiene appropriate to field procurement, e. g. , recognition of diseases and defects,

---

[1] Guidelines for the Establishment of a Regulatory Programme for Control of Veterinary Drug Residues in Foods (CAC/GL 16 - 1993) (under revision).

application of GHP in partial field dressing and transport to a game depot.

25. As wild game are killed in the field, appropriate hygienic practices immediately following death are essential to minimise contamination of edible parts. GHP should be applied to the extent practicable during bleeding, partial dressing, e. g., removal of the head, and (or) partial evisceration (where allowed by the competent authority).[1]

Bleeding and partial dressing of killed wild game in the field should include:

- bleeding and partial evisceration as soon as possible after killing (unless exempted by the competent authority for a particular species of wild game);
- partial skinning and (or) partial dressing in a manner that minimises the level of contamination of edible parts to the lowest level practicable;
- removal only of those parts of the animal that are not necessary for post-mortem inspection and judgement; and
- retention of the lungs, liver, heart and kidneys as a minimum if partial evisceration is carried out, either by natural attachment to the carcass or identified and packaged as an attachment to the carcass, unless a hunter, who is a competent person, has carried out an inspection and has not detected or suspected abnormalities.[2]

26. Game depots should not be simultaneously used for a purpose other than receiving and holding killed wild game, unless the competent authority specifies other uses and conditions.

27. Delivery of killed wild game to a game depot or an establishment should be within time limits established by the competent authority considering harvesting, environmental conditions and desired food safety outcomes. The body and other animal parts should not be frozen before dressing and post-mortem inspection in an establishment, unless unavoidable due to ambient temperatures.

5.4 HYGIENE OF FEED AND FEED INGREDIENTS

28. Feeding of animals during primary production should be subject to good animal feeding practice[3].

Records should be maintained at the manufacturing level, on the origin of feed and feed ingredients to facilitate verification.

29. There is a need for collaboration between all parties involved in production, manufacturing and use of feed and feed ingredients, so as to establish any linkage between identified hazards and the level of risk to consumers that may result from transmission through the food chain[4].

Animals should not be given feed and feed ingredients that:

- are recognised as likely to introduce zoonotic agents (including transmissible spongiform encephalopathies-TSEs) to the slaughter population; or
- contain chemical substances, (e. g., veterinary drugs, pesticides) or contaminants that could result in residues in meat at levels that make the product unsafe for human consumption.

30. The competent authority should implement appropriate legislation and controls governing the feeding of animal protein to animals where there is a likelihood of transmission of zoonotic agents, and this may in-

---

[1] Partial evisceration usually only involves removal of the gastrointestinal tract, and this aids cooling.

[2] In the case of small killed wild game, the competent authority may allow full evisceration.

[3] Codex Code of Practice on Good Animal Feeding (CAC/RCP 54 - 2004).

[4] OIE International Animal Health Code (chapters on zoonotic diseases); OIE Guidelines on antimicrobial resistance.

clude a ban on such feeding when justified by risk management. Any processed feed and feed ingredients should be subject to appropriate microbiological and other criteria according to a specified sampling plan and testing protocol, and maximum limits for mycotoxins.

5.5 HYGIENE OF THE PRIMARY PRODUCTION ENVIRONMENT

31. Primary production of animals should not be undertaken in areas where the presence of hazards in the environment could lead to an unacceptable level of such hazards in meat.

The competent authority should design and administer monitoring and surveillance programmes appropriate to the circumstances that address:

- hazards arising from animals and plants that may compromise the production of meat that is safe and suitable for human consumption;
- environmental contaminants that may result in levels in meat that make the product unsafe for human consumption; and
- ensuring that potential carriers such as water, are not significant vehicles for transmission of hazards.

Facilities and procedures should be in place to ensure that:

- housing and feeding platforms where used, and other areas where zoonotic agents and other hazards may accumulate, can be effectively cleaned, and are maintained in a sanitary condition (refer to Section 10);
- systems for active processing and (or) disposal of dead animals and waste should not constitute a possible source of food-borne hazards to human and animal health; and
- chemical hazards required for technological reasons are stored in a manner so that they do not contaminate the environment or feed and feed ingredients and thereby pose a risk to human health.

5.6 TRANSPORT

5.6.1 Transport of slaughter animals

32. Transport of slaughter animals should be carried out in a manner that does not have an adverse impact on the safety and suitability of meat. ❶

Slaughter animals require transport facilities to the abattoir that ensure that:

- soiling and cross-contamination with faecal material is minimised;
- new hazards are not introduced during transport;
- animal identification as to the place of origin is maintained; and
- consideration is given to avoiding undue stress that may adversely impact on the safety of meat (such as stress-induced shedding of pathogens).

Transport vehicles should be designed and maintained so that:

- animals can be loaded, unloaded and transported easily and with minimal risk of injury;
- animals of different species, and animals of the same species likely to cause injury to one another, are physically separated during transport;

---

❶ OIE International Animal Health Code (chapter on transport); Report of the OIE Working Group on Animal Welfare, October 2002.

• use of floor gratings, crates or similar devices limits soiling and cross-contamination with faecal material;

• where the vehicle has more than one deck, animals are protected from cross-contamination as appropriate ;

• ventilation is adequate; and

• cleaning and sanitising is readily achieved (refer to Section 10).

33. Transport vehicles, and crates where used should be cleaned and if necessary sanitised as soon as practicable after animals have been unloaded at the establishment.

5.6.2 Transport of killed wild game

34. Following killing and partial dressing in the field, the body and other parts should be transported to an establishment, including a game depot, without delay and in a manner that minimises contamination of edible parts. The use of these vehicles for this purpose should be consistent with good hygienic practice and any specific regulatory requirements.

35. Unless deemed unnecessary due to low environmental ambient temperatures, the temperature of the body should be actively reduced as quickly as possible after partial field dressing and transport.

6 PRESENTATION OF ANIMALS FOR SLAUGHTER

36. Only healthy, clean and appropriately identified animals should be presented for slaughter.

37. All animals should be screened upon arrival at the abattoir. Where abnormalities in behaviour or appearance suggest that an individual animal or a consignment of animals should be segregated, this should occur and the competent person undertaking ante-mortem inspection should be notified.

38. Ante-mortem inspection is an important pre-slaughter activity, and all relevant information on animals presented for slaughter should be utilised in meat hygiene systems.

6.1 PRINCIPLES OF MEAT HYGIENE APPLYING TO ANIMALS PRESENTED FOR SLAUGHTER

i. Animals presented for slaughter should be sufficiently clean so that they do not compromise hygienic slaughter and dressing.

ii. The conditions of holding of animals presented for slaughter should minimise crosscontamination with food-borne pathogens and facilitate efficient slaughter and dressing.

iii. Slaughter animals should be subjected to ante-mortem inspection, with the competent authority determining the procedures and tests to be used, how inspection is to be implemented, and the necessary training, knowledge, skills and ability of personnel involved.

iv. Ante-mortem inspection should be science- and risk-based as appropriate to the circumstances, and should take into account all relevant information from the level of primary production.

v. Relevant information from primary production where available and results of ante-mortem inspection should be utilised in process control.

vi. Relevant information from ante-mortem inspection should be analysed and returned to the primary producer as appropriate.

6.2 CONDITIONS OF LAIRAGE

39. Holding of animals presented for slaughter has an important effect on many aspects of slaughter, dressing and the production of meat that is safe and suitable for human consumption. The cleanliness of animals has a major influence on the level of microbiological cross-contamination of the carcass and other edible parts during slaughter and dressing. A range of measures appropriate to the animal species may be applied to ensure that only animals that are sufficiently clean are slaughtered and to assist in reducing microbiological cross- contamination.

40. Quality assurance (QA) systems implemented by the establishment operator should enhance achievement of appropriate conditions of lairage on an on-going basis.

The establishment operator should ensure conditions of lairage that include:

- facilities are operated in a way that soiling and cross-contamination of animals with food-borne pathogens are minimised to the greatest extent practicable;
- holding of animals so that their physiological condition is not compromised and ante-mortem inspection can be effectively carried out, e. g., animals should be adequately rested and not overcrowded and protected from weather where necessary;
- separation of different classes and types of slaughter animals as appropriate, e. g., separation of animals with special dressing requirements, and separation of "suspects" that have been identified as having the potential to transfer specific food-borne pathogens to other animals (refer to 6.3);
- systems to ensure that only animals that are sufficiently clean are slaughtered;
- systems to ensure that feed has been appropriately withdrawn before slaughter;
- maintenance of identification of animals (either individually, or as lots, e. g., poultry) until the time of slaughter and dressing; and
- conveying of relevant information on individual animals or lots of animals to facilitate ante- and post-mortem inspection.

41. The competent authority or the competent body should take into account QA systems properly implemented by the establishment operator, in setting the frequency and intensity of verification activities necessary to determine that the conditions of lairage are in accordance with regulatory requirements.

6.3 ANTE-MORTEM INSPECTION

42. All animals presented for slaughter should be subjected to ante-mortem inspection, by a competent person whether on an individual or a lot basis. Inspection should include confirmation that the animals are properly identified, so that any special conditions pertaining to their place of primary production are considered in the ante-mortem inspection, including relevant public and animal health quarantine controls.

43. Ante-mortem inspection should support post-mortem inspection by application of a specific range of procedures and (or) tests that consider the behaviour, demeanour and appearance, as well as signs of disease in the live animal.

Animals described below should be subject to special controls, procedures or operations imposed by the competent authority (which may include denial of entry to the abattoir) when:

- animals are not sufficiently clean;
- animals have died in transit;

• a zoonotic disease posing an immediate threat to either animals or humans is present, or suspected;

• an animal health disease subject to quarantine restrictions is present, or suspected;

• animal identification requirements are not met; or

• declarations from the primary producer, if required by the competent authority (including compliance with good veterinary practice in the use of animal medicines), are absent or inadequate.

6. 3. 1 Design of ante-mortem inspection systems

44. Ante-mortem inspection should be included as an integral component of an overarching risk-based system for the production of meat, with systems for process control (refer to Section 9) incorporating appropriate components. Relevant information on the slaughter population, e. g., animal class, health status, geographical region of origin, should be utilised in both the design and implementation of ante-mortem inspection systems.

45. Ante-mortem inspection, including procedures and tests, should be established by the competent authority according to a science and risk-based approach. In the absence of a risk-based system, procedures will have to be based on current scientific knowledge and practice.

46. Ante-mortem procedures and tests may be integrated and implemented together so as to achieve public health and animal health objectives. In such cases all aspects of ante-mortem inspection should be sciencebased and be tailored to the relevant risks.

47. Where indicated by public health concerns, measures additional to routine ante-mortem inspection may be required.

Characteristics of a risk-based ante-mortem inspection programme are:

• procedures for confirmation of proper animal identification in accordance with national legislation;

• design and application of organoleptic procedures and tests that are relevant and proportional to meat-borne risks associated with clinical signs of illness and grossly-detectable abnormalities;

• tailoring of procedures to the spectrum and prevalence of diseases and defects reasonably likely to be present in the slaughter population, taking into account the type of animal, geographical origin and primary production system;

• integration with HACCP-based process control to the extent practicable, e. g., application of objective criteria for ensuring appropriate cleanliness of animals presented for slaughter;

• on-going tailoring of procedures to information received from the primary production unit, where practicable;

• use of laboratory tests for hazards that are unaddressed by organoleptic inspection when their presence is suspected, e. g., chemical residues and contaminants; and

• return of information to the primary producer so as to seek continuous improvement in the safety and suitability status of animals presented for slaughter (refer to 6. 4).

6. 3. 2 Implementation of ante-mortem inspection

48. The competent authority should determine how ante-mortem inspection is to be implemented, including identification of the components that may be applied at primary production rather than the abattoir,

e. g. , in the case of intensively-raised poultry. [1]The competent authority should establish the training, knowledge, skills and ability requirements of all personnel involved, and the roles of the official inspector, including the veterinary inspector (refer to 9. 2). Verification of inspection activities and judgements should be undertaken as appropriate by the competent authority or competent body. The final responsibility for verifying that all regulatory requirements are met should lie with the competent authority.

The responsibilities of the establishment operator in respect of ante-mortem inspection include:

- providing verifiable information required by the competent authority with respect to ante-mortem inspection carried out at primary production;
- segregation of animals if, for example, they have recently given birth during transport or in lairages, or have recently aborted and (or) show retained foetal membranes;
- applying identification systems for individual animals or lots of animals until the time of slaughter that document the outcome of ante-mortem inspection, and after slaughter in the case of "suspect" animals;
- presentation of animals that are sufficiently clean; and
- prompt removal of animals that have died in the lairage, e. g. , from metabolic disease, stress, suffocation, with the permission of the competent person undertaking ante-mortem inspection.

49. Ante-mortem inspection at the abattoir should occur as soon, as is practicable after delivery of slaughter animals. Only animals that are judged to be sufficiently rested should proceed to slaughter, but should not be withheld from slaughter any longer than necessary. If ante-mortem inspection has occurred and there is a delay of more than 24 hours before slaughter, ante-mortem inspection should be repeated.

Ante-mortem inspection systems required by the competent authority should include the following:

- all relevant information from the level of primary production should be taken into account on an on-going basis, e. g. , declarations from the primary producers relating to the use of veterinary drugs, information from official hazard control programmes;
- animals suspected as being unsafe or unsuitable for human consumption should be identified as such and handled separately from normal animals (refer to 6. 2 and 8. 2);
- results of ante-mortem inspection are made available to the competent person undertaking postmortem inspection before animals are inspected at the post-mortem stations so as to augment final judgement. This is particularly important when a competent person undertaking ante-mortem inspection, judges that a suspect animal can proceed to slaughter under special hygiene conditions;
- in more equivocal situations, the competent person undertaking ante-mortem inspection may hold the animal (or lot) in special facilities for more detailed inspection, diagnostic tests, and (or) treatment;
- animals condemned as unsafe or unsuitable for human consumption should be immediately

---

[1] In some cases the competent authority may allow slaughter on the farm for particular classes of animal, e. g. , farmed game, and in such cases the slaughter animals should be subject to ante-mortem inspection and other hygiene controls as determined by the competent authority.

identified as such and handled in a manner that does not result in cross-contamination of other animals with food-borne hazards (refer to 8.2); and

• the reason for condemnation should be recorded, with confirmatory laboratory tests being carried out if deemed necessary. Feed back of this information to the primary producer should take place.

50. Slaughter of animals under an official or officially-recognised programme for the eradication or control of a specific zoonotic disease, e.g., salmonellosis, should only be carried out under the hygiene conditions specified by the competent authority.

6.3.3 Ante-mortem judgement categories

Ante-mortem judgement categories include:

• passed for slaughter;

• passed for slaughter subject to a second ante-mortem inspection, after an additional holding period, e.g., when animals are insufficiently rested, or are temporarily affected by a physiological or metabolic condition;

• passed for slaughter under special conditions i.e. deferred slaughter as "suspects", where the competent person undertaking ante-mortem inspection suspects that post-mortem inspection findings could result in partial or total condemnation;

• condemned for public health reasons i.e. due to: meat-borne hazards, occupational health hazards, or likelihood of unacceptable contamination of the slaughter and dressing environmentfollowing slaughter;[1]

• condemned for meat suitability reasons;

• emergency slaughter, when an animal eligible for being passed under special conditions could deteriorate if there was a delay in slaughter; and

• condemned for animal health reasons, as specified in relevant national legislation.

6.4 INFORMATION ON ANIMALS PRESENTED FOR SLAUGHTER

51. Information provided on animals presented for slaughter may be an important determinant of optimal slaughter and dressing procedures and is a prerequisite for effective design and implementation of process control by the establishment operator. The competent authority should analyse relevant information and take it into account when setting hygiene requirements for risk-based hygiene systems throughout the entire food chain (refer to 9.2).

52. The competent authority may require monitoring of animals presented for slaughter to establish baseline information on the prevalence of hazards in the slaughter population, e.g., specified meat-borne pathogens, chemical residues greater than maximum residue limits. The competent authority should design and implement these monitoring activities according to national public health goals. Scientific analysis and dissemination of results to interested parties is the responsibility of the competent authority.

So as to facilitate science- and risk-based meat hygiene throughout the entire food chain, systems should be in place that provide:

• on-going information on animals presented for slaughter for incorporation into HACCP plans

[1] The competent person may judge, after post-mortem inspection in special facilities, that edible parts of the animal can be salvaged for a particular purpose e.g. pet-food.

and (or) quality assurance (QA) programmes that are part of process control;

• information back to the primary producer on the safety and suitability status of animals presented for slaughter; and

• information to the competent authority that facilitates on-going review.

7 PRESENTATION OF KILLED WILD GAME FOR DRESSING

53. Killed wild game presented at an establishment have been subject to different harvesting, handling and transportation arrangements compared to live animals presented for slaughter. Killed wild game should undergo an appropriate inspection before dressing and full post-mortem inspection commences, so as to prevent undue contamination of the dressing environment and wastage of resources.

7.1 PRINCIPLES OF MEAT HYGIENE APPLYING TO INSPECTION OF KILLED WILD GAME PRESENTED FOR DRESSING

i. Inspection of killed wild game for safety and suitability prior to dressing should be risk-based to the extent practicable, and should take into account relevant information available from the field.

7.2 INSPECTION OF KILLED WILD GAME PRESENTED FOR DRESSING

54. The inspection should determine to the extent possible whether hygienic practice for field-harvested animals has been appropriately applied, including an assessment of cleanliness sufficient for hygienic dressing. Special measures required by the competent authority to facilitate post-mortem inspection, e. g.

correct identification and attachment of viscera separated from the animal body (refer to 5.3), should be confirmed at this time.

55. The inspection should take into account any information available from harvesting in the field, e. g.

presence of abnormalities at the time of death, geographical location. Where practicable, the results should be returned to hunters or other people involved in harvesting of wild game so as to improve their knowledge of and contribution to meat hygiene.

56. Inspection of killed wild game for safety and suitability prior to dressing should be risk-based to the extent practicable, given that the entire animal may not be presented for dressing, e. g., the gastrointestinal tract of large killed wild game will most likely have been discarded in the field. Inspection procedures prior to dressing and post-mortem inspection, will be necessarily limited in nature. They should be focused on detecting abnormalities intrinsic to field harvesting of wild game, e. g. signs of natural death or the animal being moribund at the time of death, the effects of a misplaced or expanding bullet, decomposition, and any evidence of intoxication with poisons or environmental contaminants. Systems for the implementation of inspection procedures and judgements should be based on those used for ante-mortem inspection of other classes of animals (refer to 6.3).

57. Identity of the body of the animal along with those parts required for post-mortem inspection, should be maintained until final post-mortem judgement.

8 ESTABLISHMENTS: DESIGN, FACILITIES AND EQUIPMENT

58. The principles and guidelines presented in this section are supplemental to the objectives and guidelines in Section IV of the Recommended International Code of Practice: General Principles of Food Hygiene (CAC/RCP 1 - 1969, Rev 4 2003).

59. The competent authority should allow variations in the design and construction of game depots and establishments processing killed wild game, and their facilities, where they are by necessity impermanent, as long as meat hygiene is not compromised.

8.1 PRINCIPLES OF MEAT HYGIENE APPLYING TO ESTABLISHMENTS, FACILITIES AND EQUIPMENT

i. Establishments should be located, designed and constructed so that contamination of meat is minimised to the greatest extent practicable.

ii. Facilities and equipment should be designed, constructed and maintained so that contamination of meat is minimised to the greatest extent practicable.

iii. Establishments, facilities and equipment should be designed to allow personnel to carry out their activities in a hygienic manner.

iv. Facilities and equipment that are in direct contact with edible parts of animals and meat, should be designed and constructed so that they can be effectively cleaned and monitored for their hygiene status.

v. Suitable equipment should be available for control of temperature, humidity and other factors as appropriate to the particular processing system for meat.

vi. Water should be potable except where water of a different standard can be used without leading to contamination of meat.

60. Each establishment should have appropriate facilities and equipment for competent persons to properly carry out their meat hygiene activities.

61. Laboratory facilities necessary to support meat hygiene activities may be located in the establishment or provided at a separate location.

8.2 DESIGN AND CONSTRUCTION OF LAIRAGES

62. Lairages should be designed and constructed so that they do not lead to undue soiling of the animal, cause undue stress of the animal, or otherwise adversely impact on the safety and suitability of meat derived from animals held therein.

Lairages should be designed and constructed so that:

- animals can be held without overcrowding or injury, and are not exposed to climatic stress;[1]
- there are appropriate layout and facilities for cleaning and (or) drying of animals;
- ante-mortem inspection is facilitated;

[1] In the case of poultry and farmed game birds, facilities should be available to park transport vehicles in areas that are well ventilated, and are protected from direct sunlight, inclement weather and extremes of temperature.

• floors are paved or slatted and allow good drainage;

• there is an adequate supply and reticulation of clean water for drinking and cleaning, and facilities are provided for feeding where necessary;

• there is a physical separation between lairages and areas of an abattoir where edible material may be present;

• "suspect" animals can be segregated and inspected in separate areas.[1] These areas should include facilities that are capable of secure holding of "suspect" animals pending slaughter under supervision, in a manner that precludes contamination of other animals; and

• there is an adjacent area with adequate facilities for cleaning and sanitation of transport vehicles and crates, unless there are facilities within close distance that are approved by the competent authority.

63. Special facilities may be required to handle condemned animals.

These facilities should be:

• constructed so that all parts, gut contents and faeces from condemned animals can be held under secure containment as appropriate to the circumstances; and

• constructed and equipped so as to facilitate effective cleaning and sanitation (refer to Section 10).

8.3 DESIGN AND CONSTRUCTION OF SLAUGHTER AREAS

64. Stunning and bleeding areas should be separated from dressing areas (either physically or by distance), so that cross-contamination of animals is minimised.

65. Areas for scalding, dehairing, defeathering, scraping and singeing (or similar operations) should also be appropriately separated from dressing areas.

66. Where slaughter is carried out the processing line should be designed so that there is constant progress of animals in a manner that does not cause cross-contamination.

67. Special facilities may be required to slaughter and dress "suspect" or injured animals.

Where these facilities exist they should be:

• easily accessed from pens containing "suspect" or injured animals;

• constructed with suitable facilities for hygienic storage of parts derived from "suspect" or injured animals; and

• constructed and equipped so as to facilitate effective cleaning and sanitising (refer to Section 10).

8.4 DESIGN AND CONSTRUCTION OF AREAS WHERE BODIES OF ANIMALS ARE DRESSED OR MEAT MAY OTHERWISE BE PRESENT

68. All areas and facilities where bodies of animals are dressed or meat may be present should be designed and constructed so that they facilitate GHP,[2] and contamination of meat is minimised to the greatest extent practicable.

---

[1] In the case of poultry and farmed game birds, "suspect" birds are usually slaughtered on the slaughter line under special hygiene provisions.

[2] Recommended International Code of Practice: General Principles of Food Hygiene (CAC/RCP 1 - 1969, Rev. 4 - 2003).

Rooms and other areas in which bodies of animals are dressed or meat may be present should be designed and constructed so that:

• cross-contamination during operations is minimised to the greatest extent practicable;

• effective cleaning, sanitation and maintenance can be carried out during and between periods of operation; (refer to Section 10);

• floors in areas where water is present slope sufficiently to grilled or otherwise protected outlets so as to ensure continual drainage;

• exterior doors do not open directly into the area;

• chutes separately conveying different parts of animals are fitted with inspection and cleaning hatches where these are necessary for sanitation;

• separate rooms or separated areas are used for skin-on dressing of pigs or other animals, when other classes of animals are being dressed at the same time;

• separate rooms are used for:

– emptying and cleansing of alimentary tracts, and further preparation of clean alimentary tracts, unless such separation is deemed unnecessary;

– handling of meat and inedible parts of animals after they have been so designated, unless these products are otherwise separated by time or distance;

– storage of inedible animal parts such as hides, horns, hooves, feathers and inedible fats;

• there is adequate natural or artificial lighting for hygienic process control;

• there are appropriate facilities for the preparation and storage of edible fats;

• access and harbouring of pests are effectively restricted; and

• adequate facilities are provided for secure storage of chemicals, (e. g. , cleaning materials, lubricants, branding inks) and other hazardous substances so as to prevent accidental contamination of meat.

69. Appropriately designed and insulated rooms should be available as necessary for cooling, chilling and freezing of meat.

Establishments that de-bone or otherwise cut up meat should have for this purpose:

• facilities that allow constant progress of operations or that ensure separation between different production batches;

• a room or rooms, capable of being temperature-controlled; and

• separation of the boning, cutting and primary wrapping area from the packaging area, unless hygiene measures are in place to ensure that packaging does not contaminate meat.

70. Wood may be used in rooms for curing, smoking, maturing, pickling, storage and dispatch of meat preparations and manufactured meat when essential for technological reasons, as long as meat hygiene requirements are not compromised.

71. Drainage and waste disposal systems should not be a source of contamination of meat, the potable water supply or the processing environment. All lines should be watertight and adequately trapped and vented, with catch basins, traps and sumps that are isolated from any area where bodies of animals are dressed or meat may be present.

72. Establishments should have an appropriate area, sufficiently protected from environmental contamination and capable of preventing adverse temperature variations, for dispatching meat.

8.5 DESIGN AND CONSTRUCTION OF EQUIPMENT WHERE BODIES OF ANIMALS ARE DRESSED OR MEAT MAY BE PRESENT

73. All equipment used in areas where bodies of animals are dressed or meat may be present should facilitate good hygienic practices (GHP). Equipment and containers in rooms and other areas where bodies of animals are dressed or meat may be present should be designed and constructed so that contamination is minimised. Meat should not be allowed to contact the floor and walls, or fixed structures not designed for such contact.

74. Where slaughter lines are operated, they should be designed so that there is constant progress of animal bodies, carcasses and other parts, in a manner that prevents cross-contamination between different parts of the slaughter line and between different slaughter lines. In establishments where meat preparations and manufactured meat are circulating, the layout and equipment should be designed to prevent cross contamination between products of different status and products at different production stages.

75. All rooms and other areas in which animals are dressed or meat may be present should be equipped with adequate facilities for washing hands, and should be equipped with adequate facilities for cleaning and sanitation of implements where required (refer to Section 10).

Facilities for cleaning and sanitation of equipment should:

- be designed to effectively clean and sanitise the particular equipment;
- be located convenient to work stations; and
- have waste water ducted to drains.

76. Equipment and implements for use with inedible or condemned parts of animals should be distinctively identified.

77. Establishments should be provided with adequate means of natural or mechanical ventilation so as to prevent excessive heat, humidity and condensation, and ensure that air is not contaminated with odours, dust or smoke.

Ventilation systems should be designed and constructed so that:

- air-borne contamination from aerosols and condensation droplets is minimised;
- ambient temperatures, humidity and odours are controlled; and
- air flow from contaminated areas, (e. g., slaughter and dressing areas) to clean areas, (e. g., chilling rooms for carcasses) is minimised.

78. Equipment used for heat treatment of manufactured meat and meat preparations should be fitted with all control devices necessary to ensure that an appropriate heat treatment is applied.

8.6 WATER SUPPLY [1]

79. Adequate facilities should be provided for monitoring and maintaining potability, storage, temperature control, distribution of water and for the disposal of waste water.

Equipment should be installed that provides:

- an adequate and easily accessible supply of hot and cold potable water at all times;
- hot potable water for effective sanitising of equipment, or an equivalent sanitation system;

[1] Recommended International Code of Practice: General Principles of Food Hygiene, Section 5.5 (CAC/RCP 1 – 1969, Rev. 4 – 2003).

- potable water at a temperature appropriate for hand-washing; and
- sanitising solution used according to manufacturers'specifications supplied as and where necessary;

80. Where non-potable water is supplied for various uses e. g. , fire fighting, steam production, refrigeration, reticulation systems should be designed and identified so that cross-contamination of the potable water supply is prevented.

8.7 TEMPERATURE CONTROL

81. In the absence of suitable temperature, humidity and other environmental controls, meat is particularly vulnerable to survival and growth of pathogens and spoilage micro-organisms.

82. Facilities and equipment should be adequate for:

- Cooling, chilling and (or) freezing of meat according to written specifications;
- Storage of meat at temperatures that achieve the safety and suitability requirements; and
- Monitoring of temperature, humidity, air flow and other environmental factors so as to assure that process control regimes are achieved.

83. Where steam is generated in the cooking of meat, it should be properly vented out of the area in order to minimise the potential for condensation and not be allowed to permeate into adjoining rooms.

8.8 FACILITIES AND EQUIPMENT FOR PERSONAL HYGIENE

84. Slaughter and dressing of animals and animal parts, and further handling of meat preparations and manufactured meat presents many opportunities for cross-contamination of meat by food handlers (refer to Section 11). Appropriate personal hygiene facilities are needed to minimise cross-contamination of meat from this source.

85. Facilities and equipment should be provided, designed and located so that meat safety is not compromised. Where necessary, separate amenities should be provided e. g. for staff handling live animals, condemned products (refer Section 11).

Facilities for personal hygiene should include:

- changing rooms, showers, flush toilets, hand-washing and hand-drying facilities in the appropriate locations, and separate areas for eating; and
- protective clothing that can be effectively cleaned and minimises accumulation of contaminants.

All areas in which exposed meat may be present, should be equipped with adequate facilities for washing hands that:

- are located convenient to work stations;
- have taps that are not operable by hand;
- supply water at an appropriate temperature, and are fitted with dispensers for liquid soap or other hand cleansing agents;
- include hand drying equipment where necessary, and receptacles for discarded paper towels; and
- have waste water ducted to drains.

8.9 MEANS OF TRANSPORT

Vehicles or shipping containers in which unprotected meat is transported should:

• be designed and equipped so that the meat does not contact the floor;

• have joint and door seals that prevent entry of all sources of contamination; and

• where necessary, be equipped so that temperature control and humidity can be maintained and monitored.

9 PROCESS CONTROL

86. An extensive range of hazards are associated with meat, e.g., *Salmonella* spp. and veterinary drug residues; the processing environment, e.g., *Listeria monocytogenes*; and food handlers themselves, e.g., *Staphylococcus aureus* and hepatitis viruses. Effective process control, that includes both GHP and HACCP, is necessary to produce meat that is safe and suitable for human consumption.

87. The principles and guidelines presented in this section should satisfy the general objectives and guidelines in Section V of the Recommended International Code of Practice: General Principles of Food Hygiene (CAC/RCP 1 - 1969, Rev 4 - 2003). They are developed in this section in respect of hazards in meat however they are equally applicable to suitability characteristics.

88. Many aspects of slaughter and dressing procedures have the potential to result in significant contamination of meat, e.g., hide/feather removal, evisceration, carcass washing, post-mortem inspection, trimming, and further handling in the cold chain. Systems for process control should limit microbial crosscontamination in these circumstances to as low as practicably achievable, and reflect the proportional contribution of these controls in reducing meat-borne risks to human health.

89. Ready-to-eat (RTE) products may require specific microbiological testing regimes that incorporate microbiological criteria. [1]

9.1 PRINCIPLES OF MEAT HYGIENE APPLYING TO PROCESS CONTROL

i. Production of meat that is safe and suitable for human consumption requires that detailed attention be paid to the design, implementation, monitoring and review of process control.

ii. The establishment operator has the primary responsibility for implementing systems for process control. Where such systems are applied, the competent authority should verify that they achieve all meat hygiene requirements.

iii. Process control should limit microbiological contamination to the lowest level practicable, according to a risk-based approach.

iv. HACCP should be applied wherever practicable as the system of choice for process control, and should be supported by prerequisite GHP that includes sanitation standard operating procedures (SSOPs).

---

[1] Principles for the Establishment and Application of Microbiological Criteria for Foods (CAC/GL 21 - 1997).

v. Process control should reflect an integrated strategy for control of hazards throughout the food chain, with information available from primary production and pre-slaughter being taken into account wherever possible and practicable.

vi. All bodies of animals should be subjected to post-mortem inspection that is science- and riskbased, and is tailored to the hazards and (or) defects that are reasonably likely to be present in the bodies of animals presented for inspection. ❶

vii. The competent authority should determine the procedures and tests to be used in post-mortem inspection, how that inspection is to be implemented, and the necessary training, knowledge, skills and ability required of personnel involved (including the role of veterinarians, and personnel employed by the establishment operator).

viii. Post-mortem inspection should take into account all relevant information from primary production, ante-mortem inspection, and from official or officially-recognised hazard control programmes.

ix. Post-mortem judgements should be based on: food-borne risks to human health, other human health risks, e. g., from occupational exposure or handling of meat in the home, food-borne risks to animal health as specified in relevant national legislation, and suitability characteristics.

x. Performance objectives or performance criteria for the outcome of process control and post-mortem inspection activities should be established by the competent authority wherever practicable, and should be subject to verification by the competent authority.

xi. Where appropriate, microbiological testing, for verification purposes, should be included in meat preparation and manufactured meat HACCP plans. Such testing should be relevant to the type of product and the likely risks to consumers, including vulnerable sub-populations.

xii. Competent bodies or competent persons may be engaged by the establishment operator to undertake prescribed process control activities❷, including ante-❸and post-mortem inspection, as approved by the competent authority.

xiii. Handling of ready-to-eat (RTE) products up until the point of sale to the consumer should ensure that there is no contact with non- ready-to-eat (RTE) products, and any other exposure to potential sources of microbiological contamination is minimised to the greatest extent practicable.

xiv. Voluntary or officially recognised quality assurance (QA) systems may be implemented by the establishment operator where they enhance meat hygiene activities, and they may be taken into account in the verification of regulatory requirements by the competent authority.

9.2 PROCESS CONTROL SYSTEMS

90. Effective process control requires design and implementation of appropriate systems. Industry has the primary responsibility for applying and supervising process control systems to ensure the safety and suita-

❶ Where risk assessment capability is not available, post-mortem inspection carried out according to current scientific knowledge and practice should be capable of achieving the level of consumer protection required.

❷ Prescribed process control activities may include "Officially recognised inspection systems" (CAC/GL 20 – 1995).

❸ Ante-mortem inspection as covered in Section 6. 3.

bility of meat, and these should incorporate prerequisite GHP and HACCP plans as appropriate to the circumstances.

91. A documented process control system should describe the meat hygiene activities applied (including any sampling procedures), performance objectives or performance criteria (if set), verification activities, and corrective and preventative actions.

92. Competent bodies or competent persons suitably recognised by the competent authority may be engaged by the establishment operator to undertake prescribed process control activities, including postmortem inspection. These activities should be part of HACCP or QA systems as appropriate to the circumstances.

93. Process control systems relating to food safety should incorporate a risk-based approach. Application of HACCP principles in the design and implementation of process control systems should be according to The Hazard Analysis and Critical Control Point (HACCP) System and Guidelines for its Application (CAC/RCP 1 - 1969, Rev. 4 - 2003). The Guidelines for the Design, Operation, Assessment and Accreditation of Food Import and Export Inspection and Certification Systems (CAC/GL 26 - 1997) provide general requirements for control of operations for food as they relate to international trade.

9.2.1 Sanitation Standard Operating Procedures (SSOPs)

94. Pre-operational and operational sanitation standard operating procedures (SSOPs) should minimise direct and indirect contamination of meat to the greatest extent possible and practicable. A properly implemented SSOP system should ensure that facilities and equipment are clean and sanitised prior to start of operations, and appropriate hygiene is maintained during operations. SSOP guidelines may be provided by the competent authority, which may include minimum regulatory requirements for general sanitation.

Characteristics of sanitation standard operating procedures (SSOPs) are:

- development of a written SSOP programme by the establishment that describes the procedures involved and the frequency of application;
- identification of establishment personnel responsible for implementing and monitoring SSOPs;
- documentation of monitoring and any corrective and (or) preventative actions taken, which is made available to the competent authority for purposes of verification;
- corrective actions that include appropriate disposition of product; and
- periodic evaluation of the effectiveness of the system by the establishment operator.

95. Microbiological verification of SSOPs can utilise a range of direct or indirect methods. Establishment operators should use statistical process control or other methods to monitor sanitation trends.

96. In the case of ready-to-eat (RTE) products, microbiological verification of SSOPs for food contact and non-food contact surfaces is likely to be of higher intensity than for other types of product.

9.2.2 HACCP

97. HACCP systems for production of meat are a proactive means of process control for food safety purposes. [1]Validation of a HACCP plan for meat should ensure that it is effective in meeting performance objectives or performance criteria (refer 9.2.3), taking into account the degree of variability in presence of hazards that is normally associated with different lots of animals presented for processing.

98. Verification frequency may vary according to the operational aspects of process control, the histori-

---

[1] Hazard Analysis and Critical Control Point (HACCP) System and Guidelines for its Application, (Annex to CAC/RCP 1 - 1969, Rev. 4 - 2003).

cal performance of the establishment in application of the HACCP plan, and the results of verification itself. The competent authority may choose to approve HACCP plans and stipulate verification frequencies.

99. Microbiological testing for verification of HACCP systems, e. g. for verification of critical limits and statistical process control, is an important feature of HACCP for many products.

100. Guidelines for the development of HACCP programmes to achieve pre-determined process criteria stipulated by the competent authority should be provided to establishment operators so as to guide development of process and product-specific HACCP plans. Guidelines should be developed in consultation with industry and other interested stakeholder organisations, and may be differentiated according to processing category, e. g. :

- Raw ground or comminuted e. g. pork sausage;
- Meat with secondary inhibitors / non-shelf stable e. g. cured corned beef;
- Heat treated / not fully cooked, non-shelf stable e. g. partially-cooked patties;
- Fully cooked / non-shelf stable e. g. cooked ham;
- Non-heat treated / shelf stable e. g. dry salami;
- Heat treated / shelf stable e. g. beef jerky;
- Thermally processed / commercially sterile e. g. canned meat;
- Specific ethnic processes, e. g. tandoori.

101. When developing HACCP plans for heat-treated meat preparations and manufactured meat, the establishment operator should fully document as appropriate to the process, all thermal process parameters, post-heat treatment handling, and additional preservation treatments appropriate to the intended process outcome e. g. a pasteurised product. Process parameters for cooling of heat-treated products may incorporate as appropriate to the product, rapid cooling, slow cooling, or interrupted cooling. Previously heated products should not be packaged above a minimum temperature, e. g. 4℃, unless it can be demonstrated that cooling after packaging does not compromise product safety.

102. HACCP plans for meat preparations and manufactured meat that are cooked should include monitoring and documentation of parameters that ensure appropriate internal temperatures are reached.

Internal temperatures of product should be taken as necessary to verify the adequacy of the cook.

9. 2. 3 Outcome-based parameters for process control

103. In a risk-based meat hygiene system, verification of process control is greatly strengthened by establishment of performance objectives or performance criteria for the outcome of specified activities. In most cases these will be established by the competent authority. When performance objectives or performance criteria are established, industry can use them to readily demonstrate adequate process control for food safety characteristics of meat.

104. The establishment should have a documented process control system for implementing corrective actions that will allow it to consistently meet performance objectives or performance criteria. Process review and any other corrective and preventative actions required as a result of non-compliance with performance objectives or performance criteria should be properly recorded. The competent authority should implement a system for collecting and analysing results from all establishments to the greatest extent possible, and periodically review process control trends in relation to national meat hygiene goals.

105. Where possible, performance objectives or performance criteria should objectively express the level of hazard control as derived from the application of risk analysis principles. In the absence of sufficient knowledge of risks to human health, performance objectives or performance criteria can initially be estab-

lished from baseline surveys of current performance, and subsequently modified as appropriate to reflect public health goals. Where outcome-based parameters have been established for suitability characteristics of meat, outcomes should be practically achievable and reflect consumer expectations.

106. Organoleptic parameters may also be established.

Performance objectives or performance criteria for outcomes of process control systems act to:

- facilitate validation of process control systems;
- facilitate derivation of process parameters at various steps in the food production system;
- allow maximum flexibility and technical innovation in the way the establishment operator achieves the required level of performance;
- facilitate industry-wide consistency in performance;
- provide an objective basis for outcome-driven regulatory guidelines and standards, e.g., statistical process control requirements, prevalence of Salmonella spp.;
- improve hazard control over time so as to enhance the level of consumer protection; and
- facilitate determination of the equivalence of sanitary measures.

107. Microbiological performance objectives or performance criteria, process criteria and microbiological criteria for ready-to-eat (RTE) products should be risk-based according to the category of product e.g. not heat treated and shelf stable, heat treated and shelf stable, fully cooked and not shelf stable. Microbiological verification tests should be undertaken by the establishment at a frequency appropriate to the circumstances.

The competent authority may also implement testing to verify that appropriate control is maintained by industry. HACCP plans applied by the establishment should document corrective and preventative measures to be taken in the event of positive tests for pathogens or toxins.

108. Where performance objectives or performance criteria are established as regulatory requirements e.g., guidelines for allowable levels of generic *E. coli*, standards for absence of *E. coli* O157: H7, maximum residue limits for chemicals with acute toxicity, explanation of the linkage to an appropriate level of consumer protection should be provided to all interested parties, .

109. In some circumstances a performance criterion may be established as a microbiological criterion that defines the acceptability of a production lot, e.g. based on the presence/absence or number of microbes, and (or) the quantity of their toxins or metabolites according to a specified sampling plan. [1]

110. The competent authority should, wherever practicable, recognise different risk-based meat hygiene activities within its competence, which have been demonstrated to meet at least the same risk-based meat hygiene outcomes.

9.2.4 Regulatory systems

111. The competent authority should have the legal power to set and enforce regulatory meat hygiene requirements, and has the final responsibility for verifying that all regulatory requirements are met. The competent authority should:

i. Establish regulatory systems (e.g. recall, traceback, product tracing, etc., as appropriate) and requirements, e.g. training, knowledge, skills and ability of personnel (generally at a national level).

ii. Undertake specified meat hygiene controls that are designated activities of the competent authority,

[1] Principles for the Establishment and Application of Microbiological Criteria for Foods (CAC/GL 21 - 1997).

e. g. , official sampling programmes, those aspects of ante and post-mortem activities specified by the competent authority, or official certification.

iii. Verify that process control systems implemented by the establishment operator meet regulatory requirements e. g. GHP, SSOPs, HACCP, as appropriate.

iv. Verify that competent bodies are carrying out functions as required.

v. Carry out enforcement actions as necessary.

The competent authority should verify compliance with:

- GHP requirements for: animals presented for slaughter (and killed wild game presented for dressing), establishments, facilities and equipment, process control, transport, and hygiene of personnel;
- SSOPs;
- HACCP plans;
- all regulatory requirements relating to ante- and post-mortem inspection;
- microbiological performance objectives or performance criteria, process criteria or microbiological criteria that are regulatory requirements";
- chemical residue and contaminant levels that are below maximum limits as described in relevant legislation and national sampling plans;
- official or "officially-recognised" zoonoses control programmes, e. g. , microbiological tests for *E. coli* O157: H7; and
- additional risk management measures as specified by the competent authority.

112. Verification activities may include assessment of processing activities carried out by establishment personnel, documentary checks, organoleptic inspection of edible parts and meat, taking of samples for laboratory tests and testing for pathogens, indicator organisms, residues, etc. Approval/registration/listing of an establishment may facilitate the ability of the competent authority to verify that it is operating in compliance with regulatory requirements.

113. The competent authority (s) should conduct appropriate monitoring of verification activities performed by the operator, and the nature and intensity of that monitoring should be based on risk and performance.

The distribution and retail sale of products should be included in this monitoring to an extent that the risks to the consumer are mitigated.

114. The official inspector (including the veterinary inspector) should verify compliance with the regulatory requirements and may use additional documentary checks, procedures and tests in this role. Rules governing the presence of the official inspector during ante- and post-mortem inspection, and during processing, cutting, and storage of meat, should be determined by the competent authority in relation to deployment of other competent persons, and in relation to potential risks to human health associated with the classes of animals and meat involved.

115. A national meat hygiene programme should be subject to verification by the competent authority.

Where the establishment operator does not comply with regulatory requirements, the competent authority should carry out enforcement actions that may include:

- slowing of production while the operator regains process control;
- stopping production, and withdrawing certification for meat deemed to be unsafe or unsuitable for its intended use;

• withdrawing official supervision, or accreditation of competent persons;

• ordering specified treatment, recall or destruction of meat as necessary; and

• withdrawing or suspending all or part of the approval/registration/listing of the establishment if process control systems are invalid or repeatedly non-compliant.

9.2.5 Quality assurance (QA) systems

116. Whenever there are verifiable quality assurance (QA) systems in place in the industry, the competent authority should take them into account. ❶

9.3 GENERAL HYGIENE REQUIREMENTS FOR PROCESS CONTROL

117. Process control should meet the general hygiene requirements of the Recommended International Code of Practice: General Principles of Food Hygiene. ❷

General hygiene requirements for process control should include for example:

• water for cleaning and sanitising of a standard that is appropriate for the specific purpose, and used in a manner that does not directly or indirectly contaminate meat;

• cleaning of facilities and equipment that involves disassembly where necessary, removal of all debris, rinsing of parts, application of an approved cleaner, repeat rinsing, reassembly, and further sanitizing and rinsing as appropriate;

• handling and storage of containers and equipment in a way that minimises the potential for contamination of meat;

• assembly of containers or cartons in rooms or areas where meat may be present in such a manner that there is minimal possibility of contamination; and

• controlled access of personnel to processing areas.

118. The competent authority and industry should utilise appropriately accredited or otherwise recognised laboratories when verifying process control and carrying out other meat hygiene activities. Testing of samples should utilise validated analytical methods. ❸

Laboratory testing may be required for:

• verification of process control;

• Monitoring achievement of performance objectives or performance criteria;

• residue monitoring;

• diagnosis of disease conditions affecting individual animals; and

• monitoring of zoonoses.

9.4 HYGIENE REQUIREMENTS FOR SLAUGHTER AND DRESSING

119. Only live animals intended for slaughter should be brought into an abattoir, with the exception of animals that have undergone emergency slaughter outside the slaughterhouse and have appropriate veterinary

---

❶ Guidelines for the Design, Operation, Assessment and Accreditation of Food Import and Export Inspection and Certification Systems-Section 4 "Quality Assurance" (CAC/GL 26 - 1997).

❷ Note that general requirements for control of incoming materials, use of water, packaging, documentation and records, and recall procedures are described in the recommended international code of practice: general principles of food hygiene (CAC/RCP 1 - 1969, Rev. 4 - 2003).

❸ Guidelines for the assessment of the competence of testing laboratories involved in the Import and Export Control of Food (CAC/GL 27 - 1997).

documentation.

120. No animal other than an animal intended for slaughter should enter an abattoir, with the exception of animals used for stock handling provided these animals stay in the live animal handling area of the abattoir.

121. An animal should only be slaughtered or dressed in an abattoir if a competent person is available to undertake ante- and post-mortem inspection. In cases of emergency slaughter where a competent person is not available, special provisions established by the competent authority will apply to ensure that the meat is safe and suitable for human consumption.

122. All animals brought to the slaughter floor should be slaughtered without delay, and stunning, sticking and bleeding of animals should not proceed at a rate faster than that at which bodies of animals can be accepted for dressing.

During initial dressing operations, and with due consideration to minimising contamination:

- slaughtered animals that are scalded, flamed or similarly treated should be scoured of all bristles, hair, scurf, feathers, cuticles and dirt;
- the trachea and oesophagus should remain intact during bleeding, except in the case of ritual slaughter;
- bleeding should be as complete as possible; if blood is intended for food, it should be collected and handled in a hygienic manner;
- exposure of the tongue should be done in such a way that the tonsils are not cut;
- skinning of the head may not be required for some classes of animals e. g. goats, calves, sheep, provided that heads are handled in such a way as to avoid undue contamination of meat;
- before the removal from the head of any parts intended for human consumption, the head should be clean and, except in the case of animal bodies that are scalded and dehaired, skinned to an extent sufficient to facilitate inspection and the hygienic removal of specified parts;
- lactating or obviously-diseased udders should be removed from animal bodies at the earliest opportunity;
- removal of udders should be done in such as way that the contents do not contaminate the animal bodies;
- gas skinning or dehiding (pumping of air or gas between the skin or hide and the underlying tissue to facilitate skinning) should only be permitted if it can meet required criteria for process control; and
- hides/fleeces should not be washed, de-fleshed or left to accumulate in any part of an abattoir or establishment that is used for slaughter or dressing.

123. Poultry and farmed game birds, following de-feathering, can only be effectively cleaned of dust, feathers and other contaminants by the application of potable water. Washing of the animal bodies at multiple steps in the dressing process, and as soon as possible after each contaminating step, reduces the adherence of bacteria to the skin which can minimise overall carcass contamination. (Washing after evisceration and post-mortem is also necessary for technological reasons, as this is the only method available to routinely clean carcasses before entry to the chilling process). Washing may be carried out by several methods e. g. , spraying, immersion washing.

124. Farmed ratites may have an excessive amount of dust and dirt trapped in their feathers, and this has the potential for significant contamination of the dressing area unless there is adequate separation by dis-

tance, physical barrier, or other means, e. g. , positive ventilation.

125. Once the removal of the hide/fleece has commenced, or dehairing has occurred, animal bodies should be separated from each other to avoid contact, and this should be maintained until each carcass has been inspected and judged by a competent person undertaking post-mortem inspection. (Note: While full separation of carcasses is more difficult in the case of poultry and farmed game birds, such contact should be minimised).

During dressing, and with due consideration to minimising contamination:

- where bodies of animals are skinned, this process should be completed before evisceration;
- water in scalding tanks should be managed so that it is not excessively contaminated;
- evisceration should be carried out without delay;
- discharge or spillage of any material from the oesophagus, crop, stomach, intestines, cloaca or rectum, or from the gall bladder, urinary bladder, uterus or udder, should be prevented;
- intestines should not be severed from the stomach during evisceration and no other opening should be made into an intestine, unless the intestines are first effectively tied to prevent spillage, except in the case of poultry and game birds;
- stomachs and intestines and all inedible material derived from the slaughtering and (or) dressing of bodies of animals should be removed as soon as possible from the dressing area, and processed in a manner that does not cause cross-contamination of meat;
- methods used to remove visible and microbial contamination should be demonstrated to be effective and meet other requirements as specified by the competent authority; and
- faecal and other material should be trimmed or otherwise removed from carcasses in a manner that does not result in further contamination, and which achieves appropriate performance objectives or performance criteria for process control.

126. Animal bodies and carcasses should not come into contact with surfaces or equipment unless practically unavoidable. Where use of equipment involves contact by design, e. g. , in the case of automatic eviscerating machines, the hygiene of the equipment should be appropriately maintained and monitored.

127. Where a competent person undertaking post-mortem inspection, considers that the manner in which animals are being slaughtered or dressed, or meat is further handled, will adversely affect the safety and suitability of meat, that competent person should enforce a reduction in the rate of production or the suspension of operations or other appropriate measures, as deemed necessary (refer to 9. 2. 4).

128. Establishment operators should meet the requirements of the competent authority in terms of presentation of edible parts of bodies of animals for post-mortem inspection. Parts of slaughtered animals that have been removed before post-mortem inspection is performed should remain identifiable, as belonging to a single carcass (or a group of carcasses) when required for post-mortem judgement.

129. Facilities and equipment for slaughtering and (or) dressing may be used for other purposes, e. g. for animal health emergency slaughter, provided appropriate cleaning and sanitation requirements are met.

130. The competent authority should encourage development and adoption of innovative technologies and procedures at the establishment level that reduce cross-contamination and enhance food safety, e. g. , enclosing the terminal rectal intestine in a bag and tying off.

9.5 POST-MORTEM INSPECTION

131. All carcasses and other relevant parts should be subjected to post-mortem inspection, which preferably should be part of an overarching, risk-based system for the production of meat.

132. Post-mortem inspection of carcasses and other relevant parts should utilise information from primary production and ante-mortem inspection, together with the findings from organoleptic inspection of the head, carcass and viscera, to make a judgement on the safety and suitability of parts intended for human consumption. Where the results of organoleptic inspection are insufficient to accurately judge carcasses and other relevant parts as safe or suitable for human consumption, the parts should be set aside and followed up with confirmatory inspection procedures and (or) tests.

9.5.1 Design of post-mortem inspection systems

133. Post-mortem inspection procedures and tests should be established by the competent authority according to a science- and risk-based approach. The competent authority has responsibility for establishing judgement criteria and verifying the post-mortem inspection system. In the absence of a risk-based system, procedures will have to be based on current scientific knowledge and practice.

134. Post-mortem procedures and tests may be integrated and implemented together so as to achieve public health and animal health objectives. In such cases, all aspects of post-mortem inspection should be sciencebased and be tailored to the relevant risks.

135. Relevant information on the animal population, e. g., animal type, health status, geographical region of origin, should be utilised in both the design and implementation of post-mortem inspection systems.

136. Where indicated by public health concerns, routine screening of carcasses and other relevant parts by methods other than organoleptic inspection may be required for suspected hazards, e. g., testing for *Trichinella* spp.

Characteristics of a risk-based post-mortem inspection programme are:

- design and application of organoleptic procedures and tests that are relevant and proportional to meat-borne risks associated with grossly-detectable abnormalities;
- tailoring of procedures to the spectrum and prevalence of diseases and defects reasonably likely to be present in the particular slaughter population, taking into account the type (age), geographical origin and primary production system of the slaughter animals, e. g., multiple incisions of relevant muscles in all pigs from geographical regions where *Taenia solium* is present;
- procedures that minimise cross-contamination through handling to the greatest extent practicable, and may include procedures that are limited to visual observation of carcasses and other relevant parts in the first instance if justified by risk assessment;
- inspection of non-edible parts of animals where they may play an indicator role in the judgement of edible parts;
- modification of traditional procedures where scientific investigation has shown them to be ineffective, or, of themselves, hazardous to food, e. g., routine incision of lymph nodes of young animals to detect granulomatosus abnormalities;
- application of more intensive organoleptic procedures on a routine basis when a disease or condition capable of general distribution is found in a single part of a carcass and other relevant parts, e. g., cysts of *Taenia saginata* in cattle, xanthosis;

• application of additional risk-based inspection procedures on a routine basis when live animals are positive to a diagnostic test, e. g. , tuberculin test in cattle, mallein test in horses;

• use of laboratory tests for hazards that are unaddressed by organoleptic inspection, e. g. , *Trichinella* spp. , chemical residues and contaminants;

• application of measurable outcomes of organoleptic inspection that reflect a risk-based approach;

• integration with HACCP plans for other process control activities;

• on-going tailoring of procedures to take into consideration information received from the primary producer on a lot-by-lot basis; and

• return of information to the primary producer so as to seek continuous improvement in the safety and suitability status of animals presented for slaughter (refer to 6. 4).

9. 5. 2 Implementation of post-mortem inspection

137. Post-mortem inspection should occur as soon as is practicable after slaughter of animals, or delivery of killed wild game animals. Inspection should take into account all relevant information from the level of primary production and ante-mortem inspection, e. g. information from official or officially-recognised hazard control programmes, information on animals slaughtered as "suspects" .

138. The competent authority should determine: how post-mortem inspection is to be implemented, the training, knowledge, skills and ability required of personnel involved (including the role of the official inspector, the veterinary inspector, and any personnel not employed by the competent authority), and the frequency and intensity of verification activities (refer to 9. 2. 4). The final responsibility for verifying that all post-mortem inspection and judgement requirements are met should lie with the competent authority.

139. Carcasses and other relevant parts condemned by the competent person undertaking post-mortem inspection, as unsafe or unsuitable for human consumption should be identified as appropriate and handled in a manner that does not result in cross-contamination of meat from other carcasses and relevant parts. The reason for condemnation should be recorded, and confirmatory laboratory tests may be taken if deemed necessary.

The responsibilities of the establishment operator in respect of post-mortem inspection include:

• maintenance of the identity of a carcass and other relevant parts (including blood as appropriate) until inspection is complete;

• skinning and dressing of heads to the extent necessary to facilitate inspection, e. g. , partial skinning to allow access to sub-maxillary lymph nodes, detaching of the base of the tongue to allow access to the retropharyngeal lymph nodes;

• skinning of heads to the extent necessary to allow hygienic removal of edible parts, when this is a processing option;

• presentation of a carcass and other relevant parts for inspection according to the requirements of the competent authority;

• a prohibition on establishment personnel intentionally removing or modifying any evidence of a disease or defect, or animal identification mark, prior to post mortem inspection;

• prompt removal of foetuses from the evisceration area, for rendering or other processes as allowed by the competent authority, e. g. , collection of foetal blood;

• retention in the inspection area of all carcasses and other relevant parts required for inspection, until inspection and judgement has been completed;

• provision of facilities for identifying and retaining all carcasses and other relevant parts that require more detailed inspection and (or) diagnostic tests before a judgement on safety and suitability can be made, in a manner that prevents cross-contamination of meat from other carcasses and other relevant parts;

• condemnation of parts of the carcass trimmed from the region of the sticking wound;

• routine condemnation of the liver and (or) kidneys from older animals where the competent authority has determined that there may be accumulation of heavy metals to an unacceptable level;

• use of health marks (as specified by the competent authority) that communicate the outcome of post-mortem inspection; and

• co-operation with competent persons undertaking post-mortem inspection, in all other ways necessary to facilitate effective post-mortem inspection, e. g. , access to processing records, and easy access to all carcasses and other relevant parts.

Post-mortem inspection systems, should include:

• procedures and tests that are risk-based to the extent possible and practicable (refer to 9. 5. 1);

• confirmation of proper stunning and bleeding;

• availability of inspection as soon as is practicable after completion of dressing;

• visual inspection of the carcass and other relevant parts, including inedible parts, as determined by the competent authority;

• palpation and (or) incision of the carcass and other relevant parts, including inedible parts, as determined by the competent authority according to a risk-based approach;

• additional palpation and (or) incisions, as necessary to reach a judgement for an individual carcass and other relevant parts, and under appropriate hygiene control;

• more detailed inspection of edible parts intended for human consumption compared with inspection of those parts for indicator purposes alone, as appropriate to the circumstances;

• systematic, multiple incisions of lymph nodes where incision is necessary;

• other organoleptic inspection procedures, e. g. , smell, touch;

• where necessary, laboratory diagnostic and other tests carried out by the competent authority or by the establishment operator under instruction;

• performance objectives or performance criteria for the outcomes of organoleptic inspection, if available;

• regulatory authority to slow or halt processing so as to allow adequate post-mortem inspection at all times;

• removal of specified parts if required by the competent authority, e. g. ,"specified risk materials" for BSE; and

• proper use and secure storage of equipment for health marking.

140. The competent authority and industry should record and disseminate the results of post-mortem inspection as appropriate. Notifiable human or animal health diseases and cases of non-complying residues or contaminants should be reported to national competent authorities as well as to the owner of the animal (s).

Analysis of the results of post-mortem inspection over time is the responsibility of the competent authority, and the results of such analyses should be made available to all interested parties.

9.6 POST-MORTEM JUDGEMENT

141. Post-mortem judgement of edible parts as safe and suitable for human consumption should primarily be based on food-borne risks to human health. Other risks to human health, e. g. , from occupational exposure or from handling of meat in the home, also are an important consideration. Judgements in relation to suitability characteristics of meat should reflect consumer acceptability requirements appropriate to intended end-use. [1]

142. Although outside the mandate of Codex, post-mortem inspection programmes may be utilised to identify and judge carcasses and other relevant parts according to risks to animal health, as specified in relevant national legislation.

Judgement of edible parts as safe and suitable should take into account information from the following sources:

- information from primary production (refer to Section 6);
- observations made of animals in the lairage;
- ante-mortem inspection; and
- post-mortem inspection, including diagnostic tests, where required.

143. Judgements should be based on science and risks to human health to the greatest extent possible, with guidelines being provided by the competent authority. Judgements should only be made by competent persons.

The level of training, knowledge, skills and ability required for judgement may be less in situations where edible parts demonstrating a specific abnormality are always judged to be unsafe or unsuitable for human consumption and appropriately disposed of.

144. Where the initial results of post-mortem inspection are insufficient to accurately judge edible parts as safe or suitable for human consumption, a provisional judgement should be followed up with more detailed inspection procedures and (or) tests. Pending the outcome of more detailed inspection and (or) diagnostic tests, all parts of the animal that are required for further investigation should be held under the control of the competent person undertaking these activities.

Judgement categories for edible parts include:

- safe and suitable for human consumption;
- safe and suitable for human consumption, subject to application of a prescribed process, e. g. , cooking, freezing; [2]
- held on suspicion of being unsafe or unsuitable, pending the outcome of further procedures and (or) tests;
- unsafe for human consumption but able to be used for some other purpose, e. g. , petfood, feed and feed ingredients, industrial non-food use, providing there are adequate hygiene controls to prevent any transmission of hazards, or illegal re-entry to the human food chain;

---

[1] The competent authority may take into account varying needs of different consumer populations so that suitability judgements do not distort the economics of the food supply.

[2] The competent person can instruct that following post-mortem inspection, edible parts held under suitable inventory control can be designated as safe and suitable when subjected to a particular process e. g. freezing, cooking, canning.

- unsafe for human consumption and requiring condemnation and destruction;
- unsuitable for human consumption, but able to be used for some other purpose, e. g. , pet-food, feed and feed ingredients, industrial non-food use, providing there are adequate controls to prevent illegal re-entry to the human food chain;
- unsuitable for human consumption, and requiring condemnation and destruction; and
- unsafe for animal health reasons as specified in national legislation, and disposed of accordingly. [1]

145. When edible parts are judged to be safe and suitable for human consumption subject to application of a prescribed process, the specifications for that process should be verified by the competent authority as sufficient to eliminate/reduce or adequately remove the hazard or condition of concern, e. g. , specifications for retorting, high temperature rendering and freezing.

9.7 HYGIENE REQUIREMENTS FOR PROCESS CONTROL AFTER POST-MORTEM INSPECTION

146. Operations following post-mortem inspection include all procedures until the point of retail sales, e. g. chilling of carcasses, de-boning and cutting, further preparing, processing, packaging, freezing, storing, and distribution to the point of retail sale. Particular attention needs to paid to temperature control, with temperatures of freshly slaughtered and dressed carcasses and other edible parts being reduced as rapidly as possible to a temperature that minimise the growth of micro-organisms or the formation of toxins that could constitute a risk to human health. It is also important that the cold chain is not interrupted except to the minimal extent necessary for practical operations, e. g. , handling during transportation.

147. In the case of poultry and farmed game birds, viscera or parts of viscera, apart from kidneys, should be entirely removed as soon as possible, unless otherwise permitted by the competent authority.

Meat passed as safe and suitable for human consumption should be:

- removed without delay from the dressing area;
- handled, stored and transported in a manner that will protect it from contamination and deterioration;
- held under conditions that reduce its temperature and (or) water activity as quickly as possible, unless cut up or de-boned pre-rigor; and
- held at temperatures that achieve safety and suitability objectives.

In the case of poultry or farmed game birds undergoing immersion chilling:

- the immersion chilling process should meet hygiene criteria as specified by the competent authority;
- the reduction in carcass temperature should be as rapid as possible;
- carcasses emerging from the process should have a lesser microbiological count for indicator organisms and pathogens than those entering the process; and
- sanitation requirements should include complete emptying, cleaning and sanitation of tanks as appropriate.

148. An official health mark applied to meat, wrapping or packaging, should provide recognition that

---

[1] In some circumstances, edible parts may be judged as suitable for human consumption but subject to restricted distribution because the animals were sourced from geographical areas under quarantine for animal health reasons.

the product has been produced in accordance with regulatory requirements, and should assist with trace-back to the establishment of origin if required. When used as part of an official meat hygiene programme, the health mark should include the approval/registration/listing number of the establishment, be applied in such a way that it cannot be re-used, and be legible. Other marks may denote conformance with commercial specifications, or unacceptability for human consumption, e. g. , distinctive brands for pet-food.

149. Official health marks may be applied directly to the product, wrapping or packaging, or be printed on a label affixed to the product, wrapping or packaging. In circumstances of bulk transport to another establishment for further handling, processing or wrapping, health marks may be applied to the external surface of the container or packaging.

Where carcasses, parts of carcasses or other meat is placed in a holding room:

- all requirements for hygienic control of operations must be adhered to e. g. , chiller loading rates;

stock rotation, specifications for temperature and relative humidity;

- carcasses and parts of carcasses, whether hung or placed in racks or trays, should be held in a manner permitting adequate circulation of air;
- the potential for cross-contamination via dripping of fluids should be prevented; and
- water dripping from overhead facilities and condensation should be controlled to the extent practicable, to prevent contamination of meat and food contact surfaces.

150. Rooms and equipment for cutting, mincing, mechanical separation, meat preparation and the manufacturing of meat should be designed such that activities can be carried out separately, or in such a manner that does not led to cross contamination.

151. Fresh meat intended for cutting or de-boning should be brought into work rooms progressively as needed, and should not accumulate on work tables. If fresh meat is cut or de-boned prior to reaching temperatures that are appropriate for storage and transport, it should be immediately reduced in temperature to prescribed levels.

When fresh meat is cut or de-boned pre-rigor:

- it should be transported directly from the dressing area to the cutting up or de-boning room;
- the cutting up or de-boning room should be temperature-controlled and directly linked to the dressing areas, unless the competent authority approves alternative procedures that provide an equivalent level of hygiene; and
- cutting up, de-boning and packing should be done without delay and should meet all requirements for hygienic process control.

When raw meat is minced:

- it should be obtained only from parts of animals as approved by the competent authority e. g. striated muscle and adherent fatty tissues[1];
- it should not contain bone fragments or skin;
- any grossly abnormal tissues and / or post-dressing contamination should be removed before mincing; and
- the competent authority may specify compositional criteria.

[1] Striated muscles from affected animal species should have undergone an examination from Trichinella as specified by the competent authority.

When raw meat is mechanically separated, the competent authority should:

• restrict the type of animal parts that can be used e. g. non-use of skulls;

• set compositional standards for maximum calcium content; and

• require specific labelling of the final product.

When raw meat is minced, mechanically separated or used in meat preparations:

• the competent authority can specify maximum time/temperature schedules for process control at each step of production e. g. maximum times and temperatures from chilling or freezing of raw material to the time of preparation, maximum temperatures during production, maximum times before chilling or freezing;

• unless used directly as an ingredient for meat preparations and manufactured meat, it should be immediately wrapped and (or) packaged, followed by immediate refrigeration;

• the competent authority may specify microbiological performance objectives, performance criteria, process criteria or microbiological criteria for raw materials and final product;

• establishments should have in-line magnets or other means of detecting contamination with metal fragments as appropriate; and

• it should not be refrozen after thawing.

When meat preparations or manufactured meat are handled:

• the process flow of raw meat awaiting processing and during processing should ensure uniform turnover of accumulated product and avoid possible cross-contamination, e. g. between raw materials and ready-to-eat products;

• supply and addition of non-meat ingredients should be subject to good hygienic practice and HACCP as appropriate and practicable, and may involve decontamination treatments e. g. for herbs and spices;

• products that include non-meat protein products (as defined or standardised by Codex) should be appropriately labelled[1];

• process control for non-commercially sterile products should prevent pathogen growth and toxin production during all processing activities e. g. during fermentation, partial heat treatment, drying, maturing and curing. Process criteria may include for example, correct pH after fermentation, correct time/temperature schedules during and after heating or smoking, correct moisture / protein ratio after drying, correct formulation and application of nitrite as a cure ingredient;

• if heat and (or) other processing treatments are not sufficient to ensure the stability of the product, the product should be cooled to an appropriate storage temperature and in a manner that ensures product safety is not compromised as a result of germination and subsequent growth of pathogenic sporeformers;

• product formulations e. g. distribution of antibacterial ingredients throughout cooked sausage emulsions, addition of cultures, adjustment of pH, should achieve required levels of pathogen control;

• microbiological contamination of raw meat used to produce fermented products should be as low as possible, and similarly, mechanically separated meat should only be used if appropriate time / temperature schedules to achieve product safety requirements of the competent authori-

---

[1] Codex General Standard for the Labelling of Prepackaged Food (CODEX STAN 1 - 1985, Rev. 1 - 1991).

ty are used;

• processing of shelf-stable products in hermetically sealed rigid containers should be according to Codex guidelines;[1]

• cooked products should achieve time / internal temperatures that are validated as achieving appropriate pathogen reduction, including meeting specified performance objectives, performance criteria and microbiological criteria;

• pasteurisation values or other heat processes should be validated for all heat treated chilled products in hermetically sealed containers so as to ensure that product safety is maintained to the end of shelf life, taking into account all preservation factors that may be present;

• unless the absence of trichinellae can be assured by testing or other means, process treatments for products containing striated muscle from affected animal species, either alone or in combination, should be sufficient to destroy *Trichinella* spp. ;

• contamination with *L. monocytogenes* of heat treated / non-shelf stable and non-heat treated /shelf stable products should be prevented by use of SSOPs and GHPs that are subject to routine microbiological verification;

• dried products should be protected from environmental contamination and from reabsorption of moisture; and

• processes for products containing minced, comminuted or mechanically separated meat should have in-line magnets or other means of detecting contamination with metal fragments.

Where meat is packaged or wrapped:

• packaging material should be suitable for use, stored and used in a hygienic manner; and

• cases or cartons should have a suitable inner liner or other means of protecting the meat, except that the liner or other protection may not be required if pieces of meat, such as cuts, are individually wrapped before packing.

Where meat is placed in a room for freezing:

• meat that is not in cartons should be hung or placed on racks or trays in a manner that allows adequate circulation of air;

• meat that is not in cartons should be held in a manner whereby the potential for crosscontamination via dripping of liquids is prevented;

• cartons containing meat should be stacked so as to permit adequate circulation of air; and

• meat held on trays should be placed so as to avoid contact with the base of an upper tray.

Where meat is held in a freezer room or storage facility:

• the temperature of the meat should have been reduced to an acceptable level before placement;

• exposed meat must be stored in such a way that the hygiene cannot be compromised by the presence of packaged meat or packaging material;

• meat, whether in carcass form or in cartons, should not be stacked directly on the floor and should be positioned so that there is adequate air circulation;

• the freezer store should be operated and maintained under conditions appropriate to maintaining the safety and suitability of meat;

---

[1] Recommended International Code of Hygienic Practice for Low-Acid Canned Foods CAC/RCP 23 - 1979 (Rev. 1 - 1989).

- temperatures should be continuously recorded and monitored; and
- adequate inventory control should be maintained.

152. Where raw meat is thawed for further processing, hygiene controls should be such that thawing will not result in growth of micro-organisms or the formation of toxins to the extent that they may constitute a risk to human health. Hygiene controls should include adequate drainage of liquid run-off.

153. The establishment operator should establish and implement a procedure for determining and validating the shelf life of manufactured meat and meat preparations.

154. In some circumstances ready-to-eat (RTE) products that do not meet microbiological performance objectives, performance criteria, process criteria, or microbiological criteria, may be re-processed, condemned or treated as inedible. Where appropriate, follow-up sampling should verify that re-processed ready-to-eat (RTE) products comply with regulatory microbiological requirements. When ready-to-eat (RTE) products have been contaminated subsequent to cooking and (or) other preservation treatment with pathogens such that they could pose a risk to public health, the products should be reworked or condemned without compromise.

155. Where establishments are approved, registered and (or) listed for different animal species, all operations must be controlled in terms of space or time so that there is no possibility of accidental mixing of meat from different slaughter species, and no mis-identification at the time of packaging.

9.8 HYGIENE REQUIREMENTS FOR PARTS OF ANIMALS DEEMED UNSAFE OR UNSUITABLE FOR HUMAN CONSUMPTION

156. Special hygiene measures should be applied to operations involving parts of animals deemed unsafe or unsuitable for human consumption. These measures should prevent cross-contamination to other edible parts and meat, and prevent any possibility of substitution.

Parts of animals deemed unsafe or unsuitable for human consumption should be:

- placed without delay into specifically identified chutes, containers, trolleys, or other handling facilities;
- identified by means as appropriate to the type and end use of the tissue;
- in the case of condemned material, handled in rooms reserved for that purpose and conveyed in a secure manner to a place of disposal (e.g. rendering station).

9.9 SYSTEMS FOR REMOVING PRODUCTS THAT ARE IN CIRCULATION

157. Establishments should have adequate systems that enable removal of products that are in circulation. The competent authority should verify that the systems are adequate. The competent authority should be notified when an establishment operator removes product for public health reasons. Consumers and interested parties should be notified as appropriate in these cases.

158. Removal of product requires systems that are capable of:

- Withdrawal, where measures are applied by the establishment operator to prevent the distribution, display or offer of a product that is not safe or suitable for human consumption;
- Recall, where measures are applied to return unsafe or unsuitable product that has already been supplied or made available to consumers;
- Detention, where measures are applied by the competent authority to ensure that the product is not moved or tampered with pending a decision on its disposition; it includes storage by the establishment oper-

ator in accordance with instructions from the competent authority.

159. The particular systems that are enacted in the case of a removal will depend on the specific situation and the likely risks to human health.

160. Where removal of product is necessary, the amount of product involved may be more than that from a single production or sampled lot. The competent authority should verify to the extent practicable, that the establishment has taken all steps necessary to ensure all affected product or potentially affected product is included in the removal.

Product removal systems designed by the establishment operator should:

- Incorporate identification, management and operational procedures that facilitates the rapid and complete removal of implicated lots;
- Provide for records that facilitate trace-back to the origin of the problem;
- Provide for records that facilitate investigation of any processing inputs that may be implicated;
- Be reviewed and tested periodically; and
- Include provision for communication where appropriate to the competent authority, consumers and other interested stakeholders particularly where public health issues are involved.

10 ESTABLISHMENTS: MAINTENANCE AND SANITATION

161. The principles and guidelines presented in this section are supplemental to the objectives and guidelines in Section VI of the Recommended International Code of Practice: General Principles of Food Hygiene (CAC/RCP 1-1969, Rev 4-2003).

10.1 PRINCIPLES OF MEAT HYGIENE APPLYING TO MAINTENANCE AND SANITATION OF ESTABLISHMENTS, FACILITIES AND EQUIPMENT

i. Establishments, facilities and equipment should be maintained and sanitised in such a manner that contamination of meat is minimised to the greatest extent practicable.

ii. Documented programmes for effective and appropriate maintenance and sanitation should be in place (refer to 9.2.1).

iii. Monitoring of the effectiveness of maintenance and sanitation should be included as a basic component of meat hygiene programmes (refer to 9.2.1).

iv. Special sanitation requirements should be applied to the slaughter and dressing of animals that are condemned or designated as "suspects".

10.2 MAINTENANCE AND SANITATION

162. Establishments, facilities and equipment should be kept in an appropriate state of repair and condition to facilitate all sanitation procedures and prevent contamination of meat, e.g., from metal shards, flaking plaster and chemical contaminants.

163. Sanitation standard operating procedures (SSOPs) should specify the scope of the cleaning programme, cleaning specifications, persons responsible, and monitoring and record keeping requirements.

Cleaning procedures and programmes should:

- be specified in SSOPs as appropriate to the circumstances;

• provide for removal and storage of waste;

• ensure that there is no consequential contamination of meat with detergents or sanitising agents, unless allowable under conditions of use; and

• be monitored for their effectiveness, e. g. , organoleptic checks and microbiological sampling of meat contact surfaces, and be redesigned if and when necessary.

164. Particular cleaning programmes are required for equipment used in the slaughter and dressing of carcasses e. g. , knives, saws, machine cutters, evisceration machines and flushing nozzles.

Such equipment should be:

• clean and sanitised before each new period of work;

• cleaned, and sanitised, by immersion in hot water or alternative methods, with appropriate frequency during and (or) between periods of work;

• immediately cleaned and sanitised when coming into contact with abnormal or diseased tissue that may harbour food-borne pathogens; and

• stored in designated areas in such a manner that it will not become contaminated.

165. Containers and equipment should not pass from an "inedible" area to an "edible" area before being cleaned and sanitised.

166. Pest control programmes are an essential part of maintenance and sanitation and should follow GHP as described in the Recommended International Code of Practice: General Principles of Food Hygiene. [1]

In particular:

• the programme should be properly documented and verified by the establishment operator;

• treatment of areas, rooms, facilities and equipment, with an approved pesticide should be carried out according to the conditions of use; and

• pesticides and other pest control chemicals should be kept in secure storage, with access being limited to authorised persons.

11 PERSONAL HYGIENE

167. Slaughter and dressing of animals, and handling and inspection of meat, presents many opportunities for cross-contamination. Personal hygiene practices should prevent undue general contamination, and prevent cross-contamination with human pathogens that may cause food-borne disease. The guidelines presented in this section are supplemental to the objectives and guidelines in Section Ⅷ of the Recommended International Code of Practice: General Principles of Food Hygiene (CAC/RCP 1 - 1969, Rev 4 - 2003).

168. Persons moving from rooms or areas containing raw meat to rooms or areas used for meat preparations and manufactured meat (especially when these products are cooked) should thoroughly wash, change and (or) sanitise their protective clothing as appropriate, and otherwise limit the possibility of cross-contamination to the lowest level practicable.

---

[1] Recommended International Code of Practice: General Principles of Food Hygiene (CAC/RCP 1 - 1969, Rev. 4 - 2003).

11.1 PERSONAL CLEANLINESS

169. Persons who come into direct or indirect contact with edible parts of animals or meat in the course of their work should maintain appropriate personal cleanliness and behaviour, and should not be clinically affected by communicable agents likely to be transmitted by meat.

Persons who come into direct or indirect contact with edible parts of animals or meat should:

- maintain an appropriate standard of personal cleanliness;
- wear protective clothing appropriate to the circumstances, and ensure that non-disposable protective clothing is cleaned before and during work;
- if wearing gloves during the slaughter and dressing of animals and the handling of meat, ensure that they are of an approved type for the particular activity, e. g. , chain-mail stainless steel, synthetic fabric, latex, and they are used according to specifications, e. g. , washing of hands before use, changing or sanitising gloves when contaminated;
- immediately wash and sanitise hands and protective clothing when there has been contact with abnormal animal parts that are likely to harbour food-borne pathogens;
- cover cuts and wounds with waterproof dressings; and
- store protective clothing and personal effects in locations that are separate from areas where meat may be present.

11.2 PERSONAL HEALTH STATUS

170. The establishment should maintain relevant personal health records of personnel.

Persons who come into direct or indirect contact with edible parts of animals or meat in the course of their work should:

- where necessary, have a medical examination prior to and during employment;
- not work while clinically affected by, or suspected to be carrying, communicable agents likely to be transmitted through meat; and
- be aware of and comply with reporting requirements to the establishment operator in respect of communicable agent.

12 TRANSPORTATION

171. The guidelines presented in this section are supplemental to the objectives and guidelines in Section Ⅷ of the Recommended International Code of Practice: General Principles of Food Hygiene (CAC/RCP 1-1969, Rev 3-1997, Amended 1999).

172. Due to the potential for growth of pathogenic and spoilage micro-organisms under conditions of inadequate temperature control, meat should be transported at temperatures that achieve safety and suitability objectives. Equipment for continuous monitoring and recording of temperatures should accompany transport vehicles and bulk containers wherever appropriate. Additionally, the conditions of transport should provide adequate protection from exogenous contamination and damage, and should minimise growth of pathogenic and spoilage micro-organisms.

173. If meat is inadvertently exposed to adverse temperature conditions or sources of contamination that may affect safety and suitability, an inspection should be carried out by a competent person before further

transport or distribution is allowed.

13 PRODUCT INFORMATION AND CONSUMER AWARENESS

174. Appropriate product information and adequate knowledge of food hygiene is necessary to prevent mishandling at later stages in the food chain. Pre-packaged foods should be labelled with clear instructions to enable the next person in the food chain to handle, display, store and use the product safely. Principles and guidelines for product information and consumer awareness in the context of safety and suitability of meat are described in general terms in Section IX of the Recommended International Code of Practice: General Principles of Food Hygiene (CAC/RCP 1 - 1969, Rev 4 - 2003).

175. The conditions of storage of meat preparations and manufactured meat should be clearly presented on the packaging.

176. Meat preparations and manufactured meat should, where appropriate, be specifically labelled so as to provide safe handling, refrigeration and storage instructions for consumers. Foods containing meat that have not received an adequate biocidal treatment for pathogens (e. g. containing raw meat, partially cooked meat, or products with secondary inhibitors) should be labelled with handling, refrigeration, storage, cooking and preparation statements that have been validated as sufficiently biocidal.

14 TRAINING

177. Adequate training of competent personnel is of fundamental importance in the production of meat that is safe and suitable for human consumption. The principles and guidelines presented in this section are supplemental to the objectives and guidelines in Section X of the Recommended International Code of Practice: General Principles of Food Hygiene (CAC/RCP 1 - 1969, Rev 4 - 2003).

14. 1 PRINCIPLES OF TRAINING IN MEAT HYGIENE

Persons engaged in meat hygiene activities should be trained, and (or) instructed to a required level of training, knowledge, skills, and ability. Training specified or recognised by the competent authority, should be:

i. appropriate to the activities and operations;

ii. proportional to the potential of the particular meat hygiene activity to impact on food-borne risks to human health;

iii. properly documented, including records of training programme delivery;

iv. verified as appropriate; and

v. subject to recognition by the competent authority where delivered by third parties.

14. 2 TRAINING PROGRAMMES

Training programmes should:

- provide personnel with the training, knowledge, skills and ability to carry out specified meat hygiene tasks, e. g., post-mortem inspection, verification of statistical process control, HACCP;
- provide practical training to the extent required;

- where necessary, arrange for formal testing of personnel;
- ensure that personnel involved in supervisory roles have appropriate skills;
- recognise and build on professional qualifications; and
- provide for the continuing education of competent persons.

ANNEXES

Annex I

RISK-BASED EVALUATION OF ORGANOLEPTIC POST-MORTEM INSPECTION PROCEDURES FOR MEAT

1 INTRODUCTION

1. Post-mortem meat inspection procedures are a set of food hygiene measures that are unique to the production of meat. Such procedures are regarded as a component of overall process control, which is defined as " all conditions and measures applied during the production process that are necessary to achieve safety and suitability of meat" .

2. The General Principles of Food Hygiene state that " in deciding whether a (food control) requirement is necessary or appropriate, an assessment of the risk should be made, preferably within the framework of the HACCP approach" . ❶ Many long-standing post-mortem meat inspection procedures are often complex, labour-intensive, undifferentiated for different classes of slaughtered livestock, and poorly evaluated in terms of their relative contribution to reducing food-borne risks to public health. For these reasons, competent authorities in a number of countries are carrying out investigations into the scientific basis of current procedures. ❷

3. This Annex generally applies to the evaluation of routine on-line organoleptic inspection procedures.

The performance of other inspection technologies, e. g. tissue imaging, relative to organoleptic procedures, may also be considered.

4. While risk-based evaluation of organoleptic post-mortem inspection procedures should be based on risk assessment for hazards of concern and development of performance objectives, currently few such risk assessments are available. In their absence, other sources of scientific knowledge on food-borne risks to human health e. g. human surveillance data, risk ranking processes, can be used to develop risk-based postmortem inspection procedures.

5. The principles and guidelines presented in this Annex could also be adapted to evaluation of organoleptic post-mortem inspection procedures for determining the suitability of meat.

2 OBJECTIVES OF RISK-BASED POST-MORTEM INSPECTION PROCEDURES FOR MEAT

6. A risk-based approach to post-mortem inspection for meat can achieve the following objec-

❶ Recommended International Code of Practice: General Principles of Food Hygiene (CAC/RCP 1 - 1969, Rev. 4 - 2003).

❷ Competent authorities have different approaches to defining the respective roles of industry and competent authority personnel in delivering meat hygiene activities, and this issue is not covered in this Annex.

tives：

• Determination of the level of consumer protection provided by specified post-mortem inspection procedures；

• Relative measurement of the contribution of post-mortem inspection to the overall level of control of hazards in meat (and risks to consumers), thereby allowing risk managers to allocate meat hygiene resources proportionate to their greatest benefit in reducing risk by preventing exposure to meat-borne hazards；

• Comparison of the effectiveness of different inspection procedures applied for the same purpose and in the same context, e. g. positive predictive value；

• Provision of information that allows appropriate evaluation of different risk management options e. g. regionalisation of inspection programmes, feasibility and comparative costs of different post-mortem inspection procedures, potential for cross-contamination；

• Full integration of post-mortem inspection procedures into a " production-to-consumption" approach to meat hygiene.

3 RISK ANALYSIS

3.1 RISK MANAGEMENT FRAMEWORK

7. Development and implementation of risk-based post-mortem inspection procedures should utilise a risk management framework. [1]The four components are: preliminary risk management activities, evaluation of risk management options, implementation of management decisions, and monitoring and review of decision taken. All components require effective risk communication among risk assessors, risk managers and other interested parties as necessary. Utilisation of a risk management framework is the subject of ongoing work within the Codex system, and is described in a number of Codex documents.

3.2 RISK ASSESSMENT

8. If required, a risk assessment is commissioned during preliminary risk management activities. A risk assessment consists of four steps: hazard identification, hazard characterisation, exposure assessment, and risk characterisation. The output of this process should be qualitatively integrated with all other factors relating to post-mortem meat inspection to make risk management decisions on appropriate procedures for control of hazards.

9. In the ideal situation, risk estimates will be quantified in terms of risks to human health, and risk management decisions on an appropriate level of protection (ALOP) will dictate the nature and intensity of the post-mortem inspection procedures to be applied. However, risk assessment of microbiological hazards in meat is currently limited by a lack of quantitative risk assessment models. Nevertheless, appropriate assembly of scientific information and qualitative risk characterisation as to the probable impacts on human health can provide an objective basis for de-

[1] Working Principles for Risk Analysis for Application in the Framework of the Codex Alimentarius. Codex Procedural Manual, 14th Edition.

cision-making. In any case, risk management decisions will revolve around the acceptability of the likely human health impact of differences in hazard levels brought about by different inspection procedures.

4 GENERAL PRINCIPLES FOR DEVELOPMENT OF RISK-BASED POST-MORTEM MEAT INSPECTION PROCEDURES

i. Risk-based post-mortem inspection procedures should be derived from the application of risk analysis principles.

ii. Development of risk-based post-mortem inspection procedures should:

- Involve application of a risk management framework;
- Include quantitative risk assessment where appropriate and practicable;
- Take into account all relevant information available from the food chain;
- Take into account disease prevalence;
- Take into account all relevant information from primary production and ante-mortem inspection of the animals.

iii. Inspection procedures should be evaluated for application within a specific context e. g. species and class of slaughtered animal, defined geographical region, defined animal husbandry system.

iv. Where different inspection procedures that have the same purpose and context are being evaluated:

- An objective basis for comparison of the level of control of hazards associated with these procedures, should be established;
- The efficacy of each inspection procedure in detecting abnormalities and visible contamination affecting the safety of meat should be taken into account;
- Other risk management factors should be taken into account as appropriate e. g. potential for inadvertent cross-contamination, feasibility, and practicality.

v. Where needed, representative and sufficiently large field trials should be undertaken to determine the performance attributes of specified inspection procedures e. g. sensitivity, specificity, and non-detection rates for abnormalities.

vi. Where appropriate, laboratory investigations should be designed to detect the range of hazards of possible public health importance that have been described in hazard identification.

vii. Routine application of post-mortem inspection procedures should not inadvertently increase cross-contamination with microbiological hazards.

viii. Irrespective of inspection delivery systems, the competent authority should be responsible for defining the role of personnel involved in post-mortem inspection procedures, and verifying that any risk-based regulatory requirements are met.

ix. Alternative inspection procedures (e. g. serology) may be utilised to complement post-mortem inspection, which might be reduced to visual inspection.

5 GUIDELINES FOR THE DEVELOPMENT OF RISK-BASED POST-MORTEM INSPECTION PROCEDURES

5.1 IDENTIFICATION OF THE MEAT HYGIENE ISSUES

10. A hazard identification process should be undertaken to determine the likely range of hazards of public health significance that may be present in the abnormalities or visible contamination that are the target of the inspection procedure (s) being evaluated. Following this, field trials should be undertaken to determine the performance attributes of specified inspection procedures or new technologies relative to the hazards that may be present.

5.2 FIELD TRIALS

11. Once the likely range of hazards has been established, field trials may be an appropriate means to establish the prevalence of these hazards in the animal population, the potential exposure of consumers to these hazards and the potential impact of different inspection procedures on this exposure. Field trials should be carried out under competent authority supervision and employing competent personnel. The number of animals inspected by the inspection procedures under evaluation should give a statistically valid estimate of the detection rate of abnormalities achieved by specific post-mortem inspection procedures.

12. Sampling plans should be representative of the slaughter population, and cater for known biological variation in respect of the type and prevalence of abnormalities e. g. influence of animal age, geographical region, farming type and season. Different trial designs may be employed, depending on the prevalence of abnormalities in the slaughter population, and the logistics of detailed inspection.

13. Where different post-mortem inspection procedures are being compared: all procedures should be applied to the same animals, each inspection station should be designed to provide independent results, and the trial should include enough samples so as to allow definite conclusions as to the consequences of changing inspection procedures. The possibility of target tissues acting as "indicators" for detection of abnormalities in other tissues and (or) disposition of other tissues may be included in the design of field trials.

Detailed recording of trial results is necessary, including appropriate pathological descriptions of all abnormalities detected.

14. Laboratory investigations e. g. microbiological examination and histology, should be designed to identify the range of hazards of possible public health importance that have been identified in the hazard identification process. A representative number and range of samples should be taken from abnormalities, so as to confirm the outcome of the hazard identification process and provide as much information as possible on the prevalence (and concentration) of hazards in target tissue. Trial design should include representative surveying of the prevalence (and concentration) of hazards in target tissues that are organoleptically normal, so as to provide a comparison with the prevalence (and concentration) of hazards in those tissues that are organoleptically abnormal.

5.3 SENSITIVITY

15. An understanding of the level of consumer protection that is achieved by particular inspection procedures requires knowledge of the level of control of hazards that is attained by their application. The sensitivi-

ty of post-mortem inspection procedures should be determined to establish their contribution to achieving overall public health goals.

16. The sensitivity of a post-mortem inspection procedure is the probability of identifying bodies or parts thereof that contain grossly detectable abnormalities likely to contain hazards of concern.

17. The sensitivity of an inspection procedure e. g. visual inspection, palpation, and (or) incision, should be determined within appropriate statistical limits established by the competent authority. The intended end-use of the target tissues has an important influence on the development of risk-based post-mortem inspection procedures. When selecting post-mortem inspection procedures, priority should be given to those procedures with high correlation between the detection of a specified abnormality and the presence of the hazard of concern.

5.4 RISK MANAGEMENT DECISIONS

18. Risk management decisions on the acceptability or otherwise of specified post-mortem inspection procedures will generally be based on the worst case of non-detection of abnormalities included in an appropriate statistical confidence interval. Decisions should take into account the comparative public health risks associated with:

- The prevalence (and concentration) of hazards in target tissues that are organoleptically abnormal;
- The prevalence (and concentration) of hazards in target tissues that are organoleptically normal;
- The overall prevalence (and concentration) of hazards being transmitted by all pathways throughout the production of meat.

19. In the general case, new or alternative inspection procedures should provide a level of consumer protection that is at least equivalent to that provided by existing procedures, unless there are strong mitigating factors that may influence a different risk management choice e. g. unacceptable introduction of new hazards, undue risks from occupational exposure.

20. Required regulatory outcomes for post-mortem inspection may include performance attributes expressed as limits on non-detection rates for particular abnormalities. Those performance attributes may be derived quantitatively from risk assessment models, or qualitatively from baseline surveys of current performance.

21. Where detailed information on the health status of slaughtered animals is available from primary production, risk-based post-mortem inspection procedures may be modified on a lot-by-lot basis, with the competent authority having responsibility for determining the frequency and extent of the procedures.

22. The competent authority should regularly analyse results of post-mortem inspection at both the establishment and national level, and provide appropriate feedback to establishments and other interested parties on the performance of risk-based post-mortem inspection procedures. The competent authority could consider an incentive for improving the system, e. g. recognition of performance, decreased farm inspection frequency, additional change of inspection procedures, etc.

23. The competent authority may change presentation requirements and the sequence of inspection procedures as a result of scientific evaluation of different post-mortem inspection procedures, and allow introduction of new inspection tools e. g. mirrors. Alternative technologies for detecting abnormalities e. g. tissue imaging, should be acceptable to the competent authority if validated as being as effective as current procedures.

Annex Ⅱ

VERIFICATION OF PROCESS CONTROL OF MEAT HYGIENE BY MICROBIO LOGICAL TESTING

1 INTRODUCTION

1. Microbiological testing at specific points in the food chain is an important tool for verifying a risk-based approach to food safety. Specification of food safety microbiological outcomes establishes appropriate levels of consumer protection, while providing maximum flexibility to industry in terms of the detailed process control systems that are employed.

2. The General Principles of Food Hygiene❶state that "in deciding whether a (food control) requirement is necessary or appropriate, an assessment of the risk should be made, preferably within the framework of the HACCP approach", and any microbiological specifications "should be based on sound scientific principles and state, where appropriate, procedures, analytical methods and action limits"❷. Process control is defined as "all conditions and measures applied during the production process that are necessary to achieve safety and suitability of meat".

3. Where appropriate, microbiological performance objectives or performance criteria should be included in verification of process control.

4. As described in this Annex, microbiological performance objectives or performance criteria are different from microbiological criteria. The latter are used for judging the acceptability of a product or food lot. ❸Although not included in the scope of this Annex, microbiological testing of meat may also be used to assess suitability.

2 VERIFICATION OF PROCESS CONTROL BY MICROBIOLOGICAL TESTING

5. A preventative, HACCP-based approach should be regarded as the most effective means of ensuring microbiological process control. Once process control has been validated, verification by microbiological testing can be important to assure that required food safety outcomes are being met on an on-going basis.

Verification by microbiological testing for process control purposes should be implemented where meaningful in terms of consumer protection.

6. Verification of process control of meat by microbiological testing provides a tool for:

• Assessing the adequacy and efficacy of establishment process control in relation to faecal and other contamination;

❶ Recommended International Code of Practice General Principles of Food Hygiene (CAC/RCP 1 - 1969, Rev. 4 - 2003).

❷ Specifications for microbiological testing in relation to the outcome of SSOPs are not regarded as microbiological performance objectives or performance criteria for process control.

❸ Principles for the Establishment and Application of Microbiological Criteria for Foods. (CAC/GL 21 - 1997).

- Assuring the level of control of specified hazards of public health importance;
- Facilitating development of process criteria at a specified step or combination of steps that achieve microbiological performance objectives or performance criteria;
- Identifying the need for review and redesign of HACCP plans;
- Objective comparison of the outcome of different process control systems in different situations;
- Provision of assurances by competent authorities.

3 PRINCIPLES FOR THE ESTABLISHMENT OF MICROBIOLOGICAL TESTING REQUIREMENTS

i. Establishment of microbiological testing requirements should take into account all information available throughout the food chain, including the health status of live animals relative to public health.

ii. Microbiological testing requirements should be: hazard-, product- and process-specific, reasonably achievable, and applied only at those points in the food chain specified. When validating the testing requirements, account should be taken of the likelihood of uneven distribution of micro-organisms in the sampled unit and the inherent variability of the analytical procedure.

iii. Microbiological testing requirements should be based on scientific analysis and advice, and, where sufficient data is available, developed from risk analysis. Where a food safety objective based on the required level of consumer protection has been established, the relationship between the food safety objective (FSO) and performance objectives (POs) or performance criteria (PCs) should be specified.

iv. The stringency of microbiological testing requirements should be proportional to human health risk.

v. In the absence of sufficient knowledge of risks to human health, microbiological testing requirements should initially be established from baseline surveys of current industry performance, and subsequently be modified as appropriate to reflect public health goals.

Sampling plans for baseline surveys should be representative of the slaughter population, and cater for known biological variation in respect of hazards in the raw material supply e. g. influence of geographical region, farming type and season.

vi. Microbiological testing requirements should be based on micro-organisms that are indices of the presence of hazards to human health, or the pathogen itself, in the food specified.

vii. Establishment of microbiological testing requirements, including performance objectives or performance criteria should be the responsibility of competent authorities, in consultation with relevant interested parties, and may consist of guidelines or regulatory standards.

viii. The competent authority should verify compliance with microbiological testing requirements where they are specified in regulation e. g. , microbiological statistical process control requirements, standards for *Salmonella* spp.

4 IMPLEMENTATION OF A PROGRAMME FOR VERIFICATION OF PROCESS CONTROL BY MICROBIOLOGICAL TESTING

4.1 SPECIFICATIONS

7. A standardised random sampling plan should be developed, including specification of the process

step, product, size and type of sample, time and date of sampling, collection methods and transport. Sampling and testing at multiple steps in the food chain may provide greater information on process control and allows for a more targeted response to non-compliance by the establishment and the competent authority.

8. Sampling of tissue may be destructive e. g. by excision, or non-destructive e. g. by swabbing or sponging. No method will recover all the flora present on the surface. As non-destructive sampling will recover only a proportion of those recovered by the destructive method, microbiological testing requirements specified in this manner should be established in relation to the type of sampling used.

9. For practical reasons, microbiological testing requirements are unlikely to be verified on an on-going basis as part of a HACCP plan. However, microbiological verification should be conducted with sufficient frequency to ensure effectiveness of any process criteria that are part of a HACCP plan. These criteria should be measurable in real time, will most likely constitute critical limits at critical control points in HACCP plans, and may be subject to microbiological verification as appropriate.

10. In the case of indicator micro-organisms e. g. generic *Escherichia coli*, Enterobacteriaciae and total viable counts (aerobic plate counts), the presence and / or concentration of these indicator organisms should reflect states or conditions that indicate process control or lack of process control. In the case of specific hazards[1] (e. g. *Salmonella* spp. on carcasses, *Listeria monocytogenes* in ready-to-eat products), the prevalence will generally be reflective of hazards arising pre-slaughter (e. g. *Salmonella* present on hides of incoming animals) and at specific steps during product processing.

11. The competent authority should provide flexibility in regulation so that the most effective verification systems can be established at the establishment level e. g. provision for alternative carcass sampling sites if an establishment can identify that they are equally as effective in assessing carcass contamination than those specified. Similarly, flexibility should be provided by the competent authority with regard to the number of units comprising the sample or testing against alternative indicator micro-organisms as long as the procedure can provide equivalent guarantees.

12. Alternative approaches to microbiological testing that are properly validated should be established where they offer practical advantages.

4.2 FREQUENCY OF SAMPLING

13. There is no single method for determining the frequency of sampling. For slaughter and dressing establishments frequency of sampling may be fixed in relation to the particular process or may be based on throughput of animals. In addition to ensuring randomness, variables to be taken into account at the establishment level include: source of raw materials, type and nature of the meat process, and volume of production.

14. Sampling frequency should be increased or decreased according to performance. Once results show that the HACCP-based procedures are providing a consistent level of acceptable performance, subsequent microbiological testing must be sufficient to ensure that process control is maintained.

4.3 LABORATORY ANALYSIS

15. Methods for detection and enumeration should be practical, accurate, reproducible, sensitive and

[1] Ongoing work in CCFH and JEMRA with respect to foodborne pathogens should also be taken into account.

selective. Only methods for which the reliability and reproducibility have been validated should be used. Inter-laboratory testing should be a feature of a microbiological verification programme. In cases of dispute, recognised reference methods should be used.

16. To allow meaningful analysis and to permit objective comparison of different control systems, methods for the computation of results should be specified, including handling of pooled/individual results, calculation of mean results (e. g. log means) from groups of samples from the same carcass or different carcasses.

4.4 REGULATORY APPLICATION

17. Regulatory requirements in terms of microbiological testing may be specified in several ways. For indicator organisms, two or three class attribute sampling plans that specify limits for numbers of microorganisms (m and M) may be useful, in other situations variable sampling plans may be useful. Two class plans should be applied for pathogen criteria. Where requirements are set according to current industry performance, percentile values may be used e. g. 80th percentile for m and 98th percentile for M, a variety of statistical approaches can be used.

18. Effective systems should be in place for distribution and sharing of information from the establishment to all interested parties, as appropriate, so as to maintain and improve process control of meat.

19. The competent authority should regularly analyse results at both the establishment and national level, and provide appropriate feedback to establishments and other interested parties.

20. Additional to verification of process control, the results of microbiological testing may be used to establish on-farm controls e. g. intensive measures to reduce the prevalence of *Salmonella* spp. in fattening pigs.

21. In situations of non-compliance with microbiological requirements, actions should be specified. Regulatory and (or) establishment responses should be proportional to test results as well as the public health impact of specific pathogens. Where detailed information on the status in relation to public health, of animals destined for slaughter, is available from primary production, e. g. in the case of *Salmonella* spp. in fattening pigs and broiler chickens in some intensive production systems, responses in relation to process control at the establishment level, may include consideration of pre-slaughter levels of hazards.

22. The competent authority should consider microbiological results in conjunction with public health and other relevant information when taking regulatory action. Regulatory intervention and (or) sanctions may be necessary when validated controls are not being properly implemented.

23. In cases of repeated non-compliance, the competent authority in addition to other actions, should require the establishment operator to review and revise the HACCP plan and may specify an increased sampling frequency to verify that the required level of process control is restored.

鸡肉中弯曲杆菌和沙门氏菌控制导则

GUIDELINES FOR THE CONTROL OF *CAMPYLOBACTER* AND *SALMONELLA* IN CHICKEN MEAT

(*CAC/GL 78 - 2011*)

目录

1 前言

1. 弯曲杆菌感染和沙门氏菌感染是两种最常报道的全球性食源性疾病，而鸡肉则被认为是最重要的传播媒介之一。此疾病带来的负担和控制成本在很多国家都非常显著，人畜共患弯曲杆菌感染和沙门氏菌感染[1]还可能严重影响国家之间的贸易。

2. 本导则应用了食品法典微生物风险管理（MRM）的实施原则和准则（CAC/GL 63－2007）中提倡的一种风险管理框架（RMF）。以“初步风险管理活动”和“识别和风险管理方案的选择”为代表的控制措施，指导食物加工链中的每一步发展。后面的“执行”和“监测”部分构成了RMF的全部应用组件。

3. 本导则构建在食品法典系统已经出版的一般食品卫生条款之上，为针对与公众卫生相关的鸡肉中弯曲杆菌和沙门氏菌制定可能的控制措施。文本中，导则落实了国际食品法典委员会（CAC）的承诺，制定基于健全的科学和风险评估的标准[2]。单步或多步可能执行的控制措施如下：

- 基于良好卫生操作（GHP）。实际上它们一般是定性的，并建立在实证科学和经验的基础之上。它们通常又是约定俗成的，国家之间可能存在显著差异。
- 基于危害分析。它们是根据控制食物加工链中某一步（或系列步骤）中危害的可能水平制定的，对弯曲杆菌或沙门氏菌传播或富集有定量基础，并可以通过控制该步骤中危害的有效性进行验证。基于危害分析的控制措施的成效需要通过特定的风险评估确定；尽管如此，任何能显著减少病原体传播或富集的措施都对人类健康颇有益处[3]。

4. 基于危害控制定量水平提出控制措施的案例，在制定导则时已经通过了严谨的科学评估和审查。这些案例仅作为示例，它们的使用和批准可能在各个国家之间存在不同。将它们引入导则，可以说明一种定量方法对减少食物加工链危害的价值，当使用基于网络的决策工具时，根据特定食品加工链步骤和根据国情选择的控制措施可以得出公众健康保护的相近水平。

5. 本导则通过流程图表示，从而加强从初级生产到消费方法在食品安全中的实际运用。这些图：

- 表明弯曲杆菌和沙门氏菌控制措施的不同和相同之处；
- 说明食物加工链中各个步骤使用的控制措施之间的关系；
- 对基于GHP的控制措施就科学论证/验证而言的数据差异；
- 促进个人企业和国家层面HACCP计划的发展；
- 协助判断不同国家间应用鸡肉控制措施的等效性[4]。

6. 因此，该导则为其在国家（和个人企业的初级生产和加工）层面上的使用提供灵活性。

2 目的

7. 本导则的主要目的是为了给政府和业界提供控制鸡肉中弯曲杆菌和沙门氏菌的信息，从而

---

[1] 仅为公共卫生相关的人类致病病原体。本文中所提到的沙门氏菌和弯曲杆菌仅指人类致病病原体。

[2] 食品法典委员会2008—2013年战略计划“促进最广泛的科学原则和风险分析的应用”和第一个原则声明有关食品安全风险评估“适当的情况下，食品法典委员会做出的健康和安全方面的决定和建议，应根据风险评估”。法典程序手册。

[3] JEMRA，2002年。鸡蛋和肉鸡中的沙门氏菌风险评估。粮农组织/世界卫生组织微生物风险评估系列第2号。粮农组织/世界卫生组织微生物风险评估专家委员会。JEMRA，2009年。肉鸡中弯曲杆菌风险评估技术报告。粮农组织/世界卫生组织微生物风险评估系列第12号。粮农组织/世界卫生组织微生物风险评估专家委员会。

[4] 法典：与食品检查和认证系统相关的卫生措施等效性判决准则（CAC/ GL53－2003）。

减少这种来源的食源性疾病，同时确保国际食品贸易公平。该导则提供了科学合理的国际化工具，强化用于根据国内风险管理决策使用基于 GHP 和基于危害的方法控制鸡肉中弯曲杆菌和沙门氏菌。

8. 本导则不是为了在国际贸易中为鸡肉弯曲杆菌和沙门氏菌设置定量限。相反，导则只是遵循国际食品法典肉类卫生操作规程（CAC/RCP 58 - 2005）的例子并为各国提供一个“开放的”可以用来设置适合本国情况控制措施的框架。

3 本导则的范围和使用

3.1 范围

9. 本导则适用于控制所有可能污染鸡肉（原鸡）及引起食源性疾病的弯曲杆菌和沙门氏菌。首要的重点是鸡肉包括整鸡和块鸡，但是不包括内脏。该准则也适用于其他种类的鸡，如下完蛋的鸡，具体视情况而定。

10. 本导则适用于使用典型“工业”系统生产的鸡肉从“初级生产到消费”食物加工链的所有步骤。本文档中主要用于环境可调节鸡舍系统的生物安全条款，也适用于其他鸡舍系统。

3.2 使用

11. 本导则根据“初级生产至消费”食物加工链方法控制鸡肉中弯曲杆菌和沙门氏菌提供特定指导，为流程中的每一步或者多步提供可行的控制措施。该导则是对操作规程——《食品卫生一般原则》（CAC/RCP 1 - 1969）、《肉类卫生操作规程》（CAC/RCP 58 - 2005）、《速冻食品处理和加工操作规程》（CAC/RCP 8 - 1976）及《良好动物饲养操作规程》（CAC/RCP 54 - 2004）的补充，并应与它们结合使用。

本导则酌情参考了这些一般和总体的规定，本导则不再重复他们的内容。

12. 本导则系统地阐述了基于 GHP 控制措施及基于危害控制措施的实例。GHP 是选择基于危害控制措施的先决条件。基于危害控制措施的实例仅限于那些作为有效的商业用途并已进行过科学评估的控制措施。如果对特定控制措施为提及定量结果，应注意其对弯曲杆菌和沙门氏菌的效果可能有所不同。各个国家应注意这些基于危害控制措施仅是示例性的，应重新审查参考文献以便于应用。控制措施的定量结果报告仅针对特定研究条件，需要在当地商业条件下进行验证，才能为减少风险提供有效估算[1]。政府和业界对特定食品加工程序应用 HACCP 原则时可以通过对基于危害的控制措施的选择来决定关键控制点（CCPs）的决策。

13. 本导则中的很多基于危害的控制措施是通过使用化学去污剂来减少肉鸡胴体中弯曲杆菌和（或）沙门氏菌的传播和（或）富集。这些控制措施包括相关化学去污剂在初级生产到加工食物加工链中的使用，将提交主管部门酌情通过。同时本导则不排除选择任何其他不包含在实例中的危害控制措施。

14. 应用本导则的灵活性也是很重要的内容。主要是为了政府风险管理者和业界在设计和执行食品安全控制系统时使用。

15. 本导则有利于判断不同国家对鸡肉的不同食品安全控制系统的等效性。

---

[1] 粮农组织/世卫组织 2009 年。鸡肉中沙门氏菌和弯曲杆菌的技术会议。2009 年 5 月 4 ~ 8 日，意大利罗马。

4 定义

批	群的子集。指一组同一时间一起送至屠宰场的鸡
肉鸡	选择性地培养原鸡，主要用于产肉而不是产蛋的鸡
鸡	原鸡
竞争排斥❶	对家禽中定义❷或未定义的菌群进行管理，以防止肠道病原体在肠道定植，包括沙门氏菌
柳条箱	用于运输活鸡的柳条箱
流行病学单位	一组具有定义流行病学关系的动物，具有感染相同病原体的可能性。这有可能是因为他们处于相同的环境中（如一圈中的动物），或者因为相同的管理操作。通常是一群。尽管如此，流行病学单位也可能是一组如属于同一村庄的居民的动物，或者是使用同一组公用动物操作设备的。这些流行病因病或者病原菌株而异
企业	饲养动物的地方
群	在人类控制下饲养在一起的同一种动物或者是群居的野生动物。根据陆生规程，一群通常被视为一个流行病学单元
单元	指一种便于装载和卸载柳条箱/笼子的结构
线上再加工	额外的清洗步骤（代替修整或线下清洗）可用于控制排泄物或摄取物的污染
部分分群	一个生长群中部分鸡出笼
分群	一个生长群中全部鸡出笼

5 控制鸡肉中弯曲杆菌和沙门氏菌的适用原则

16. 在肉类卫生操作规程（CAC/RCP 58 – 2005）第四章肉类卫生总则中介绍了肉类良好卫生操作的总原则。本导则中特别考虑了两条原则：

i. 从初级生产到消费过程中，控制鸡肉中弯曲杆菌和沙门氏菌应该尽可能并恰当地包含食品安全风险分析原则。

ii. 主管部门应尽可能实际地制定风险管理指标❸，客观反映鸡肉中弯曲杆菌和沙门氏菌控制水平，从而达到公共健康目标。

6 风险概况

17. 风险概况是使用 RMF 处理食品安全事件时，“初级风险管理活动”的重要部分。能为风险管理者和同行在为个体食品生产加工企业量身设计食品安全控制系统时提供科学信息。

18. 本导则的内容是根据肉鸡中沙门氏菌和弯曲杆菌两条额外的风险概况确定的：

- 肉鸡（雏鸡）中沙门氏菌的食品安全风险概况，2007 年 6 月❹；

---

❶ 此定义是直接从 OIE 陆生动物卫生法典中引用。www. oie. int。

❷ 益生菌定义为竞争排斥产品。

❸ 微生物风险管理（MRM）的实施原则和准则 CAC/GL 63 – 2007。

❹ ftp：//ftp. fao. org/codex/ccfh40/fh40rpsl. pdf。

- 肉鸡（雏鸡）中弯曲杆菌的食品安全风险概况，2007 年 6 月[1]。

7 初级生产到消费中的控制措施

19. 本导则包含了一个“初级生产到消费”的流程环节，由此来确定食物加工链中所有步骤可以应用的控制措施。由此便于使用一种系统方法来确定和评价所有可行的控制措施。考虑食物加工链的所有步骤有利于制定控制措施的不同组合。这在国家之间的初级生产到消费系统存在差异，风险管理者需要灵活选择适用于国家范围的风险管理办法时尤其重要。

7.1 应用控制措施的通用流程图

20. 通用流程图如下。

21. 不同单位的流程可能有区别，但应相应地符合 HACCP 方案设计。

流程图 1：初级生产到消费

主要生产过程（第 1 ~ 11 步）

1. 管理祖代[2]种鸡群
2. 将蛋送往孵化场
3. 父代种鸡孵化场
4. 将早期雏鸡送往父代种鸡场
5. 管理父代种鸡群
6. 将蛋运输至孵化场
7. 孵化场
8. 将早期雏鸡送往生长棚
9. 管理鸡群
10. 分群(整体或部分)[3]
11. 运输至屠宰场

加工过程（第 12 ~ 14 步）

12. 屠宰场接收
13. 宰前检查
14. 屠宰

---

[1] ftp：//ftp. fao. org/codex/ccfh40/fh40rpcb. pdf。

[2] 步骤 1 ~ 4 也适用于曾祖代种鸡和优质繁殖种群。

[3] 可以包括宰前检查。

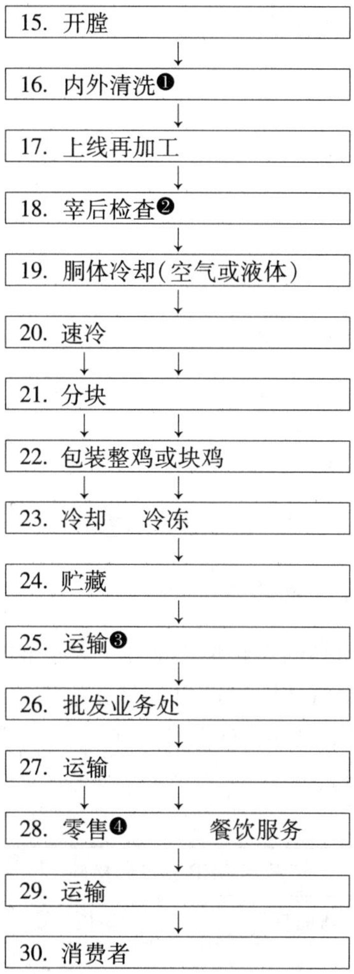

流程图2：第14步——屠宰

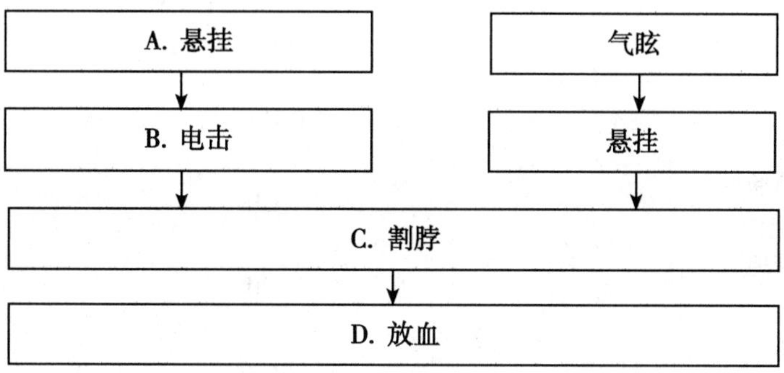

流程图3：第15步——开膛[5,6]

---

❶ 可以在整个过程中进行。

❷ 可以在内部清洗和外部清洗前进行。

❸ 可能会直接供应零售业餐饮服务业。

❹ 包括贮存。

❺ 此工艺步骤是通用的，并且可适当调整指令。

❻ 在开膛过程中清洗或漂洗可在多个步骤中进行。

A. 浸烫
↓
B. 脱毛
↓
C. 去头
↓
D. 关节切割
↓
E. 重新悬挂(可选)
↓
F. 开膛
↓
G. 内脏去除
↓
H. 鸡嗉去除
↓
I. 剖开颈部 / 颈侧皮瓣切除

7.2 本导则特定流程步骤控制措施的可行性

22. 下列表格是为了说明已经识别的食物加工链不同部分的每一步流程中，相关的弯曲杆菌与（或）沙门氏菌特定控制措施。控制措施用√指出，具体细节见该导则或 OIE 陆生动物卫生法典[1]的 GHP。空白单元格表示此流程步骤中弯曲杆菌和（或）沙门氏菌的特定控制措施还未得到确认。

流程步骤中特定控制措施的可行性。

流程步骤

流程步骤	基于 GHP 的控制措施		基于危害的控制措施	
	弯曲杆菌	沙门氏菌	弯曲杆菌	沙门氏菌
1. 祖代种鸡群 ↓		OIE + √		
2. 运往孵化场 ↓		OIE + √		
3. 父代孵化 ↓		OIE + √		
4. 运往父代养殖场 ↓		OIE		
5. 父代种鸡群管理 ↓		OIE		
6. 运往孵化场 ↓		OIE + √		
7. 孵化 ↓		OIE + √		
8. DOC 至生长棚 ↓		OIE		
9. 管理鸡群 ↓		OIE + √	√	

[1] 参考网址：www. oie. int。

（续表）

流程步骤	基于 GHP 的控制措施		基于危害的控制措施	
	弯曲杆菌	沙门氏菌	弯曲杆菌	沙门氏菌
10. 分群 ↓		OIE		
11. 运往屠宰场 ↓	√	OIE		
12. 屠宰场接收 ↓		√		
13. A－M 检验 ↓				
14. 屠宰 ↓				
15. 开膛 ↓				√
16. 内外清洗 ↓			√	√
17. 线上再加工 ↓			√	√
18. P－M 检验 ↓				
19. 胴体冷却 ↓	√	√	√	√
20. 速冷 ↓			√	√
21. 分割 ↓		√		
22. 包装 ↓		√	√	√
23. 冷却或冷冻 ↓			√	
24. 贮藏 ↓		√		
25. 运输 ↓				
26. 零售 ↓		√		
27. 运输 ↓				
28. 零售或餐饮业 ↓		√	√	√
29. 运输 ↓				
30. 消费者 ↓		√	√	√

8 第1步至第11步的控制措施（初级生产）

23. 这些初级生产导则是对下述的补充，并结合使用：

- OIE 陆生动物卫生规程（仅适用于沙门氏菌）：
  - 第6.4章“家禽生产中的生物安全程序”。
  - 第6.5章“家禽中沙门氏菌的预防、检测和控制”。
- 《良好动物饲养操作规程》(CAC/RCP 54－2004)。
- 《肉类卫生操作规程》(CAC/RCP 58－2005)。

注：本导则并未提供 OIE 陆生动物卫生规程和动物饲养文档的具体条文。

8.1

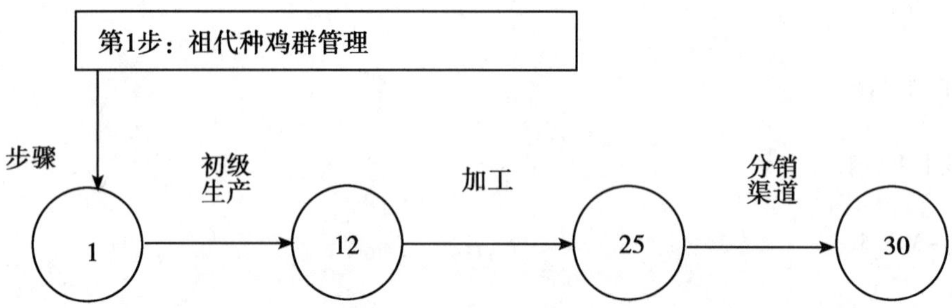

8.1.1 基于 GHP 的控制措施

24. 结合应用生物安全措施和人员卫生措施来加强对祖代种鸡群弯曲杆菌和沙门氏菌的控制。这种特殊的结合方式在国家层面应该通过与利益相关方的协商采纳。

<u>针对沙门氏菌</u>

25. 应该保证饲养鸡群远离沙门氏菌疾病传播。

26. 如果发现鸡群有沙门氏菌阳性反应，则应按照 OIE 陆生动物卫生规程 19 第6.5章“家禽中沙门氏菌的预防、检测和控制”执行。

27. 饲料的处理、贮藏和分销应最大限度地减少沙门氏菌的出现。饲养饲料最好能只用饲料运输专用的工具运输。

28. 通过主管部门批准允许使用类似活性和灭活疫苗，竞争性排他，水和饲料添加剂等控制措施，例如，有机酸或甲醛。

8.2

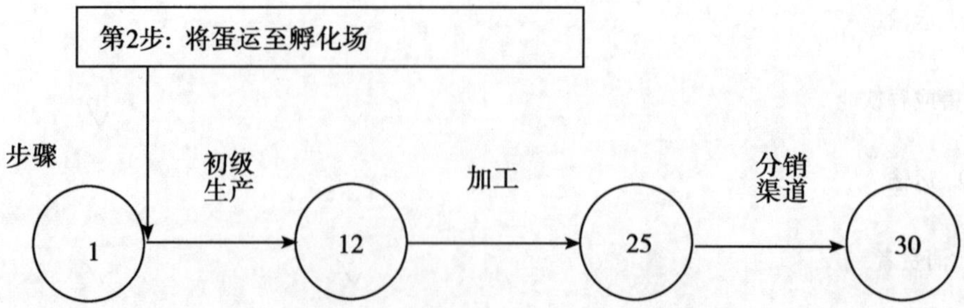

8.2.1 基于 GHP 的控制措施

针对沙门氏菌

29. 只有来自沙门氏菌阴性鸡群的蛋才能被运往孵化场。如果这不可行，则应将来自沙门氏菌阳性鸡群的蛋与其他鸡蛋分开运输。

8.3

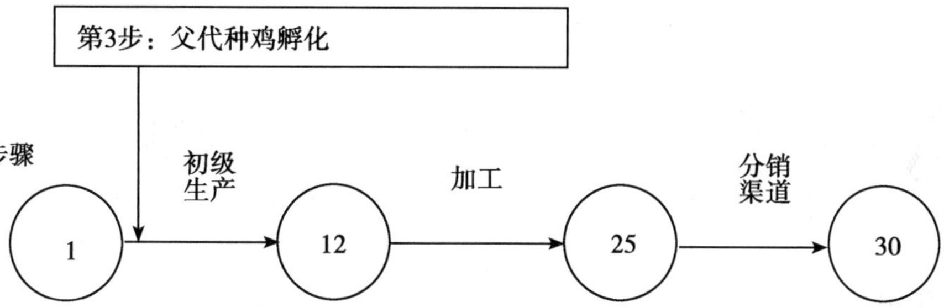

8.3.1 基于 GHP 的控制措施

针对沙门氏菌

30. 如果可能，只有沙门氏菌呈阴性鸡群的鸡蛋才能被孵化。

31. 如果不可避免要使用已经被污染鸡群的蛋，则应与其他鸡蛋分开并单独孵化。应该追溯受感染鸡群的污染并对控制措施进行重新审查。

8.4

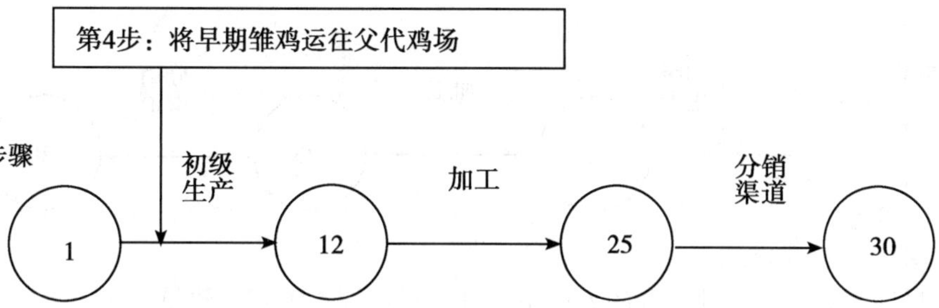

8.4.1 基于 GHP 的控制措施

32. 运输早期雏鸡至父代种鸡群的人员不应进入任何饲养家畜的建筑，在装载和卸载的过程中应避免交叉污染。

8.5

第5步：父代种鸡群管理

33. 该步骤中使用第 1 步使用的控制措施。

8.6

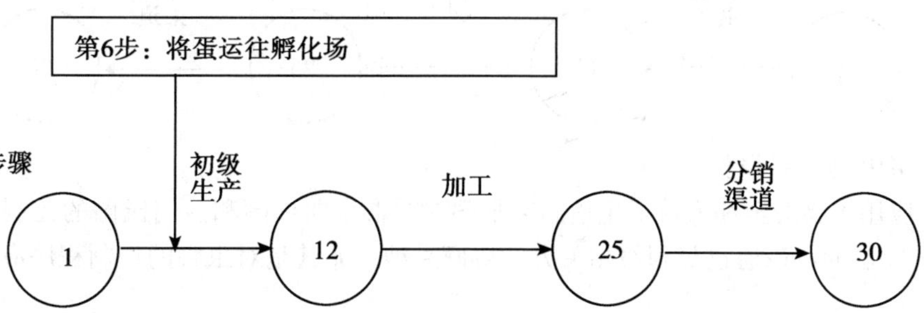

针对沙门氏菌

34. 只有来自沙门氏菌阴性鸡群的蛋才能被运往孵化场。如果不可行，则应将来自沙门氏菌阳性鸡群的蛋与其他鸡蛋分开运输。

8.7

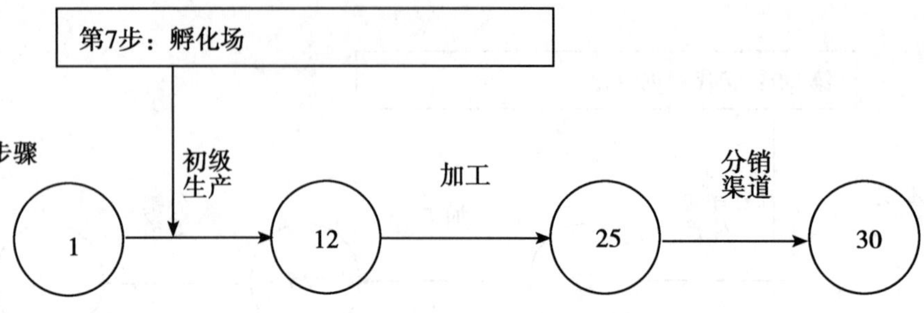

8.7.1 基于GHP的控制措施

35. 如果不可避免要使用已经被污染鸡群的蛋，则应与其他鸡蛋分开并单独孵化，同时应将其雏鸡与其他鸡群分离。应该追溯受感染鸡群的污染，并对控制措施进行重新审查。

8.8

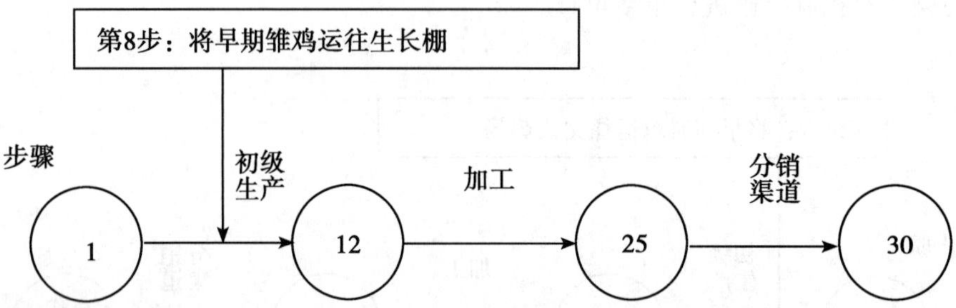

8.8.1 基于GHP的控制措施

36. 运输早期雏鸡至父代种鸡群的人员不应进入任何饲养家畜的建筑。

37. 人员应该遵循适合的生物安全程序由此避免在装载和卸载的过程中交叉污染。所有的活禽运输的柳条箱和单元应该在再次使用前最大可能地清洗、消毒和干燥。

8.9

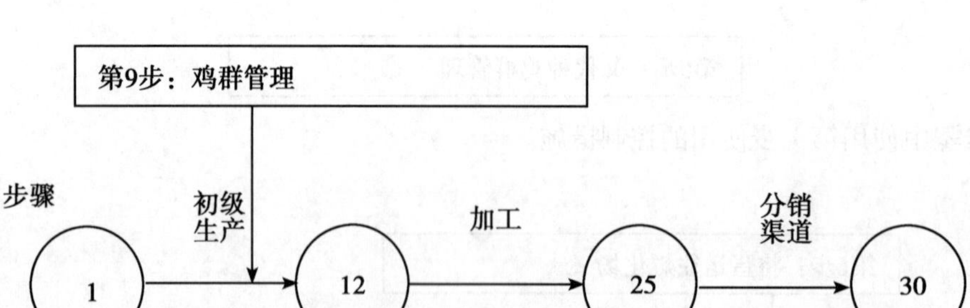

8.9.1 基于GHP的控制措施

38. 结合应用生物安全和人员卫生措施来加强对鸡群弯曲杆菌和沙门氏菌的控制。这种特殊的结合方式在国家层面应该通过与利益相关方的协商采纳。尤其是对虫害的控制程序应该根据当地情况制定。

<u>针对沙门氏菌</u>

39. 特定控制措施如竞争排斥细菌、屠宰前饮用水中的有机酸及有机酸或者是饲料中的甲醛可以通过主管部门允许使用。

8.9.2 基于危害的控制措施

<u>针对弯曲杆菌</u>

40. 使用防蚊蝇纱减少或防止蚊蝇侵扰肉鸡棚，能将受弯曲杆菌感染鸡群从 51.4% 降低到 15.4% 。

8.10

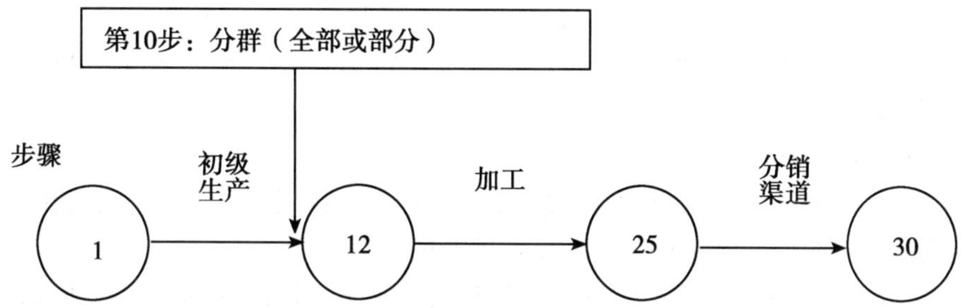

8.10.1 基于危害的控制措施

41. 尽可能进行全部分群。当全部分群不可行而部分分群可行时，应特别注意须严格保证使用的抓捕器和设备的生物安全和卫生。

42. 最好能对部分分群的鸡棚在当天能在全部分群前预先进行抓捕。

43. 喂食时间间歇期，应使用乳酸等水添加剂来降低鸡嗉污染。

8.11

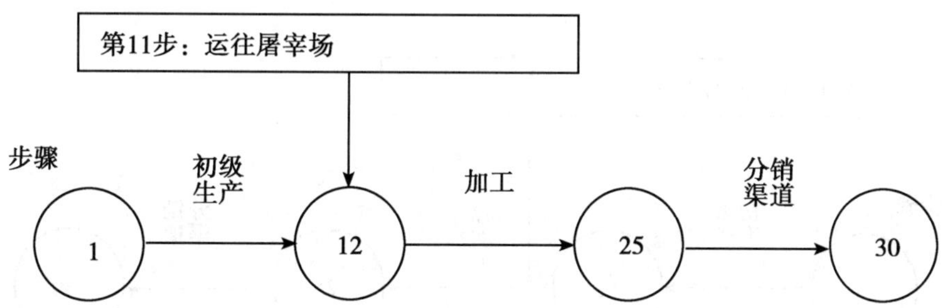

8.11.1 基于 GHP 的控制措施

<u>针对弯曲杆菌和沙门氏菌</u>

44. 所有运输活禽的柳条箱及单元应该在再次使用前尽最大可能地清洗、消毒和干燥。

9 第12步至第24步的控制措施（加工）

9.1

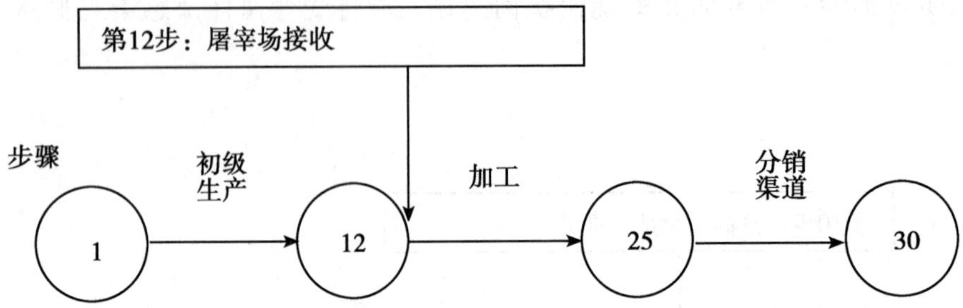

9.1.1 基于GHP的控制措施

45. 如果符合国家规定的情况，应及时提供鸡群的信息，特别是关于沙门氏菌和（或）弯曲杆菌状况，由此实现禽肉的后期屠宰和（或）渠道的处理。

46. 如果可行，鸡群应在停止喂食8～12小时后进行屠宰，以减少胴体被粪便及食物污染的可能性。

47. 应最小化鸡的紧张状态，如使用昏暗的灯光、最小化处理及避免延误处理。

针对沙门氏菌

48. 如果鸡群在屠宰时呈沙门氏菌阳性那么应该最小化与其他鸡群的交叉污染，如在当天最后或者全部一天进行屠宰，如果是在工作周到最后一天或几天屠宰则更好，或者是通过其他有效的干预措施。

9.2

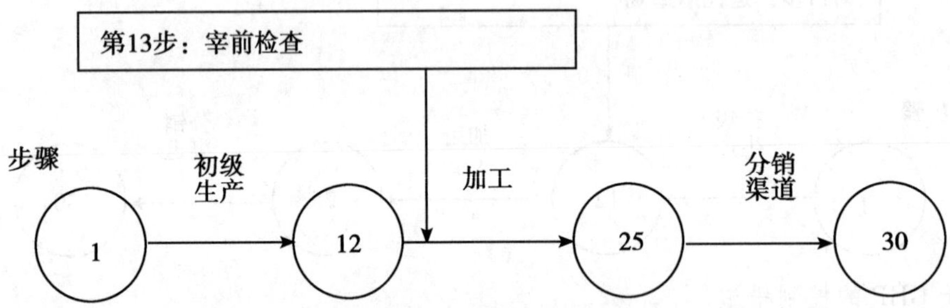

9.2.1 基于GHP控制措施

49. 不应加工濒死的、不健康的或者其他不适宜的鸡。

50. 如果到达即死、濒死的、不健康的或者其他不适宜的鸡的数量超过了预期水平，加工者应该通知相关责任人，如主管部门、农场主、兽医、捕鸡者或者运输公司，如此才能作出恰当的预防和（或）纠正措施。

9.3

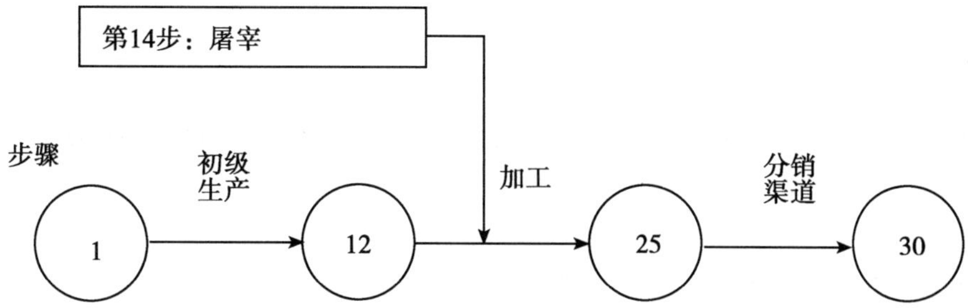

9.3.1 基于 GHP 的控制措施

51. 阳性鸡群应根据国家食品安全政策转入特定的加工和（或）处理。

52. 在悬挂活禽时应采用最小化应激处理，如使用蓝光、平静胸肌及合适的传送带速度。

53. 放血应在浸烫前全部完成，以防吸入沸水，同时能减少血液进入浸烫器。

9.4

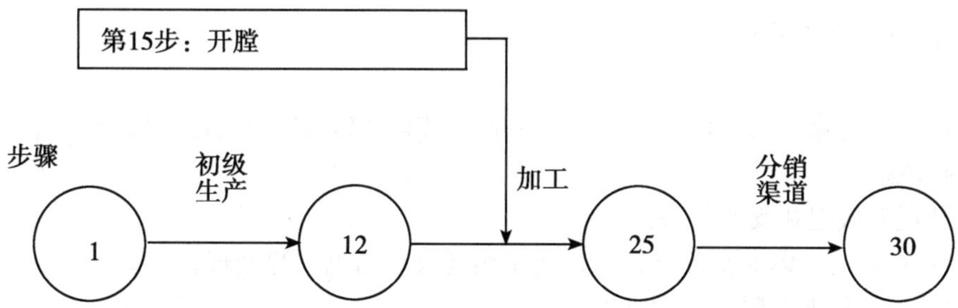

9.4.1 基于 GHP 控制措施

54. 为了最小化对胴体的污染[1]，控制措施应包括：

- 用足够的饮用水流水冲洗；
- 修整；
- 处置或者再处理被过多粪便污染的胴体；
- 使用主管部门批准的化学去污剂；
- 使用主管部门批准的其他物理方法。

55. 控制措施可以在关键控制步骤中单独或者与结合使用。多重控制措施并非总是添加剂。

56. 如果需要再次悬挂胴体，最好能进行机械操作以减少交叉污染。

57. 所有掉落的鸡须没收或者由根据主管部门决定的特定条件进行重新加工。所有掉落的产品应采用合适的纠正措施，例如，修整或重新清洗。

9.4.1.1 浸烫

58. 可通过以下措施最小化浸烫过程的污染：

- 使用对向流；
- 对高流速水适当搅拌；
- 采用最佳水温[2]以控制弯曲杆菌和沙门氏菌的生长；

---

[1] 胴体清洗会减少，但不能完全消除肉鸡及禽肉中沙门氏菌和弯曲杆菌污染。

[2] 考虑到适用性要求（不影响鸡皮外观）。

- 使用批准的❶化学物质，例如，pH 调节剂。

59. 设计可以最小化污染的浸烫加工控制系统时，应该考虑其他因素：

- 搅拌程度；
- 使用多级罐；
- 预煮清洗系统；
- 在处理间歇提高温度并保持足够长的时间，保证杀灭浸烫器中的弯曲杆菌和沙门氏菌；
- 罐体应在浸烫结束后放空并清洗；
- 罐体应至少每天进行清洗和消毒；
- 应对重复使用/循环水执行卫生措施。

9.4.1.2 脱毛

60. 应最小化脱毛过程中的交叉污染：

- 宰杀前应适当禁食；
- 防止羽毛在设备前堆积；
- 持续地冲洗设备和胴体；
- 定期调整和维护设备；
- 特别注意运动机件的清洗；
- 定期检查和替换拔毛机指。

9.4.1.3 去头

61. 去头应防止鸡嗉中的杂物漏出。头应向下拉以减少鸡嗉破裂引起的污染。

9.4.1.4 内脏去除

62. 最小化内脏破裂和粪便传播：

- 减少一批鸡的个体大小差异，尽量使用相同大小的鸡一起处理；
- 仪器设备的仔细调整及日常维护。

9.4.1.5 去除鸡嗉

63. 鸡嗉应以尽可能减少胴体污染的方式去除。

9.4.2 基于危害控制措施

<u>针对沙门氏菌</u>

64. 以 20 ~ 50mg/kg 的氯水喷雾处理肉鸡胴体能减少沙门氏菌传播，在肉鸡脱毛和去除内脏时喷洒，可分别使阳性肉鸡胴体率从 34% 减少到 26%，从 45% 减少到 36%。

65. 将胴体浸泡在三磷酸钠溶液（TSP）中能减少沙门氏菌传播，可以将沙门氏菌阳性胴体率从 72% 降至 4%。

9.5

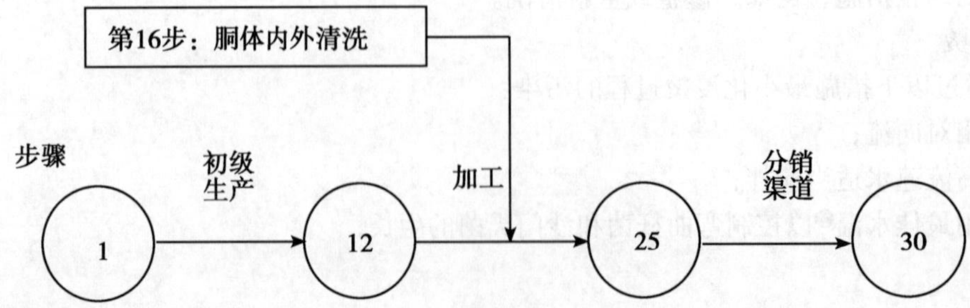

❶ 需要主管部门批准的加工助剂。

9.5.1 基于 GHP 控制措施

66. 胴体的内外应该彻底清洗，通过足够的水压来去除可见污染物。应使用合适的设备来保证水与胴体的直接接触。可以使用安装在流水线上刷洗设施来帮助去除胴体内外的污染物。

9.5.2 基于危害控制措施

针对弯曲杆菌

67. 装有 1～3 个含 25～35mg/kg 氯水的清洗器的胴体清洗系统能降低弯曲杆菌的生长水平，能降低整体漂洗样品的弯曲杆菌水平 0.5log10 CFU/ml。使用酸化亚氯酸钠（ASC）或 TSP 能更低地降低弯曲杆菌的生长水平，分别能平均降低整体清洗样品的 1.3log 10CFU/ml 或 1.0log 10CFU/ml。

针对沙门氏菌

68. 在内外清洗时使用 20～50mg/kg 的氯水喷洒能有效减少沙门氏菌阳性肉鸡胴体的传播，从 25% 降至 20%。在此基础上进行第二次内外清洗则能将沙门氏菌阳性肉鸡胴体率从 16% 降至 12%。

9.6 [❶]

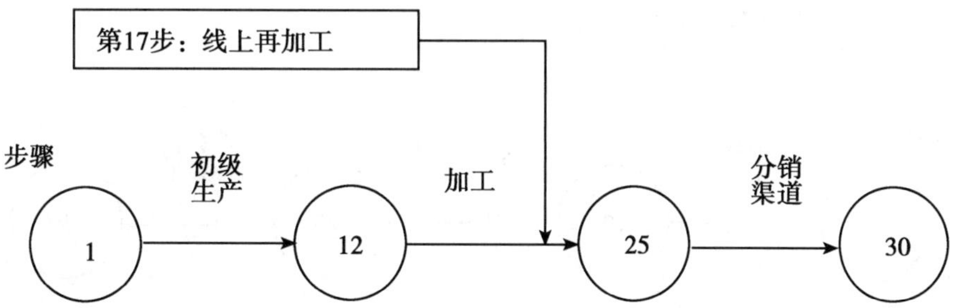

9.6.1 基于危害控制措施

针对弯曲杆菌和沙门氏菌

69. 使用线上再加工 ASC 喷雾系统能降低胴体上 2.1log 10CFU/ml 的弯曲杆菌，减少沙门氏菌阳性胴体传染，从 37% 至 10%。

70. 将胴体浸泡在 10% TSP 中能降低颈部皮肤上 1.7log 10CFU/g 的弯曲杆菌，而颈部皮肤上的沙门氏菌从 1.92log 10CFU/g 降低到检测限以下水平。

针对沙门氏菌

71. 工业设施中使用 ASC（750mg/kg，pH 值为 2.5，喷雾）将胴体中沙门氏菌的传播从大约 50% 降低至检测限以下。在另一工业设施中的沙门氏菌减少了 18%（700～900mg/kg，pH 值为 2.5，喷雾）。

72. 预冷 ASC 喷雾将胴体中沙门氏菌传播从 17% 降至 9%。将胴体部分浸泡在 ASC 中，能将沙门氏菌传播从 29% 降至 1%。

73. 在胴体冷却之前马上用 8%～12% TSP 进行喷雾可以将沙门氏菌传播从 10% 降至 3%。

❶ 主管部门批准的。

9.7

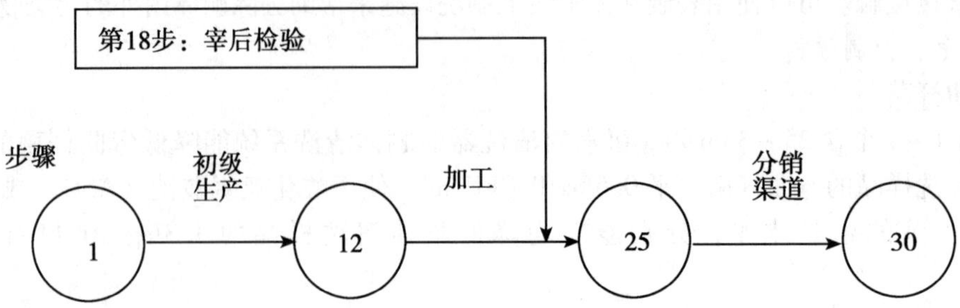

9.7.1 基于 GHP 控制措施

74. 流水线速度及光线强度应该适宜对胴体进行宰后检验，包括可见污染物、感官缺陷及相关肉眼病理学。

9.8

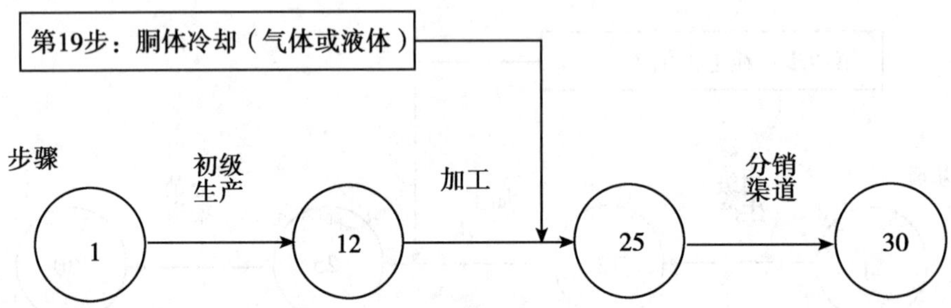

9.8.1 基于 GHP 控制措施

75. 鸡肉应使用气体或液体尽快冷却，以抑制胴体上的微生物生长。冷却系统的设计和运行能确保胴体离开冷却器时能到达目标温度。

9.8.1.1 空气冷却

76. 如果在冷却过程中使用水喷雾来防止胴体在气体冷却过程中干燥，则应最小化交叉污染。

9.8.1.2 液体冷却

77. 如果考虑到控制弯曲杆菌和沙门氏菌的必要性，则需在冷却水❶中添加加工助剂。这些加工助剂应是主管部门批准的，可以包括或者包含于：

- 游离氯（例如，由氯气、次氯酸钠、次氯酸钙片剂或电解生成的次氯酸）
- 有机酸（例如，柠檬酸、乳酸或过乙酸）
- 其他氧化剂（例如，过氧化氢、过氧酸、二氧化氯、酸化亚氯酸钠）

78. 直接在冷却罐里使用氯可能不能作为净化剂直接作用于污染的胴体上。但是，能通过向水中添加氯，以保持水中有足够的游离氯，从而抑制弯曲杆菌和沙门氏菌生长，防止重新附着和交叉污染。

79. 水（包括再循环水）应为饮用水，冷却系统应由一个或多个罐体组成。可以使用冷水或加冰。水流应为对向流，可以搅拌帮助冷却和清洗。

80. 冷却后，胴体上任何多余的水应该流干，以保证胴体在加工链后续步骤最小化的交叉

❶ 粮农组织/世界卫生组织审查各种加工助剂：使用含氯消毒剂在粮食生产和粮食加工中的优点和风险。2009 年粮农组织/世卫组织。

污染。

9.8.2 基于危害控制措施

针对弯曲杆菌

81. 强气压冷（吹冷）可以减少鸡胴体中的弯曲杆菌 0.4log 10CFU/胴体。

82. 浸冷可以将洗净胴体的弯曲杆菌浓度减少 1.1～1.3log 10CFU/ml。

针对沙门氏菌

83. 使用以 20mg/kg 或 34mg/kg 氯或者 3mg/kg 或 5mg/kg 二氧化氯处理过的水进行浸冷可分别将沙门氏菌的传播从 14% 控制至 2%（20mg/kg Cl_2）、5%（34mg/kg Cl_2）、2%（3mg/kg ClO_2）和 1%（5 mg/kg ClO_2）。

9.9

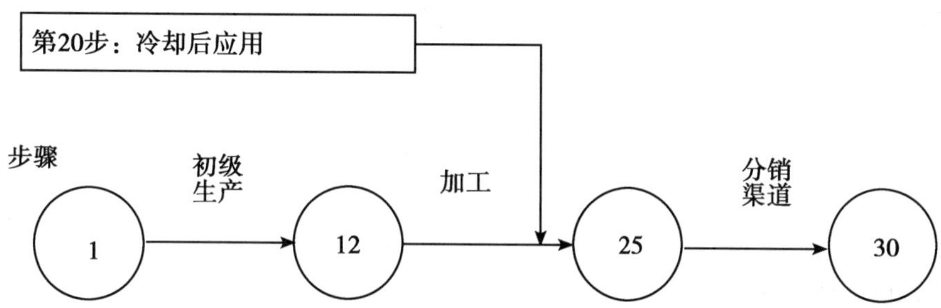

9.9.1 基于危害控制措施

针对弯曲杆菌

84. 将胴体浸入 60～800mg/kg ASC（pH 值为 2.5～2.7）15 秒后立即速冷，能将胴体样品中的弯曲杆菌减少 0.9～1.2log 10CFU/ml。

针对沙门氏菌

85. 使用 ASC（750mg/kg，pH 值≈2.5，浸蘸）速冷能将沙门氏菌的传播从 16% 降至检测限 5 以下。

86. 使用 20～50mg/kg 氯水进行喷雾能将沙门氏菌阳性胴体感染从 10% 降至 4%。

87. 使用二氧化氯生成系统，将胴体浸蘸 5mg/kg 二氧化氯进行速冷，能将沙门氏菌传播减少 15%～25%。

88. 在旋转冷却后立刻用 10% TSP 对胴体进行速喷能将沙门氏菌感染率从 50% 降至 6%。

9.10

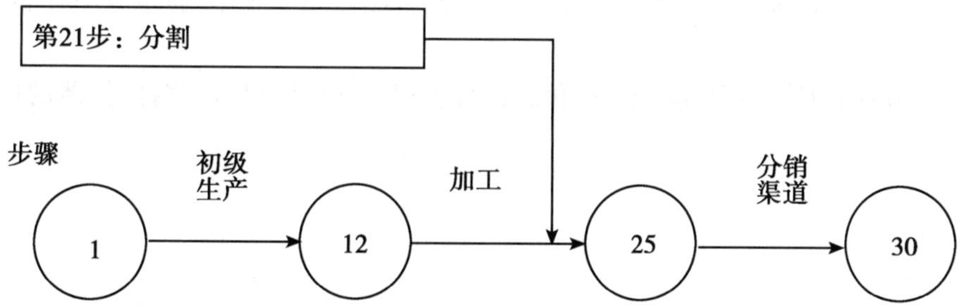

9.10.1 基于 GHP 控制措施

针对沙门氏菌

89. 冷却后的胴体应存放在温度可控的环境中，并立刻处理，可以加冰以抑制沙门氏菌生长。

9.11

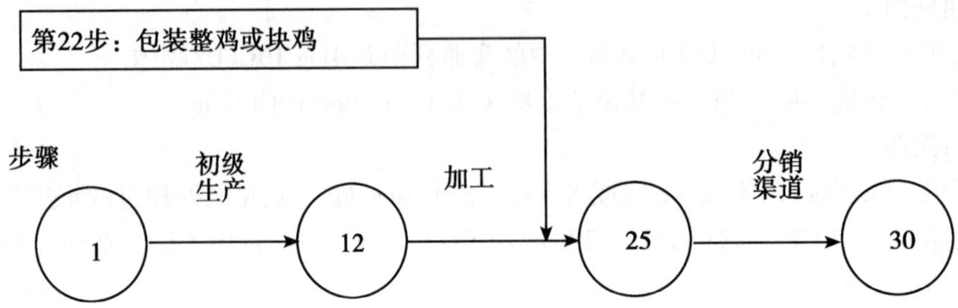

9.11.1 基于GHP控制措施

90. 包装时要注意不要被包装的外部污染，例如，使用真空包装或吸收垫。

91. 预包装用于消费者烹饪的鸡肉产品应该标识[1]符合各国情况的安全的处理、烹饪及贮藏操作说明。

针对沙门氏菌

92. 冷却后的胴体应存放在温度可控的环境中，并立刻处理，可以添加冰块以抑制沙门氏菌生长。

9.11.2 基于危害的控制措施

针对弯曲杆菌和沙门氏菌

93. 对加热、冷却或冷冻的胴体使用伽马射线或电子束[2]能有效的杀灭弯曲杆菌和沙门氏菌。使用辐照必须遵循主管部门确认和批准过的水平。

9.12

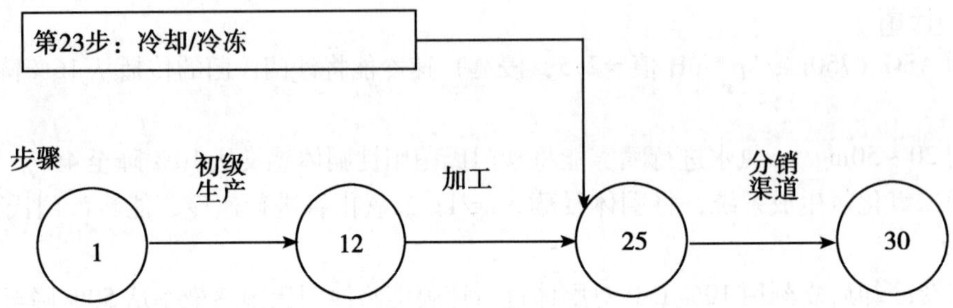

9.12.1 基于风险的控制措施

针对弯曲杆菌

94. 将自然污染的胴体在－20℃冷冻贮存31天后能将弯曲杆菌的量从0.7减少到2.9log 10CFU/g。

95. 对去皮的胸脯肉片使用持续的二氧化碳进行表面冷冻表明可以将弯曲杆菌的量降低0.4log 10CFU/片。

[1] 请参阅预包装食品标签通用标准（CODEX STAN1－1985）和世卫组织的“预防食源性疾病：食品安全五大关键”。

[2] 参考辐照食品通用标准（CODEX STAN106－1983）。

9.13

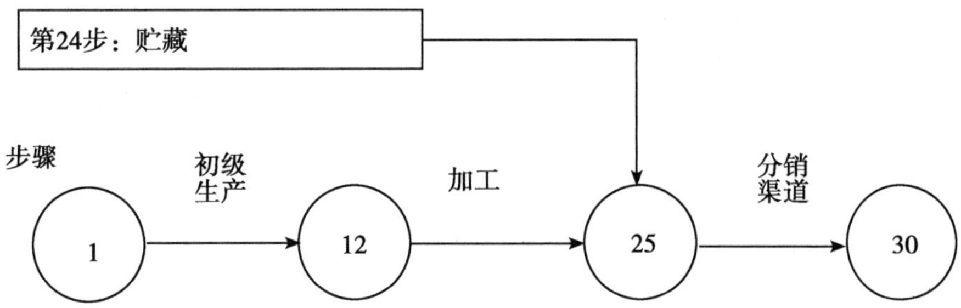

9.13.1 基于 GHP 的控制措施

<u>针对沙门氏菌</u>

96. 产品应该在贮藏在能抑制沙门氏菌生长的温度[❶]。

10 第 25 步至第 30 步的控制措施（分销渠道）

97. 针对运输所有方面的基于 GHP 的控制措施，参考了操作规程——食品卫生一般原则（CAC/RCP 1－1969）和肉类卫生操作规程（CAC/RCP 58－2005）。

10.1

第25步：运输

10.2

第26步：批发处

<u>针对沙门氏菌</u>

98. 产品应该贮藏在能抑制沙门氏菌生长的温度。

10.3

第27步：运输

10.4

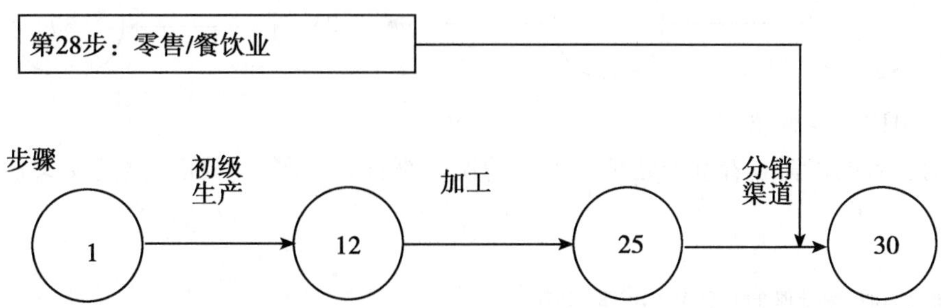

❶ 如果发生温度控制不当，改变包装气压不能防止沙门氏菌的增长。

10.4.1 基于GHP的控制措施

10.4.1.1 零售

99. 使用卫生措施防止生鸡肉与其他食品的交叉污染。

100. 零售商应分开放置生肉与熟肉。

101. 在处理生鸡肉前后都应对手进行清洗和清洁。零售商也应该为处理过生鸡肉的顾客提供清洗。

102. 零售时对顾客单独挑选的产品应尽量使用真空包装。陈列柜台里应备有外包装袋以便顾客能将购买的鸡肉和其他商品隔离。

10.4.1.2 餐饮业

103. 基于GHP的控制措施，也参考了大众餐饮业预烹调和烹调食品卫生操作规范（CAC/RCP39－1993）。

104. 取出解冻和冷冻的鸡肉时应尽量避免微生物的滋生并防止交叉污染。[1] 清洗生鸡胴体可能会带来污染。

105. 餐饮业操作者应该通过全面的食品安全培训以清楚生鸡肉与熟鸡肉的区别，并能从始至终进行分离。

106. 餐饮业操作者应该能通过采取卫生措施来尽量避免生鸡肉与手，接触表面与器皿之间的交叉污染，并防止污染其他食品。

针对沙门氏菌

107. 产品应该贮藏在能抑制沙门氏菌生长的温度。

10.4.2 基于危害的控制措施

针对弯曲杆菌和沙门氏菌

108. 鸡肉应该按照能同时以7log倍数减少弯曲杆菌和沙门氏菌的方法进行烹饪。[2]

10.5

第29步：运输

10.6

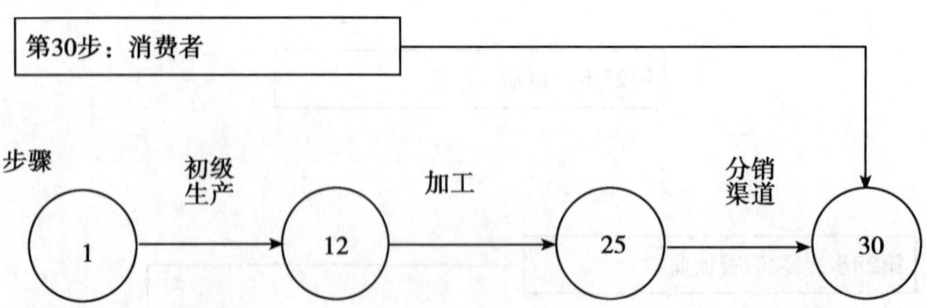

10.6.1 基于GHP的控制措施

109. 对消费者的培训应着重于处理、手部清洗、烹饪、贮藏、解冻、避免交叉污染及避免滥

---

[1] 参考速冻食品加工和处理准则（CAC/RCP8－1976）。

[2] 烹饪鸡肉能彻底消除弯曲杆菌和沙门氏菌。已证明：烹制鸡肉最低内部温度至165 ℉（74℃）不需保持时间，将至少减少7log 10倍的弯曲杆菌和沙门氏菌。

用温度。WHO 食品安全五大关键[1]能协助此过程。

110. 特别重视所有烹饪食物的人员，尤其是为孩子、老人、孕妇及病人烹饪的人。

111. 上述信息应通过多种途径传播给消费者，例如，国家媒体、健康护理专家、食品卫生培训师、产品标签、小册子、学校课程及烹饪示范。

112. 尽量不要在厨房里清洗生鸡肉，这样可以避免对其他食物与人和食品接触面的污染。如果必须要清洗生鸡胴体或鸡肉，则应采取尽量避免其他食品以及其他能与人及食品接触表面的污染。

113. 消费者在处理过生鸡肉后，应对食品接触面进行清洗和消毒，这样可以显著减少对厨房潜在交叉污染可能。

针对沙门氏菌

114. 产品应该贮藏在能抑制沙门氏菌生长的温度。

10.6.2 基于危害的控制措施

针对沙门氏菌和弯曲杆菌

115. 鸡肉应该按照能同时以 7log 倍数减少弯曲杆菌和沙门氏菌[2]的方法进行烹饪。

11 基于风险的控制措施

116. GHP 为大部分的食品安全控制系统提供了基础。如果可能及可行，食品安全控制系统应结合基于危害的控制措施与风险评估。使用微生物风险管理（MRM）的实施原则和准则（CAC/GL 63－2007）提倡的风险管理框架（RMF）程序能细化基于风险控制措施的识别和执行。

117. 当使用本导则指导针对弯曲杆菌和沙门氏菌的基于 GHP 和基于危害的控制措施时，主管部门根据国家情况制定应用于食物加工链中单步或多步的基于风险的控制措施才是首要的职责。业界将根据基于风险的控制措施来促进工程控制体系的应用。

11.1 制定基于风险的控制措施

118. 如果可能及可行，主管部门应根据国情制定针对弯曲杆菌和沙门氏菌的控制措施。

119. 使用符合目标的风险模拟工具探究风险管理选项及风险管理决策。

120. 风险管理者需要知道所选风险模拟工具的功能和局限性[3]。

121. 当制定基于风险的控制措施时，主管部门可以使用本文件中一般食物加工链中某些步骤使用相似的水平危害控制定量例子，作为同行评议的科学依据。

122. 主管部门应该根据一种科学健全与透明的方法计算出风险管理指标代表法定的控制措施。

11.2 基于网络决策工具的可用性

123. FAO/WHO 根据 JEMRA 已经开发出一款基于网络的决策支持工具[4]，探究制定符合国情[5]的生鸡肉食物加工链中弯曲杆菌和沙门氏菌的基于风险控制措施的可能性。

---

[1] http：//www.who.int/foodsafety/consumer/5keys/en/。

[2] 烹饪鸡肉能彻底消除弯曲杆菌和沙门氏菌。已证明：烹制鸡肉最低内部温度至 165 ℉（74℃）不须保持时间，将至少减少 7log 10 倍的弯曲杆菌和沙门氏菌。

[3] 进行微生物风险评估的原则和指导方针（CAC/ GL30－1999）。

[4] 粮农组织/世界卫生组织关于鸡肉中沙门氏菌和弯曲杆菌的技术会议后启动。罗马 5 月 4～8 日 2009 年。试用 2009 年 11 月。再审查 2010 年 4 月。

[5] www.mramodels.org。

124. 基于网络控制工具可以用于估算相对风险降低与（或）排序：

- 对食物加工链（从初级生产到消费）的特定步骤执行特定控制措施；
- 对食物加工链的不同步骤组合使用控制措施的特定组合。

对本文件中不同的食物加工链集合进行模拟

125. 业界在设计企业特定的食品安全程序时也可以使用决策支持工具，具体的控制措施，可能会有所不同。

126. 根据国情使用决策支持工具的人员应该：

- 对引用的科学数据的符合性责任；
- 应注意风险模拟时不可避免的及结合风险管理者的不确定性，使用基于网络的工具是用于探究风险管理选项及告知管理者决策，而不只是提供一个规定的数据库；
- 不强行使用该工具进行特定的科学假设。

12 控制措施的执行

127. 执行涉及执行选择的控制措施，制定执行计划，对控制措施决策的交流、确定执行规定的框架及机构，及评价控制措施是否恰当执行的评估程序。控制措施在执行前应该先进行验证。

12.1 控制措施的验证

128. 参考食品安全控制措施的验证准则（CAC/GL 69－2008）。

注：基于 GHP 的控制措施无需验证。

12.2 验证之前

129. 在对针对弯曲杆菌和沙门氏菌基于危害控制措施验证之前，应先完成以下事项：

- 识别要进行验证的特定措施。包括主管部门批准的措施，如果某些措施已经通过验证是适合于特定商业用途的，那么就不必再进行验证；
- 识别主管部门或业界给出的任何食品安全的结果及目标。业界可能为设定比主管部门更严格的目标。

12.3 验证

130. 业界和（或）主管部门对措施进行验证。

131. 如果对针对弯曲杆菌和（或）沙门氏菌基于危害的控制措施进行验证，则需要证据来证明针对特定的目标或结果该措施有效。可以使用单一或多重措施。食品安全控制措施的验证准则（CAC/GL 69－2008）为验证程序提供了更细节的建议（第四章）。

12.4 执行

132. 参考《肉类卫生操作规程》（CAC/RCP 58－2005）第 9.2 章。

12.4.1 业界

133. 业界主要负责过程控制系统的执行、文件编制、应用和监督，以保证鸡肉的安全性和适合性，并且可以根据国内政府要求和业界特定情况结合考虑 GHP 和验证过的针对弯曲杆菌和（或）沙门氏菌的控制措施（HACCP）。

134. 编制的处理控制系统应该描述适用的行为，包括任何抽样程序、特定目标如运行目标或运行标准、针对弯曲杆菌和（或）沙门氏菌的设置、业界验证行为、纠正及预防措施。

135. 主管部门为业界制定处理控制系统并提供合适的导则及其他执行工具。

12.4.2 规定系统

136. 主管部门可选择提供针对 GHP 和 HACCP 的规定程序控制系统，不规定验证的频率。对设定以控制弯曲杆菌和（或）沙门氏菌控制为特定目标的 HACCP 系统验证时应要求微生物测试。

137. 主管部门可以决定使用权威机构来负责针对业界处理控制系统的特定验证活动。当这样的情况发生，主管部门应规定执行特定的功能。

12.5 控制措施的确证

138. 参考《肉类卫生操作规程》第 9.2 章（CAC/RCP 58－2005）和《食品安全控制措施的验证准则》（CAC/GL 69－2008）第四章。

12.5.1 业界

139. 业界认证应能证明所有针对弯曲杆菌和（或）沙门氏菌的控制措施已经按计划执行。验证应包括处理行为的检查、文档校对、针对弯曲杆菌和（或）沙门氏菌测试的抽样。

140. 验证频度可以根据过程控制的运行情况、设立和验证结果本身的历史表现进行调整变化。

12.5.2 监督系统

141. 主管部门和（或）权威机构应该核实业界所有的监督控制措施都是遵循恰当的针对弯曲杆菌和（或）沙门氏菌控制的监督要求执行的。

13 监控和审查

142. 对食品安全控制系统进行监控和审查是应用风险管理框架（RMF）的必要组成部分。它能促进过程控制的验证朝着公共健康目标进步。

143. 在食物加工链中恰当控制对弯曲杆菌和（或）沙门氏菌水平的信息有很多作用，如验证和（或）核实食品控制措施的结果，监控符合基于危害和基于风险的监管目标，帮助优化减少食源性疾病的监管能力。系统性地审查监控信息使主管部门和利益相关者能就食品安全控制系统的整体有效性作出决策，并作出必要的改进。

13.1 监控

144. 应酌情使用随机抽样和靶向抽样，对食物加工链中恰当的步骤[1]实施监控。利用针对肉鸡中弯曲杆菌和（或）沙门氏菌的监控系统的例子应包括：

- 对饲养场和孵化场进行抽样（例如，环境、血液、粪便）检测沙门氏菌状况；
- 在鸡送往屠宰场之前进行粪便抽样以便于确定鸡群状况，并对特定步骤如热处理或冷冻的阳性鸡只进行合理安排和规定渠道；
- 在鸡送往屠宰场时进行盲肠和泄殖腔取样进行弯曲杆菌的流行病学调查以确定屠宰鸡群的状况；
- 在初级加工过程（一般是指液体或气体冷却之后）末对清洗过的整鸡、颈部皮肤或其他取样由此验证遵循基于危害监管或符合公司绩效目标；
- 对零售产品抽样进行污染物测定属于后处理；
- 全国或区域性调查能确定污染物基准线水平也能协助计算出食物加工链的监管行为目标。

---

[1] 在禽类中检测沙门氏菌的建议是在世界动物卫生组织公布的陆生动物卫生守则第 6.5 章“预防、检测和控制家禽沙门氏菌”。

145. 监管监控程序应该由相关利益方协商制定，选择最具成本效益的资源用于收集和测试样品。考虑到数据监测在风险管理中的重要性，采样和测试应该在国家基础上标准化，并有质量保证。

146. 监测系统收集的数据类型应与输出结果相匹配❶。

147. 监测信息应提供及时，例如，有关的利益相关者到生产者，加工行业，消费者。

148. 在可能的情况下，食物加工链的监测信息应结合人类从健康监测数据和食物来源归属的数据，以验证基于风险的控制措施，并验证实现减少风险目标的进展情况。综合反应的活动包括：

- 人类的沙门氏菌和弯曲杆菌病的临床监测；
- 包括疫情和零星病例的流行病学调查。

13.2 审查

149. 弯曲杆菌和沙门氏菌的监测数据应总结，并定期提供风险管理的决策和行动的有效性信息。弯曲杆菌和沙门氏菌的监测结果应与主管部门共享，使信息可以被收集汇总并做趋势分析。

150. 有关过程步骤中监测数据的定期审查应用做选择具体的控制措施，并为验证提供基础。

151. 从食物加工链监测中获得的信息，应与公众健康监控、食物来源归属数据、撤出和召回数据相结合，用来评估和审查控制措施的有效性。

152. 危害或风险的监控表明，监管绩效目标未实现时，风险管理策略和（或）控制措施应该加以审查。

13.2.1 公共卫生目标

153. 各个国家在设置针对食源性弯曲杆菌和沙门氏菌的公共卫生目标❷及进行评价程序时，应考虑监测和审查的结果。结合来源归属及人类健康监测数据对食物加工链进行监测是重要组成部分。

❶ 微生物列举和分类通常提供风险管理的目的多于存在与否的测试。

❷ 国际组织如世界卫生组织为建立和实施公共卫生提供了指导监测方案。世卫组织全球食源性感染网络（GFN）http://www.who.int/salmsurv/en/。

GUIDELINES FOR THE CONTROL OF *CAMPYLOBACTER* AND *SALMONELLA* IN CHICKEN MEAT

(*CAC/GL 78 - 2011*)

Table of contents

1 INTRODUCTION

1. Campylobacteriosis and salmonellosis are the two most frequently reported food borne diseases worldwide and chicken meat is considered to be one of the most important food vehicles. The burden of the diseases and the cost of control measures are highly significant in many countries and contamination with zoonotic *Campylobacter* and *Salmonella*[1] has the potential to severely disrupt trade between countries.

2. The Guidelines apply a risk management framework (RMF) approach as advocated in the Codex *Principles and Guidelines for the Conduct of Microbiological Risk Management* (*MRM*) (CAC/GL 63 – 2007). "Preliminary Risk Management Activities" and "Identification and Selection of Risk Management Options" are represented by the guidance developed for control measures at each step in the food chain. Following sections on "Implementation" and "Monitoring" complete application of all the components of the RMF.

3. The Guidelines build on general food hygiene provisions already established in the Codex system and develop potential control measures specific for *Campylobacter* and *Salmonella* of public health relevance in chicken meat. In this context, the Guidelines give effect to the Codex Alimentarius Commission (CAC) commitment to developing standards that are based on sound science and risk assessment[2]. Potential control measures for application at single or multiple steps are presented in the following categories:

- Good hygienic practice (GHP) -based. They are generally qualitative in nature and are based on empirical scientific knowledge and experience. They are usually prescriptive and may differ considerably between countries.

- Hazard-based. They are developed from scientific knowledge of the likely level of control of a hazard at a step (or series of steps) in a food chain, have a quantitative base in the prevalence and (or) concentration of *Campylobacter* or *Salmonella*, and can be validated as to their efficacy in hazard control at the step. The benefit of a hazard-based measure cannot be exactly determined without a specific risk assessment; however, any significant reduction in pathogen prevalence and / or concentration is expected to provide significant human health benefit. [3]

4. Examples of control measures that are based on quantitative levels of hazard control have been subjected to a rigorous scientific evaluation and review in development of the Guidelines. Such examples are illustrative only and their use and approval may vary amongst member countries. Their inclusion in the Guidelines illustrates the value of a quantitative approach to hazard reduction throughout the food chain and, where the web-based decision tool is applied, the likely level of public health protection that may result from particular food-chain scenarios and choices of control measures at the national level.

5. The Guidelines are presented in a flow diagram format so as to enhance practical application of a pri-

---

[1] Human pathogens of public health relevance only. For the purposes of this document, all references to *Salmonella* and *Campylobacter* relate only to human pathogens.

[2] Objective 2 "Promoting widest application of scientific principles and risk analysis" of the Codex Strategic Plan 2008 – 2013 and the first Statement of Principle relating to the Role of Food Safety Risk Assessment "Health and safety aspects of Codex decisions and recommendations should be based on a risk assessment, as appropriate to the circumstances" Codex Procedural Manual.

[3] JEMRA, 2002. Risk Assessments of *Salmonella* in Eggs and Broiler Chickens. FAO/WHO Microbial Risk Assessment Series No. 2. Joint FAO/WHO Expert Committee for Microbial Risk Assessment. JEMRA, 2009. Risk Assessment of *Campylobacter* spp in Broiler Chickens, Technical Report. FAO/WHO Microbial Risk Assessment Series No. 12 Joint FAO/WHO Expert Committee for Microbial Risk Assessment.

mary production-to-consumption approach to food safety. This format:

- Demonstrates differences and commonalities in approach for control measures for *Campylobacter* and *Salmonella*;
- Illustrates relationships between control-measures applied at different steps in the food chain;
- Highlights data gaps in terms of scientific justification / validation for GHP-based control measures;
- Facilitates development of HACCP plans at individual premises and national levels;
- Assists in judging the equivalence[1] of control measures for chicken meat applied in different countries.

6. In doing so, the Guidelines provide flexibility for use at the national (and individual primary production and processing) level.

2 OBJECTIVES

7. The primary objective of these Guidelines is to provide information to governments and industry on the control of *Campylobacter* and *Salmonella* in chicken meat to reduce foodborne disease from this source whilst ensuring fair practices in the international food trade. The Guidelines provide a scientifically sound international tool for robust application of GHP- and hazard-based approaches to control of *Campylobacter* and *Salmonella* in chicken meat according to national risk management decisions.

8. It is not the intention of the Guidelines to set quantitative limits for *Campylobacter* and *Salmonella* in chicken meat in international trade. Rather, the Guidelines follow the example of the overarching Codex *Code of Hygienic Practice for Meat* (CAC/RCP 58 - 2005) and provide an "enabling" framework which countries can utilise to establish control measures appropriate to their national situation.

3 SCOPE AND USE OF THE GUIDELINES

3.1 Scope

9. These Guidelines apply to control of all *Campylobacter* and *Salmonella* that may contaminate chicken meat (*Gallus gallus*) and cause food borne disease. The primary focus is on chicken meat in the form of broiler carcasses and portions, with the exclusion of offals. These Guidelines can be applied to other classes of chickens, egs. end-of-lays, as appropriate.

10. The Guidelines apply to all steps in a "primary production-to-consumption" food chain for chicken meat produced in typical "industrial" systems. While the biosecurity provisions in this document have been developed primarily for controlled-environment housing systems they also have applicability to other housing systems.

3.2 Use

11. The Guidelines develop specific guidance for control of *Campylobacter* and *Salmonella* in chicken

[1] Codex *Guidelines on the Judgement of Equivalence of Sanitary Measures Associated with Food Inspection and Certification Systems* (CAC/GL 53 - 2003).

meat according to a "primary production-to-consumption" food chain approach, with potential control measures being considered at each step, or group of steps, in the process flow. The Guidelines are supplementary to and should be used in conjunction with the *Code of Practice - General Principles of Food Hygiene* (CAC/RCP 1 - 1969), the *Code of Hygienic Practice for Meat* (CAC/RCP 58 – 2005), the *Code of Practice for the Processing and Handling of Quick Frozen Foods* (CAC/RCP 8 – 1976) and the *Code of Practice on Good Animal Feeding* (CAC/RCP 54 – 2004).

These general and overarching provisions are referenced as appropriate in the Guidelines and their content is not duplicated in these Guidelines.

12. The Guidelines systematically present GHP-based control measures and examples of hazard-based control measures. GHP is a pre-requisite to making choices on hazard-based control measures. Examples of hazard-based control measures are limited to those that have been scientifically evaluated as being effective under conditions of commercial use. Where no quantifiable outcome is mentioned for a specific control measure, it should be kept in mind that the effect may be different between *Salmonella* and *Campylobacter*.

Countries should note that these hazard-based control measures are indicative only and the references provided should be reviewed to assist application. The quantifiable outcomes reported for control measures are specific to the conditions of particular studies and would need to be validated under local commercial conditions to provide a meaningful estimate of hazard reduction[1]. Government and industry can use choices on hazard-based control measures to inform decisions on critical control points (CCPs) when applying HACCP principles to a particular food process.

13. Several hazard-based control measures as presented in these Guidelines are based on the use of chemical decontaminants to reduce the prevalence and (or) concentration of *Campylobacter* and (or) *Salmonella* in broiler carcasses. The use of these control measures, including chemical decontaminants where relevant, in the primary production-to-consumption food chain, is subject to approval by the competent authority, where appropriate. Also these Guidelines do not preclude any other choice of a hazard-based control measure that is not included in the examples.

14. Provision of flexibility in application of the Guidelines is an important attribute. They are primarily intended for use by government risk managers and industry in the design and implementation of food safety control systems.

15. The Guidelines should be useful when judging the equivalence of different food safety measures for chicken meat in different countries

4 DEFINITIONS

Batch	A subset of a flock. A group of chickens sent together to a slaughterhouse at the same time
Broiler	Birds of the species *Gallus gallus* selectively bred and reared for their meat rather than eggs
Chicken	Birds of the species *Gallus gallus*
Competitive exclusion[2]	The administration of defined[3] or undefined bacterial flora to poultry to prevent gut colonisation by enteropathogens, including *Salmonella*

[1] FAO/WHO, 2009. Technical Meeting on *Salmonella* and *Campylobacter* in chicken meat. 4 – 8 May 2009, Rome, Italy.

[2] This definition is taken directly from the OIE *Terrestrial Animal Health Code*. www. oie. int.

[3] Probiotics are defined competitive exclusion products.

(续表)

Crate	Container used to transport live chickens
Epidemiological unit[1]	A group of animals with a defined epidemiological relationship that share approximately the same likelihood of exposure to a pathogen. This may be because they share a common environment (e. g. animals in a pen), or because of common management practices. Usually, this is a herd or a flock. However, an epidemiological unit may also refer to groups such as animals belonging to residents of a village, or animals sharing a communal animal handling facility. The epidemiological relationship may differ from disease to disease, or even strain to strain of the pathogen
Establishment[1]	The premises in which animals are kept
Flock[1]	A number of animals of one kind kept together under human control or a congregation of gregarious wild animals. For the purposes of the Terrestrial Code, a flock is usually regarded as an epidemiological unit
Module	A structure containing crates / cages that facilitates loading and unloading
On-line Reprocessing	Additional washing step that may be used (instead of trimming or washing off-line) as a control measure for faecal or ingesta contamination
Partial depopulation	Incomplete harvest of chickens from a growing flock
Total depopulation	Full harvest of chickens from a growing flock

5 PRINCIPLES APPLYING TO CONTROL OF *CAMPYLOBACTER* AND *SALMONELLA* IN CHICKEN MEAT

16. Overarching principles for good hygienic practice for meat are presented in the *Code of Hygienic Practice for Meat* (CAC/RCP 58 - 2005) section 4: *General Principles of Meat Hygiene*. Two principles that have particularly been taken into account in these Guidelines are:

i. The principles of food safety risk analysis should be incorporated wherever possible and appropriate in the control of *Campylobacter* and *Salmonella* in chicken meat from primary production to consumption

ii. Wherever possible and practical, Competent Authorities should formulate risk management metrics[2] so as to objectively express the level of control of *Campylobacter* and *Salmonella* in chicken meat that is required to meet public health goals.

6 RISK PROFILES

17. Risk profiles are an important part of "Preliminary Risk Management Activities" when applying a RMF to a food safety issue. They provide scientific information to risk managers and industry in the design of food safety control systems that are tailor-made to individual food production and processing systems.

18. The contents of these Guidelines are predicated on two extensive risk profiles on *Salmonella* and *Campylobacter* in broiler chicken:

- Food Safety Risk Profile for *Salmonella* species in broiler (young) chicken, June 2007[3];

---

[1] This definition is taken directly from the OIE *Terrestrial Animal Health Code*. www. oie. int.

[2] *Principles and Guidelines for the Conduct of Microbiological Risk Management* (MRM) CAC/GL 63 - 2007.

[3] ftp: //ftp. fao. org/codex/ccfh40/fh40rpsl. pdf.

- Food Safety Risk Profile for *Campylobacter* species in broiler (young) chicken, June 2007[1].

7　PRIMARY PRODUCTION-TO-CONSUMPTION APPROACH TO CONTROL MEASURES

19. These Guidelines incorporate a "primary production-to-consumption" flow diagram approach so as to identify all steps in the food chain where control measures can potentially be applied. It facilitates a systematic approach to the identification and evaluation of all potential control measures. Consideration of all steps in the food chain allows different combinations of control measures to be developed. This is particularly important where differences occur in primary production and processing systems between countries and risk managers need the flexibility to choose risk management options that are appropriate in the national context.

7.1　Generic flow diagram for application of control measures

20. A generic flow diagram is presented in sequence on the following pages.

21. Individual premises will have variations in process flow and should adapt design of HACCP plans accordingly.

Process Flow Diagram 1: Primary production to Consumption

Production (Steps 1 - 11)

1. Manage grandparent[2] flocks
↓
2. Transport eggs to hatchery
↓
3. Parent Hatchery
↓
4. Transport day-old chicks to parent farms
↓
5. Manage parent flocks
↓
6. Transport eggs to hatchery Primary
↓
7. Hatchery
↓
8. Transport day-old chicks to grower sheds
↓
9. Manage chickens[3]
↓
10. Depopulate (full or partial)[3]
↓
11. Transport to slaughterhouse

See diagram 2

12. Receive at slaughterhouse
↓
13. Ante-mortem inspection
↓
14. Slaughter

[1] ftp://ftp.fao.org/codex/ccfh40/fh40rpcb.pdf.

[2] Steps 1 - 4 also apply to great grandparents and elite breeding flocks.

[3] May include ante-mortem inspection.

See diagram 3

15. Dress
↓
16. Inside/ Outside wash[1]
↓
17. On-line Reprocessing
↓
18. Post-mortem inspection[2]
↓
19. Chill carcass(air or immersion)
↓
20. Post-chill applications
↓ ↓
21. Portion
↓ ↓
22. Pack whole carcass or portions
↓ ↓
23. Chill Freeze
↓
24. Storage
↓
25. Transport[3]
↓
26. Wholesale premises[4]
↓
27. Transport Distribution
↓ ↓
28. Retail[4] Food service[4] Channels
↓
29. Transport
↓
30. Consumer

Processing (Steps 12 – 24)

Distribution Channels (Steps 25 – 30)

Process Flow Diagram 2: Step 14 – Slaughter

A. Hang → B. Electrical Stun → C. Neck cutting

Gas Stun → Hang → C. Neck cutting

C. Neck cutting → D. Bleed Out

Process Flow Diagram 3: Step 15 – Dress[5,6]

---

[1] May occur throughout the process.

[2] May occur before the inside / outside wash.

[3] May go direct to retail / food service.

[4] Including storage.

[5] These process steps are generic and the order may be varied as appropriate.

[6] Washing/rinsing may take place at a number of steps during dressing.

A. Scalding
↓
B. Defeathering
↓
C. Head-pulling
↓
D. Hock-cutting
↓
E. Re-hanging(optional)
↓
F. Venting
↓
G. Evisceration
↓
H. Crop removal
↓
I. Neck-cracking / cutting of neck flap

7.2 Availability of control measures at specific process flow steps addressed in these Guidelines

22. The intent of the following table is to illustrate where specific control measures for *Campylobacter* and (or) *Salmonella* have been identified in relation to each of the process flow steps at different sections of the food chain. Control measures are indicated by a tick and their details are provided in these Guidelines or the OIE *Terrestrial Animal Health Code*[1] in the case of GHP. A blank cell means that a specific control measure for *Campylobacter* and (or) *Salmonella* has not been identified for the process flow step.

Availability of Specific Control Measures at Steps in the Process Flow

Process Step	GHP-based control measures		Hazard-based Control Measures	
	Campylobacter	*Salmonella*	*Campylobacter*	*Salmonella*
1. Grand Parent Flocks ↓		OIE + ✓		
2. Transport to Hatchery ↓		OIE + ✓		
3. Parent Hatchery ↓		OIE + ✓		
4. Transport to Parent Farms ↓		OIE		
5. Manage Parents ↓		OIE		
6. Transport to Hatchery ↓		OIE + ✓		
7. Hatchery ↓		OIE + ✓		
8. DOC to Grower Sheds ↓		OIE		

[1] Refer to web site: www. oie. int.

（续表）

Process Step	GHP-based control measures		Hazard-based Control Measures	
9. Manage Chickens ↓		OIE +√	√	
10. Depopulate ↓		OIE		
11. Transport to Slaughterhouse ↓	√	OIE		
12. Receive at Slaughterhouse ↓		√		
13. A-M Inspection ↓				
14. Slaughter ↓				
15. Dress ↓				√
16. Inside / Outside Wash ↓			√	√
17. On-line Reprocessing ↓			√	√
18. P-M Inspection ↓				
19. Chill Carcass ↓	√	√	√	√
20. Post-Chill Applications ↓			√	√
21. Portion ↓		√		
22. Pack ↓		√	√	√
23. Chill or Freeze ↓			√	
24. Storage ↓		√		
25. Transport ↓				
26. Wholesale ↓		√		
27. Transport ↓				
28. Retail or Food Service ↓		√	√	√
29. Transport ↓				
30. Consumer		√	√	√

8 CONTROL MEASURES FOR STEPS 1 TO 11 (PRIMARY PRODUCTION)

23. These Guidelines on primary production are supplementary to, and should be used in conjunction with, the:

- OIE *Terrestrial Animal Health Code*19 (applies to *Salmonella* only):
  - Chapter 6.4 "Biosecurity Procedures in Poultry Production", and
  - Chapter 6.5 "Prevention, Detection and Control of *Salmonella* in Poultry".
- *Code of Practice on Good Animal Feeding* (CAC/RCP 54 -2004).
- *Code of Hygienic Practice for Meat* (CAC/RCP 58 -2005).

Note: specific provisions from the OIE *Terrestrial Animal Health Code* and Animal Feed documents are not provided in these Guidelines.

8.1

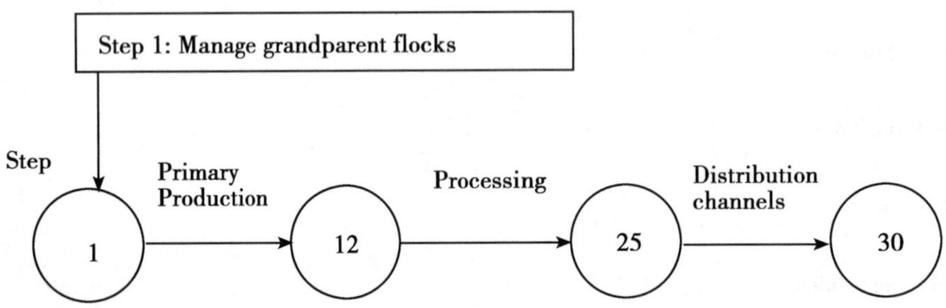

8.1.1 GHP-based control measures

24. Control of *Campylobacter* and *Salmonella* in grandparent flocks is strengthened by the application of a combination of biosecurity and personnel hygiene measures. The particular combination of control measures adopted at a national level should be determined in consultation with relevant stakeholders.

For *Salmonella*

25. The breeder flock should be kept free from *Salmonella* to prevent transmission of infection.

26. Where a flock is found to be *Salmonella*-positive a range of responses, detailed in the OIE *Terrestrial Animal Health Code*19, Chapter 6.5 "Prevention, Detection and Control of Salmonella in Poultry", should be taken.

27. Feed should be treated, stored and delivered in a manner that minimises the presence of *Salmonella*. Breeder feed should preferably be delivered in dedicated vehicles used only for feed transports.

28. The use of control measures such as live and inactivated vaccines, competitive exclusion and some water and feed additives e.g. organic acids or formaldehyde may require approval by the competent authority, to permit their use.

8.2

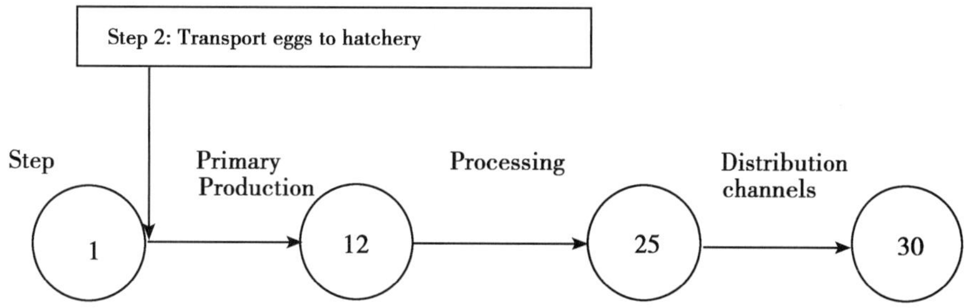

8.2.1 GHP-based control measures

For *Salmonella*

29. Only eggs from *Salmonella*-negative flocks should be sent for hatching. When this is not practical, the eggs from *Salmonella*-positive flocks should be transported separately from other eggs.

8.3

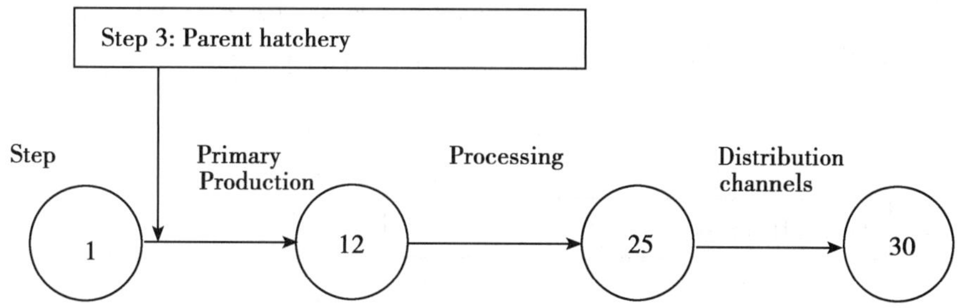

8.3.1 GHP-based control measures

For *Salmonella*

30. If possible, only eggs from *Salmonella*-negative flocks should be hatched.

31. Where the use of eggs from flocks that are known to be contaminated is unavoidable, they should be kept separate and hatched separately from eggs from other flocks. Trace back of contamination to the infected breeding flocks should be performed and control measures should be reviewed.

8.4

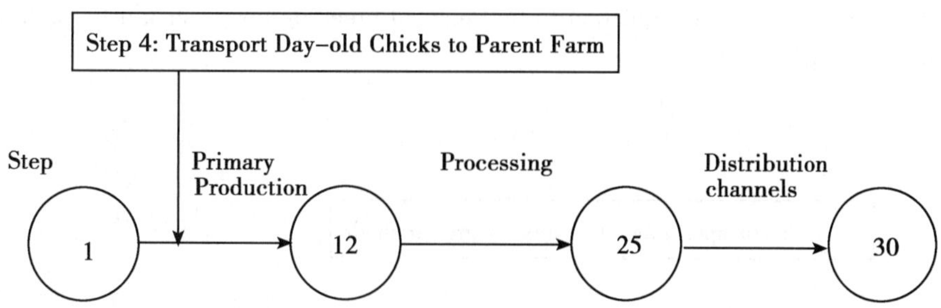

8.4.1 GHP-based control measures

32. Personnel involved in the transportation of day-old chicks to parent flocks should not enter any livestock buildings and should prevent cross contamination of day old chicks during loading and unloading.

8.5

Step 5: Manage parent flocks

33. The control measures described at Step 1 apply at this Step.

8.6

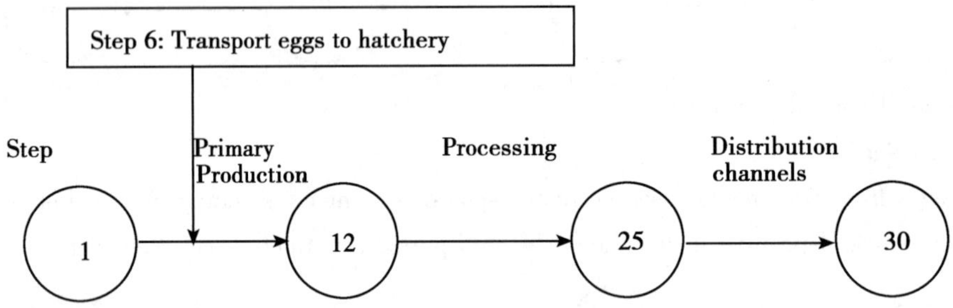

For *Salmonella*

34. Only eggs from *Salmonella*-negative flocks should be sent for hatching. When this is not practical, the eggs from *Salmonella*-positive flocks should be transported separately from other eggs.

8.7

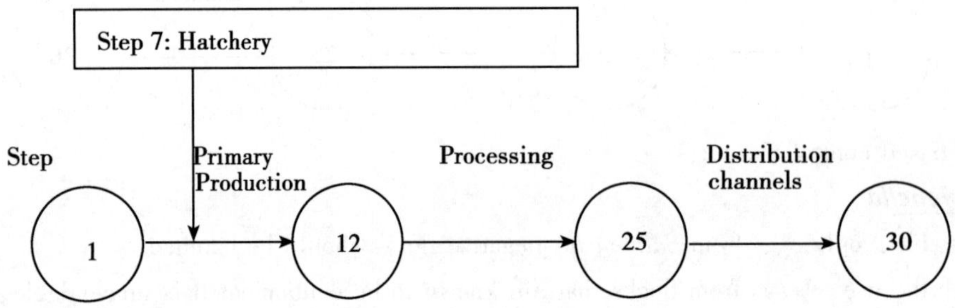

8.7.1 GHP-based control measures

For *Salmonella*

35. Where the use of eggs from flocks that are known to be contaminated is unavoidable, they should be kept separate and hatched separately from eggs from other flocks and the chicks should be kept isolated from other flocks. Trace back of contamination to the infected breeding flocks should be performed and control measures should be reviewed.

8.8

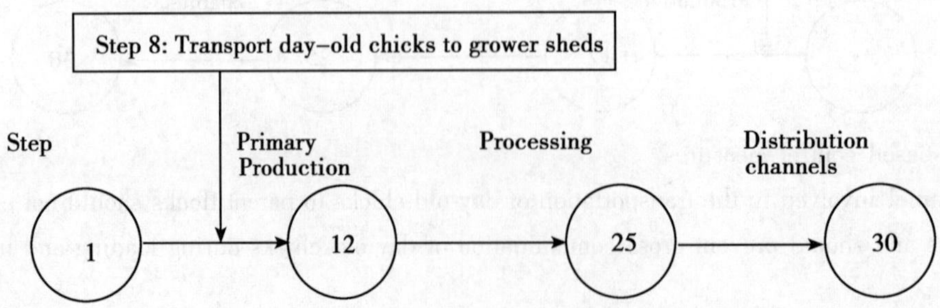

8.8.1 GHP-based control measures

36. Personnel involved in the transportation of day-old chicks should not enter any livestock buildings.

37. Personnel should follow appropriate biosecurity procedures to avoid cross contamination of day old chicks during loading and unloading. All live bird transport crates and modules should be cleaned, disinfected and dried to the greatest extent practicable before re-use.

8.9

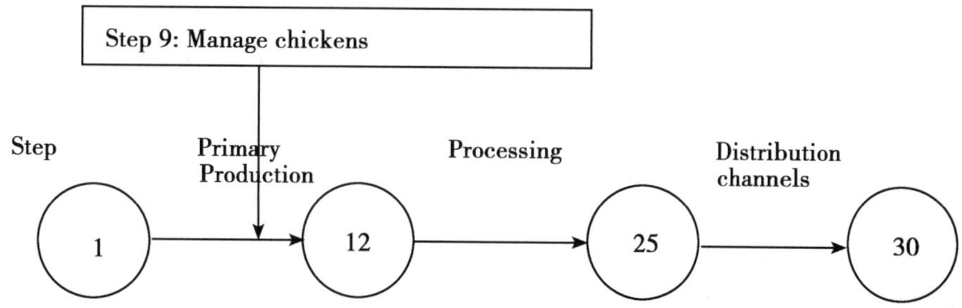

8.9.1 GHP-based control measures

38. Control of *Campylobacter* and *Salmonella* in flocks is strengthened by the application of a combination of biosecurity and personnel hygiene measures. The particular combination of control measures adopted at national level should be determined in consultation with relevant stakeholders. In particular, a pest control programme should be designed according to local conditions.

For *Salmonella*

39. The use of specific control measures such as competitive exclusion bacteria, organic acids in preslaughter drinking water and organic acids or formaldehyde in feed, may require approval by a competent authority to permit their use.

8.9.2 Hazard-based control measures

For *Campylobacter*

40. The use of fly screens to reduce or eliminate fly infestation in broiler houses has been shown to decrease the percentage of *Campylobacter* spp. -positive flocks from 51.4% to 15.4%.

8.10

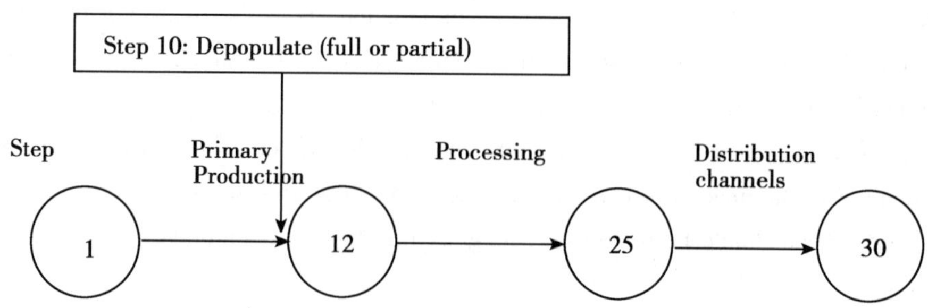

8.10.1 GHP-based control measures

41. Full depopulation of the flock should be carried out where possible. Where this is not practicable and partial depopulation is practised, particular attention should be paid to strict biosecurity and hygiene of catchers and the equipment they use.

42. It is preferable that sheds being partially depopulated are scheduled for catching ahead of those be-

ing fully depopulated on the same day.

43. When feed withdrawal is practised, water additives such as lactic acid may be used to lower post-harvest crop contamination.

8.11

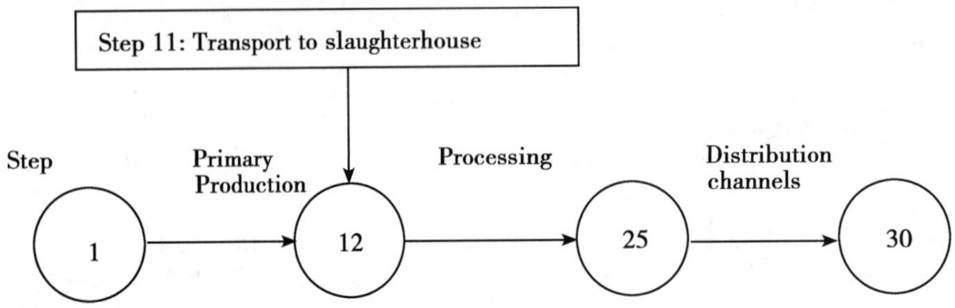

8.11.1 GHP-based control measures

For *Campylobacter* and *Salmonella*

44. All live bird transport crates and modules should be cleaned, disinfected and dried to the greatest extent practicable, before reuse.

9 CONTROL MEASURES FOR STEPS 12 TO 24 (PROCESSING)

9.1

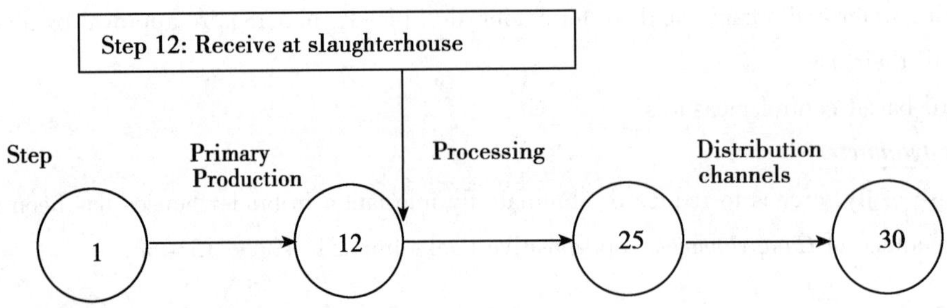

9.1.1 GHP-based control measures

45. Where appropriate to the national situation, information about the flock, in particular about *Salmonella* and (or) *Campylobacter* status should be provided in a timely manner to enable logistic slaughter and (or) channelling of poultry meat to treatment.

46. Flocks, where practical, should be slaughtered after 8 – 12 hours feed withdrawal in order to reduce the likelihood of contamination of carcasses by faecal material and ingesta.

47. Stress to chickens should be minimised, e. g. by dim lighting, minimal handling and avoiding delays in processing.

For *Salmonella*

48. If flocks that are positive for *Salmonella* are presented for slaughter this should be done in a manner that minimises cross contamination to other flocks, e. g. by slaughtering them at the end of the day, or all on one day and preferably the last day (s) of the working week or through other effective interventions.

9.2

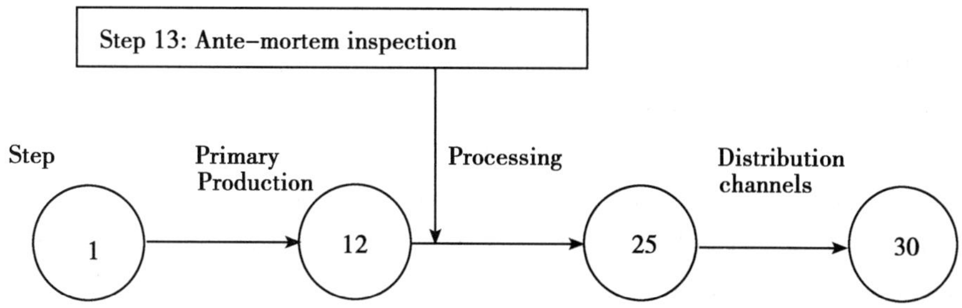

9.2.1 GHP-based control measures

49. Moribund, unhealthy or otherwise unsuitable chickens should not be processed.

50. Where numbers of chickens that are dead on arrival, moribund, unhealthy or otherwise unsuitable for processing exceed expected levels, the processor should notify the relevant responsible person, e.g. the competent authority, the farmer, veterinarian, catcher or transportation company, so that appropriate preventative and (or) corrective action can be taken.

9.3

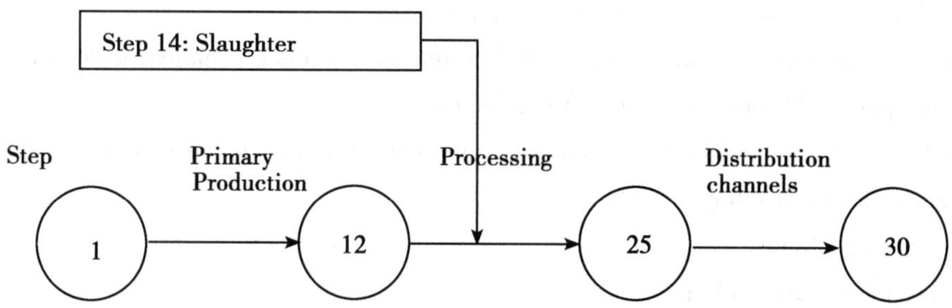

9.3.1 GHP-based control measures

51. Positive flocks may be diverted for specific processing and (or) treatment according to national food safety policies.

52. Measures should be taken to minimise bird stress at live hanging, e.g. use of blue light, breast comforter, suitable line speed.

53. Bleeding should be substantially completed before scalding in order to prevent inhalation of scald water and to reduce the amount of blood entering the scalder.

9.4

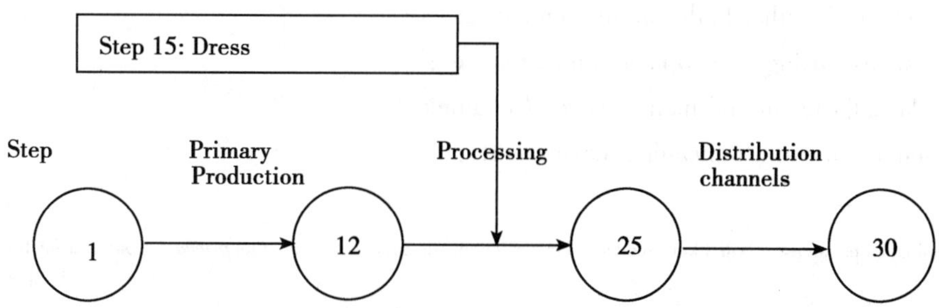

9.4.1 GHP-based control measures

54. So as to minimise contamination[1] of carcasses, control measures may include:

- Washing with abundant potable running water;
- Trimming;
- Disposal or reprocessing of carcasses with extensive faecal contamination;
- Use of chemical decontaminants approved by the competent authority;
- Use of other physical methods approved by the competent authority.

55. These control measures can be applied alone or in combination at key process steps. Multiple control measures may not always be additive.

56. Where re-hang of carcasses is necessary, it is preferable that this is done mechanically so as to reduce cross-contamination.

57. All chickens which drop on the floor should be condemned, or reprocessed under specific conditions as determined by the competent authority. Any dropped product should trigger corrective actions as appropriate, such as trimming and re-washing.

9.4.1.1 Scalding

58. Contamination during scalding can be minimised by:

- The use of counter-current flow;
- High flow rates of water with adequate agitation;
- Having an optimum scalding temperature[2] to minimise levels of *Campylobacter* and *Salmonella*;
- Use of approved[3] chemicals e. g. pH regulators.

59. Other factors that should be taken into account when designing process control systems that minimise contamination during scalding include:

- Degree of agitation;
- Use of multi-staged tanks;
- Pre-scald wash systems;
- Raising the temperature at processing breaks high enough for a long enough time to kill.

***Campylobacter* and *Salmonella* in the scalders**

- Tanks being emptied and cleaned at end of a processing period;
- Tanks being cleaned and disinfected at least daily;
- Hygiene measures applied to reused/recycled water.

9.4.1.2 Defeathering

60. Cross contamination at defeathering can be minimised by:

- Ensuring appropriate fasting of chickens prior to slaughter;
- Prevention of feather build-up on equipment;
- Continuous rinsing of equipment and carcasses;
- Regular adjustment and maintenance of equipment;
- Particular attention to cleaning moving parts;

---

[1] Decontamination of carcasses will likely reduce, but not eliminate *Salmonella* and *Campylobacter* bacteria on broiler carcasses and broiler meat.

[2] Taking into consideration, suitability requirements (i. e. not affecting the skin).

[3] The competent authority may require processing aids to be approved.

- Regular inspection and replacement of plucker fingers.

9. 4. 1. 3 Head pulling

61. Head pulling should be carried out in such a manner that leakage from the crop is prevented. Heads should be pulled downwards to reduce contamination due to crop rupture.

9. 4. 1. 4 Evisceration

62. Rupture of the viscera and spread of faeces can be minimised by:

- Limiting size variation in batches so that birds of similar sizes are processed together;
- Careful adjustment and regular maintenance of machinery.

9. 4. 1. 5 Crop removal

63. Where possible, crops should be extracted in a manner that is likely to limit carcass contamination.

9. 4. 2 Hazard-based control measures

For *Salmonella*

64. Spray applications of 20 – 50 mg/kg chlorinated water following defeathering and carcass evisceration have been shown to reduce the prevalence of *Salmonella*-positive broiler carcasses from 34% to 26% and from 45% to 36% respectively.

65. Immersion in Tri Sodium Phosphate (TSP) has been shown to reduce prevalence of *Salmonella*positive carcasses from 72% to 4%.

9. 5

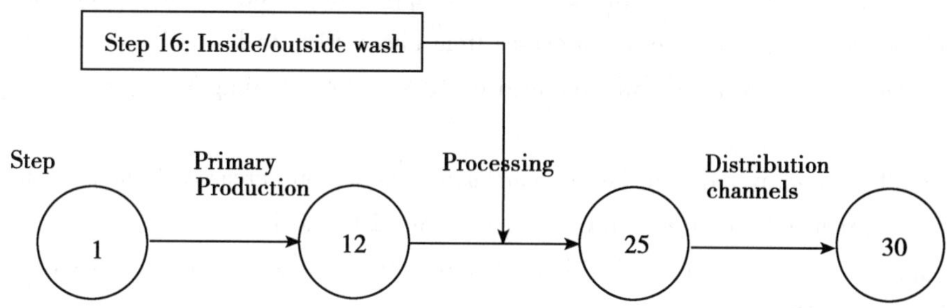

9. 5. 1 GHP-based control measures

66. The inside and outside of all carcasses should be thoroughly washed, using pressure sufficient to remove visible contamination. Appropriate equipment should be used to ensure direct water contact with the carcass. The removal of contaminants may be aided by the use of brushing apparatus installed in line with the inside/outside wash.

9. 5. 2 Hazard-based control measures

For *Campylobacter*

67. Carcass washing systems with 1 – 3 washers using water with 25 – 35mg/kg total chlorine have been shown to reduce levels of *Campylobacter* by about 0. 5log10 CFU/ml of whole carcass rinse sample. Postwash sprays using Acidified Sodium Chlorite (ASC) or TSP may further reduce *Campylobacter* levels by an average of 1. 3 log10 CFU/ml or 1. 0 log10 CFU/ml of whole carcass rinse sample respectively.

For *Salmonella*

68. Inside/outside washing using a spray application of 20 – 50 mg/kg chlorinated water has been shown to reduce the prevalence of *Salmonella*-positive broiler carcasses from 25% to 20%. A second inside/outside washing following upon the first resulted in a reduction of *Salmonella*-positive broiler carcasses from

16% to 12%.

9.6

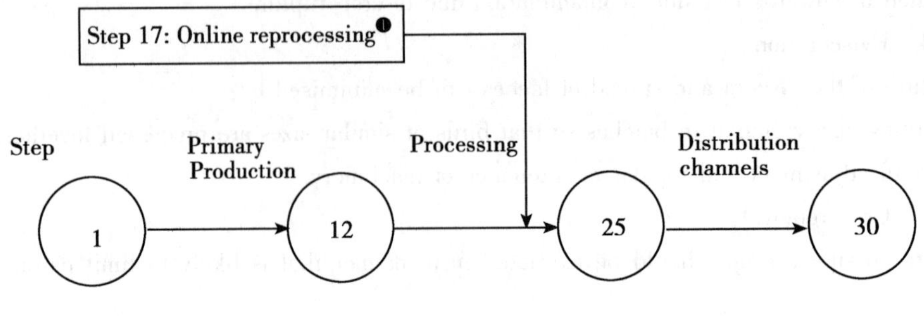

9.6.1 Hazard-based control measures

For *Campylobacter* and *Salmonella*

69. An on-line reprocessing spray system incorporating ASC has been shown to reduce *Campylobacter* in the whole carcass rinse sample by about 2.1 log10 CFU/ml and to reduce the prevalence of *Salmonella*positive carcasses from 37% to 10%.

70. Dipping carcasses in 10% TSP reduced *Campylobacter* by 1.7 log10 CFU/g neck skin and the MPN of *Salmonella* was reduced from 1.92 log10 CFU/g neck skin to undetectable levels.

For *Salmonella*

71. The use of ASC (750mg/kg, pH 2.5, spray application) has in one industrial setting been shown to reduce *Salmonella* prevalence on carcasses from about 50% to levels below detection. In another industrial setting *Salmonella* prevalence was reduced by 18% (700 – 900mg/kg, pH 2.5, spray application).

72. A pre-chill ASC spray reduced the *Salmonella* prevalence on carcasses from 17% to 9%. Dipping carcass parts in ASC reduced the *Salmonella* prevalence from 29% to 1%.

73. Spray application of 8% – 12% TSP immediately before carcass chilling was shown to reduce *Salmonella* prevalence from 10% to 3%.

9.7

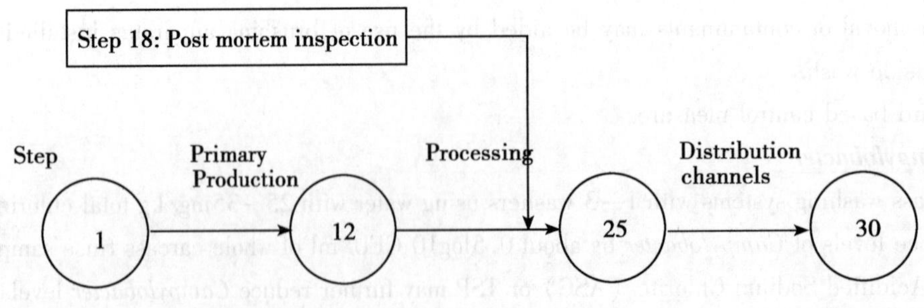

9.7.1 GHP-based control measures

74. Line speeds and the amount of light should be appropriate for effective post-mortem inspection of carcasses for visible contamination, organoleptic defects and relevant gross pathology.

❶ Where approved by the Competent Authority.

9.8

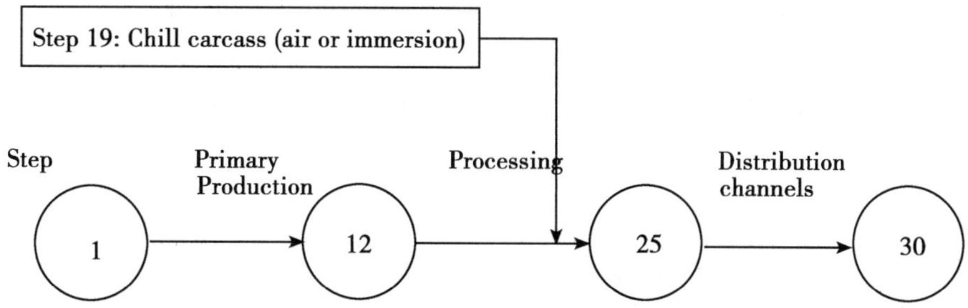

9.8.1 GHP-based control measures

75. Chicken meat should be chilled, using air or immersion chilling, as quickly as possible to limit the growth of micro-organisms on the carcass. Design and operation of chilling systems should ensure that the target temperature of chilled carcasses is achieved by the time carcasses exit the chiller.

9.8.1.1 Air chilling

76. If water sprays are used during air chilling to prevent desiccation of carcasses, they should be arranged to minimise cross contamination.

9.8.1.2 Immersion Chilling

77. Where considered necessary for control of *Campylobacter* and *Salmonella*, processing aids may be added to the chiller water[1]. These should be approved by the competent authority and may include, among others:

- Free chlorine (as produced by chlorine gas, sodium-hypochlorite, calcium hypochlorite tablets or electrolytically generated hypochlorous acid);
- Organic acids (e.g. citric, lactic or peracetic acid);
- Other oxidants (e.g. hydrogen peroxide, peroxy acids, chlorine dioxide, acidified sodium chlorite).

78. The use of chlorine in the chill tank may not act as a decontaminating agent by acting directly on the contaminated carcass. However, there would be a washing off effect by the water itself, and the addition of chlorine at a level sufficient to maintain a free residual in the water would then inactivate *Campylobacter* and *Salmonella* washed off, preventing re-attachment and cross-contamination.

79. Water (including recirculated water) should be potable and the chilling system may comprise of one or more tanks. Chilled water can be used or ice may be added to it. Water flow should be counter-current and may be agitated to assist cooling and washing action.

80. Following chilling, any excess water should be allowed to drain away from the carcasses to minimise cross-contamination of carcasses at subsequent steps in the processing chain.

9.8.2 Hazard-based control measures

For *Campylobacter*

81. Forced air chilling (blast chilling) may reduce the concentration of *Campylobacter* on chicken carcasses by 0.4 log10 CFU/carcass.

82. Immersion chilling has been shown to reduce concentrations of *Campylobacter* by 1.1 – 1.3 log10

[1] A variety of processing aids are reviewed in: FAO/WHO: Benefits and Risks of the Use of Chlorine-containing Disinfectants in Food Production and Food Processing. FAO/WHO 2009.

CFU/ml of carcass rinse.

For *Salmonella*

83. Immersion chilling in water treated with 20mg/kg or 34 mg/kg chlorine or 3mg/kg or 5 mg/kg chlorine dioxide reduced *Salmonella* prevalence from 14% in controls to 2% (20mg/kg Cl_2), 5% (34mg/kg Cl_2), 2% (3mg/kg ClO_2) and 1% (5 mg/kg ClO_2) respectively.

9.9

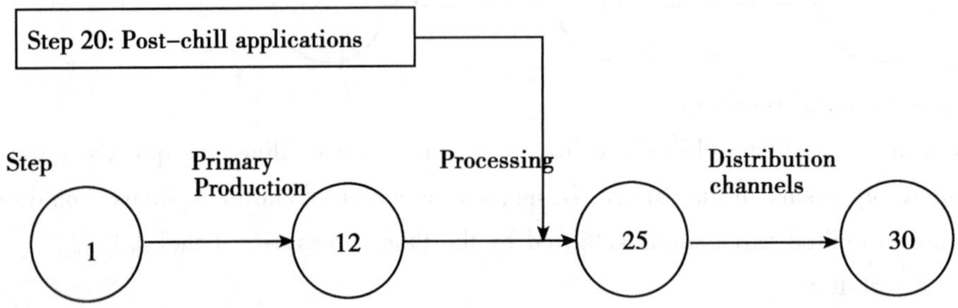

9.9.1 Hazard-based control measures

For *Campylobacter*

84. Immersing whole carcasses in 600 – 800mg/kg ASC at pH 2.5 to 2.7 for 15 seconds immediately postchill, has been shown to reduce *Campylobacter* by 0.9 – 1.2 log10 CFU/ml of whole carcass rinse sample.

For *Salmonella*

85. The use of ASC (750 mg/kg, pH ≈ 2.5, immersion dip) post-chill has been shown to reduce prevalence of *Salmonella* positive carcasses from 16% to a level below detection. ❶

86. Spray applications of 20 – 50 mg/kg chlorinated water have been shown to reduce the prevalence of *Salmonella*-positive carcasses from 10% to 4%.

87. A chlorine dioxide generating system applied as a dip at 5mg/kg post-chill resulted in 15% – 25% reduction in *Salmonella* prevalence. ❶

88. Spraying carcasses immediately after spin chilling with 10% TSP resulted in a reduction of *Salmonella* prevalence from 50% to 6%.

9.10

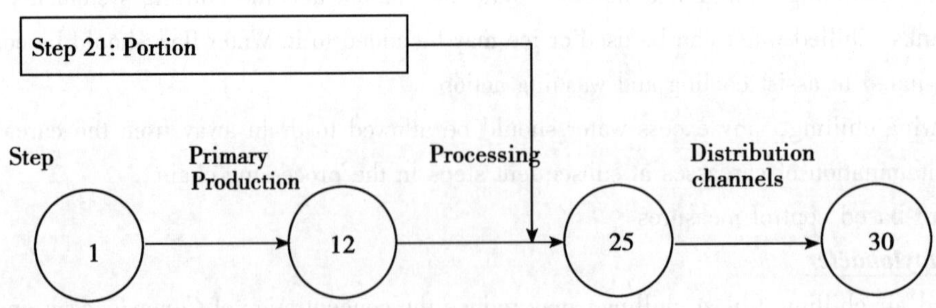

9.10.1 GHP-based control measures

For *Salmonella*

89. Chilled carcasses should be held in temperature controlled environments and processed as soon as

❶ FAO/WHO, 2009. Technical Meeting on *Salmonella* and *Campylobacter* in chicken meat. 4 – 8 May 2009, Rome, Italy.

possible, or with the addition of ice to minimise the growth of *Salmonella*.

9. 11

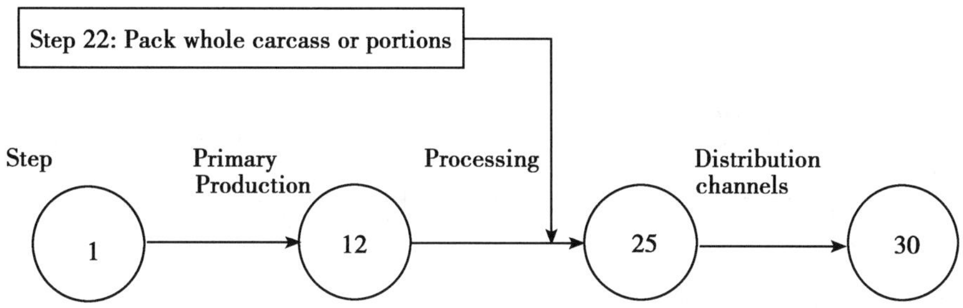

9. 11. 1 GHP-based control measures

90. Care should be taken when packaging to minimise external contamination of the pack, e. g. by use of leakproof packaging or absorbent pads.

91. Pre-packed chicken products intended to be cooked by the consumer should be labelled❶ with safe handling, cooking and storage instructions as appropriate to the National situation.

For *Salmonella*

92. Chilled carcasses should be held in temperature controlled environments and processed as soon as possible or with the addition of ice to minimise the growth of *Salmonella*.

9. 11. 2 Hazard-based control measures

For *Campylobacter* and *Salmonella*

93. Various doses of Gamma rays or electron beams❷ applied to warm, chilled, or frozen carcasses have been shown to be effective at eliminating *Campylobacter* and *Salmonella*. Where irradiation is permitted, levels should be validated and approved by the competent authority.

9. 12

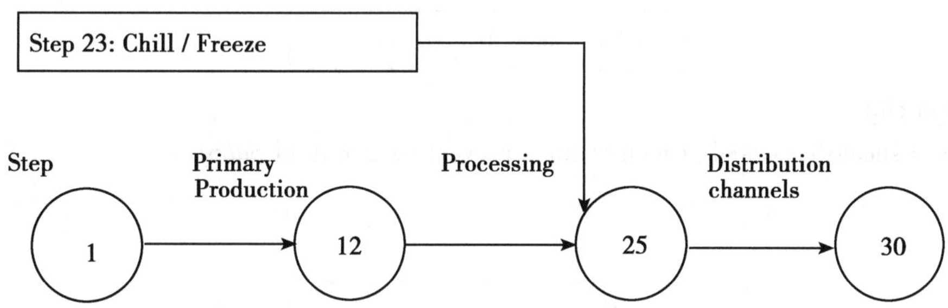

9. 12. 1 Hazard-based control measures

For *Campylobacter*

94. Freezing of naturally contaminated carcasses followed by 31 days of storage at -20 degrees C has been shown to reduce *Campylobacter* by 0. 7 to 2. 9 log10 CFU/g.

95. Crust freezing using continuous carbon dioxide belt freezing of skinless breast fillets has been shown to give a reduction of *Campylobacter* of 0. 4 log10 CFU/fillet.

---

❶ Refer to *General Standard for the Labelling of Pre-packaged Foods* (CODEX STAN 1 – 1985) and WHO's "Prevention of food-borne disease: Five keys to safer food".

❷ Refer to *General Standard for Irradiated Foods* (CODEX STAN 106 – 1983).

9.13

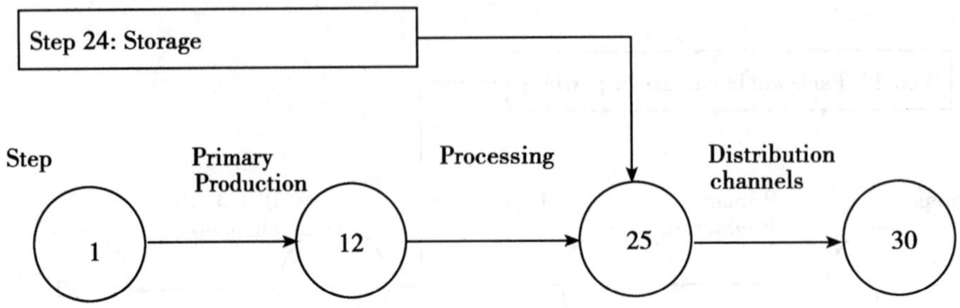

9.13.1 GHP-based control measures

For *Salmonella*

96. Products should be stored at temperatures preventing growth of *Salmonella*.[1]

10 CONTROL MEASURES FOR STEPS 25 TO 30 (DISTRIBUTION CHANNELS)

97. For GHP-based control measures for all aspects of transport, refer to the *Code of Practice - General Principles of Food Hygiene* (CAC/RCP 1 - 1969) and the *Code of Hygienic Practice for Meat* (CAC/RCP 58 - 2005).

10.1

Step 25: Transport

10.2

Step 26: Wholesale Premises

For *Salmonella*

98. Products should be stored at temperatures preventing growth of *Salmonella*.

10.3

Step 27: Transport

[1] Packaging in modified atmosphere does not prevent growth of *Salmonella* if temperature abuse occurs.

10. 4

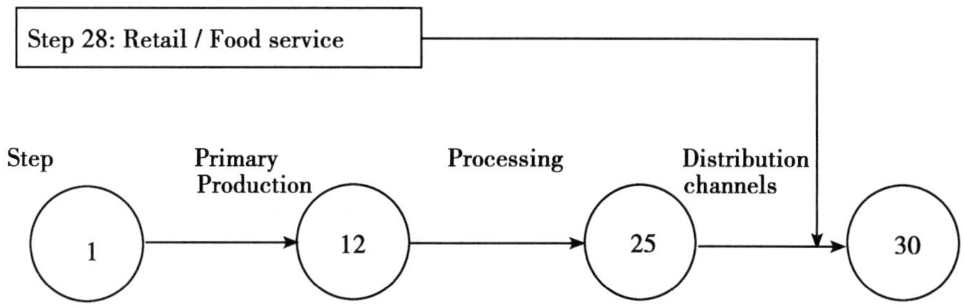

10. 4. 1 GHP-based control measures

10. 4. 1. 1 Retail

99. Hygiene measures should be in place to prevent cross-contamination between raw chicken meat and other food.

100. Retailers should separate raw and cooked products.

101. Hands should be washed and sanitized before and after handling raw chicken meat. Retailers may also provide customers with the means to sanitise hands after handling raw chicken meat packs.

102. Where product is packed at retail for individual selection by customers, packs should be leak-proof where possible. Extra packaging should be supplied at the display counter to allow customers to separate chicken from other purchases.

10. 4. 1. 2 Food service

103. For GHP-based control measures, also refer to the *Code of Hygienic Practice for Precooked and Cooked Foods in Mass Catering* (CAC/RCP 39 – 1993).

104. Thawing of frozen chicken should be carried out in a manner that minimises the potential for growth of microorganisms and prevent cross contamination. [1]Washing of raw chicken carcasses should not be carried out as it is likely to spread contamination.

105. Food service operators should be fully trained in and aware of the differences between raw and cooked chicken products in relation to food safety and ensure separation at all times.

106. Food service operators should have hygiene measures in place that minimise cross-contamination between raw chicken and hands, contact surfaces and utensils, and should prevent contamination of other foods.

For *Salmonella*

107. Products should be stored at temperatures preventing growth of *Salmonella*.

10. 4. 2 Hazard-based control measures

For *Campylobacter* and *Salmonella*

108. Chicken meat should be cooked according to a process that is capable of achieving at least a 7 log reduction in both *Campylobacter* and *Salmonella*. [2]

---

[1] Refer to the *Code of Practice for the Processing and Handling of Quick Frozen Foods* (CAC/RCP 8 – 1976).

[2] Cooking chicken meat thoroughly will eliminate *Campylobacter* and *Salmonella*. It has been shown that cooking chicken meat to 165°F (74°C) minimum internal temperature, with no hold time, will give at least a 7 log10 reduction in both *Campylobacter* and *Salmonella*.

10.5

Step 29: Transport

10.6

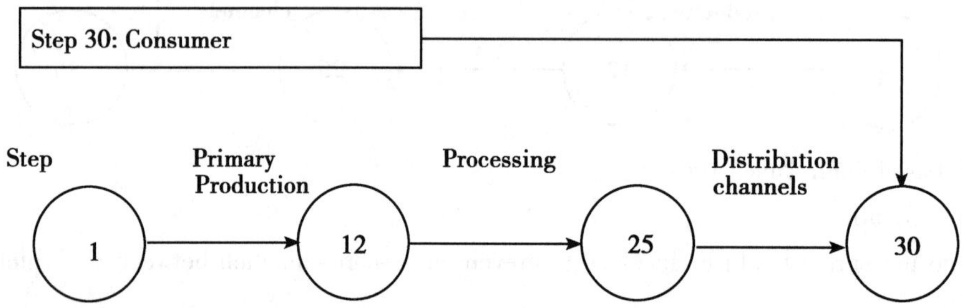

10.6.1 GHP-based control measures

109. Consumer education should focus on handling, hand washing, cooking, storage, thawing, prevention of cross contamination, and prevention of temperature abuse. The WHO Five keys to safer food[1] assists in this process.

110. Special attention should be paid to the education of all persons preparing food, and particularly to persons preparing food for the young, old, pregnant and immuno-compromised.

111. The above information to consumers should be provided through multiple channels such as national media, health care professionals, food hygiene trainers, product labels, pamphlets, school curriculae and cooking demonstrations.

112. Washing of raw chicken in the kitchen should be discouraged so as to minimise the possibility of contamination of other foods and surfaces that come in contact with food and humans. Where deemed necessary washing of raw chicken carcasses and (or) chicken meat, should be carried out in a manner which minimises the possibility of contamination of other foods and surfaces that come in contact with other foods and humans.

113. Consumers should wash and disinfect food contact surfaces after raw chicken preparation to significantly reduce the potential for cross-contamination in the kitchen.

<u>For *Salmonella*</u>

114. Products should be stored at temperatures preventing growth of *Salmonella*.

10.6.2 Hazard-based control measures

<u>For *Salmonella* and *Campylobacter*</u>

115. Chicken meat should be cooked according to a process that is capable of achieving at least a 7 log reduction in both *Campylobacter* and *Salmonella*[2].

11 RISK-BASED CONTROL MEASURES

116. GHP provides the foundation for most food safety control systems. Where possible and practicable,

[1] http://www.who.int/foodsafety/consumer/5keys/en/.

[2] Cooking chicken meat thoroughly will eliminate *Campylobacter* and *Salmonella*. It has been shown that cooking chicken meat to 165°F (74°C) minimum internal temperature, with no hold time, will give at least a 7 log10 reduction in both *Campylobacter* and *Salmonella*.

food safety control systems should incorporate hazard-based control measures and risk assessment.

Identification and implementation of risk-based control measures can be elaborated by application of a risk management framework (RMF) process as advocated in the *Principles and Guidelines for the Conduct of Microbiological Risk Management* (MRM) (CAC/GL 63 - 2007).

117. While these guidelines provide generic guidance on development of GHP-based and hazard-based control measures for *Campylobacter* and *Salmonella*, development of risk-based control measures for application at single or multiple steps in the food chain are primarily the domain of competent authorities at the national level. Industry may derive risk-based measures to facilitate application of process control systems.

11.1 Development of risk-based control measures

118. Competent authorities operating at the national level should develop risk-based control measures for *Campylobacter* and *Salmonella* where possible and practical.

119. Risk modelling tools used to explore risk management options and contribute to risk management decisions should be fit for purpose.

120. The risk manager needs to understand the capability and limitations of risk modelling tools they have selected[1].

121. When developing risk-based control measures, competent authorities may use the quantitative examples of the likely level of control of a hazard at certain steps in the generic food chain in this document, as a peer-reviewed scientific resource[2].

122. Competent authorities formulating risk management metrics[3] as regulatory control measures should apply a methodology that is scientifically robust and transparent.

11.2 Availability of a web-based decision tool

123. FAO/WHO through JEMRA has developed a web-based decision support tool[4] for exploring the potential for development of risk-based control measures for *Campylobacter* and *Salmonella* in the raw chicken meat food chain at the national level. [5].

124. This web-based tool can be used to estimate relative risk reduction and (or) ranking consequential to:

- implementation of a specific control measure at a particular step in the food chain (from primary production through to consumption);
- implementation of a particular combination of control measures at different steps in the food chain;
- modelling of different food chain scenarios to that presented in this document.

125. Industry may also make use of the decision support tool when designing premises-specific food safety programmes that may differ in availability of specific control measures.

126. The user of the decision support tool at the national level should:

- Take responsibility for the appropriateness of the scientific data that is introduced;

---

1 *Principles and Guidelines for the Conduct of Microbiological Risk Assessment* (CAC/GL 30 - 1999).

2 FAO/WHO, 2009. Technical Meeting on *Salmonella* and *Campylobacter* in chicken meat. 4 - 8 May 2009, Rome, Italy.

3 *Principles and Guidelines for Conduct of Microbiological Risk Management* (MRM) CAC/GL 63 - 2007.

4 Initiated after FAO/WHO Technical Meeting on *Salmonella* and *Campylobacter* in chicken meat. Rome 4 - 8 May 2009. Trialed November 2009. Reviewed April 2010.

5 www.mramodels.org.

- Be aware of the uncertainty that inevitably accompanies risk modelling and in conjunction with the risk manager, use the web-based tool to *explore* risk management options and *inform* risk management decisions, rather than provide a prescriptive base;
- Not use the tool to impose specific scientific assumptions.

12 IMPLEMENTATION OF CONTROL MEASURES

127. Implementation8 involves giving effect to the selected control measure (s), development of implementation plan, communication on the decision on control measure (s), ensuring regulatory framework and infrastructure for implementation, and evaluation process to assess whether the control measure (s) have been properly implemented. Validation of control measures should be carried out prior to their implementation.

12.1 Validation of Control Measures

128. Refer to the *Guidelines for the Validation of Food Safety Control Measures* (CAC/GL 69 - 2008).

Note: GHP-based control measures are not subject to validation.

12.2 Prior to Validation

129. Prior to validation of the hazard-based control measures for *Campylobacter* and (or) *Salmonella*, the following tasks should be completed:

- Identification of the specific measure or measures to be validated. This would include consideration of any measures approved by the competent authority and whether any measure has already been validated in a way that is applicable and appropriate to specific commercial use, such that further validation is not necessary;
- Identification of any existing food safety outcome or target, established by the competent authority or industry. Industry may set stricter targets than those set by the competent authority.

12.3 Validation

130. Validation of measures may be carried out by industry and (or) the competent authority.

131. Where validation is undertaken for a measure based on hazard control for *Campylobacter* and (or) *Salmonella*, evidence will need to be obtained to show that the measure is capable of controlling *Campylobacter* and (or) *Salmonella* to a specified target or outcome. This may be achieved by use of a single measure or a combination of measures. The *Guidelines for the Validation of Food Safety Control Measures* (CAC/GL 69 - 2008) provides detailed advice on the validation process (section Ⅵ).

12.4 Implementation

132. Refer to section 9.2 of the *Code of Hygienic Practice for Meat* (CAC/RCP 58 - 2005).

12.4.1 Industry

133. Industry has the primary responsibility for implementing, documenting, applying and supervising process control systems to ensure the safety and suitability of chicken meat, and these should incorporate GHP and validated measures for control of *Campylobacter* and (or) *Salmonella* (HACCP) as appropriate to national government requirements and industry's specific circumstances.

134. The documented process control systems should describe the activities applied including any sampling procedures, specified targets e. g. performance objectives or performance criteria, set for *Campylobacter* and (or) *Salmonella*, industry verification activities, and corrective and preventive actions.

135. The competent authority should provide guidelines and other implementation tools to industry as appropriate, for the development of the process control systems.

12. 4. 2 Regulatory systems

136. The competent authority may choose to approve the documented process control systems for GHP and HACCP and stipulate verification frequencies. Microbiological testing requirements should be provided for verification of HACCP systems where specific targets for control of *Campylobacter* and (or) *Salmonella* have been stipulated.

137. The competent authority may choose to use a competent body to undertake specific verification activities in relation to the industry's process control systems. Where this occurs, the competent authority should stipulate specific functions to be carried out.

12. 5 Verification of Control Measures

138. Refer to section 9. 2 of the *Code of Hygienic Practice for Meat* (CAC/RCP 58 – 2005) and section IV of the *Guidelines for the Validation of Food Safety Control Measures* (CAC/GL 69 – 2008).

12. 5. 1 Industry

139. Industry verification should demonstrate that all control measures for *Campylobacter* and (or) *Salmonella* have been implemented as intended. Verification should include observation of processing activities, documentary checks, and sampling for *Campylobacter* and (or) *Salmonella* testing as appropriate.

140. Verification frequency should vary according to the operational aspects of process control, the historical performance of the establishment and the results of verification itself.

12. 5. 2 Regulatory systems

141. The competent authority and (or) competent body should verify that all regulatory control measures implemented by industry comply with regulatory requirements as appropriate for control of *Campylobacter* and (or) *Salmonella.*

13 MONITORING AND REVIEW

142. Monitoring and review of food safety control systems is an essential component of application of a risk management framework (RMF). It contributes to verification of process control and demonstrating progress towards achievement of public health goals.

143. Information on the level of control of *Campylobacter* and *Salmonella* at appropriate points in the food chain can be used to for several purposes e. g. to validate and (or) verify outcomes of food control measures, to monitor compliance with hazard-based and risk-based regulatory goals, and to help prioritise regulatory efforts to reduce foodborne illness. Systematic review of monitoring information allows the competent authority and relevant stakeholders to make decisions in terms of the overall effectiveness of the food safety control systems and make improvements where necessary.

13.1 Monitoring

144. Monitoring should be carried out at appropriate steps[1] in the food chain using randomized or targeted sampling as appropriate. Examples of the utility of monitoring systems for *Campylobacter* and (or) *Salmonella* in broiler chickens may include:

- Sampling (e. g. environmental, blood, faecal) of breeders and hatcheries for determination of general *Salmonella* status;
- Faecal sampling of chickens prior to delivery to slaughter to determine flock status and permit logistic scheduling and (or) channelling of positive chickens for specific processing steps e. g. to heat treatment or freezing;
- Caecal or cloacal sampling for *Campylobacter* at delivery to determine slaughter flock status for epidemiological investigations;
- Whole bird rinse, neck skin or other sampling at the end of primary processing (normally after immersion or air chilling) to verify compliance with hazard-based regulatory or company performance goals;
- Sampling of retail product to determine contamination trends post-processing;
- National or regional surveys for establishing baseline levels of contamination and assisting in formulation of regulatory performance goals within the food chain.

145. Regulatory monitoring programmes should be designed in consultation with relevant stakeholders, with the most cost-efficient resourcing option being chosen for collection and testing of samples. Given the importance of monitoring data in risk management, sampling and testing components should be standardized on a national basis and be subject to quality assurance.

146. The type of data collected in monitoring systems should be appropriate for the outcomes sought[2].

147. Monitoring information should be made available to relevant stakeholders in a timely manner e. g. to producers, processing industry, consumers.

148. Wherever possible, monitoring information from the food chain should be combined with human health surveillance data and food source attribution data to validate risk-based control measures and verify progress towards risk-reduction goals. Activities supporting an integrated response include:

- Surveillance of clinical salmonellosis and campylobacteriosis in humans;
- Epidemiological investigations including outbreaks and sporadic cases.

13.2 Review

149. Monitoring data on *Campylobacter* and *Salmonella* and associated risks should be reviewed on a periodic basis to provide information on the effectiveness of risk management decisions and actions. Results from *Campylobacter* and *Salmonella* spp. should be shared with competent authorities so that the information could be integrated in trend analysis.

150. Periodic review of monitoring data at relevant process steps should be used to inform future decisions on selection of specific control measures, and provide a basis for their validation.

---

[1] Recommendations on surveillance in poultry flocks for *Salmonella* are provided in the OIE *Terrestrial Animal Health Code*, Chapter 6.5 "Prevention, Detection and Control of *Salmonella* in Poultry".

[2] Enumeration and sub-typing of microorganisms generally provides more information for risk management purposes than presence or absence testing.

151. Information gained from monitoring in the food chain should be integrated with public health surveillance, food source attribution data, and withdrawal and recall data, where available to evaluate and review the effectiveness of control measures.

152. Where monitoring of hazards or risks indicates that regulatory performance goals are not being achieved, risk management strategies and (or) control measures should be reviewed.

13.2.1 Public health goals

153. Countries should consider the results of monitoring and review when setting public health goals37 for food-borne campylobacteriosis and salmonellosis and when evaluating progress. Monitoring of the food chain in combination with source attribution and human health surveillance data are important components.

37 International organisations such as WHO provide guidance for establishing and implementing public health monitoring programmes. WHO Global Foodborne Infections Network (GFN) http://www.who.int/salmsurv/en/.